THE COMPLETE WORKS OF
THE GAWAIN=POET

THE COMPLETE WORKS OF
THE GAWAIN=POET

Gawain

In a Modern English Version with a Critical Introduction
by John Gardner

Woodcuts by Fritz Kredel

THE UNIVERSITY OF CHICAGO PRESS
Chicago & London

THE UNIVERSITY OF CHICAGO PRESS, CHICAGO 60637
THE UNIVERSITY OF CHICAGO PRESS, LTD., LONDON

Designed by Adrian Wilson

International Standard Book Number: 0-226-28329-1 (clothbound);
0-226-28330-5 (paperbound)
Library of Congress Catalog Card Number: 65-17291

For my father and mother

Open your eyes therefore, prick up your spiritual ears, open your lips, and apply your heart, that you may see your God in all creatures, may hear Him, praise Him, love and adore Him, magnify and honor Him, lest the whole world rise against you.

—BONAVENTURA

PREFACE

My object in translating and commenting on these poems has been to make generally accessible as much as I could of the technical ingenuity, the music, the narrative subtlety and vigor, the dramatic power, and the symbolic complexity to be found in the original Middle English. One knows before one begins a verse translation of this kind that one cannot hope for more than partial success. Inevitably, since it is impossible to carry all of a great poet's effects from one language into another, one is forced to make choices about what to keep and what to dismiss; and, recognizing this from the start, one is tempted to begin by devising for oneself a set of rules on what is to be most important to preserve, what next most important, and so on. But such rules are of little use, at least to me, for what seems most important in one place seems less important in another, and in the end one has no choice but to let the poetry take one where it will. I can therefore describe the method of these translations only in the following very general terms.

I have often translated freely, exaggerating the poet's images and the connotative effects of his language in order to make images, puns, and the like available to a reader less familiar than the fourteenth-century reader presumably was with, for instance, hawking, hunting, chess, and feudal etiquette. I have sometimes quite drastically altered lines in order to reproduce by indirection effects I could not get otherwise—which of course means that the reader is at the mercy of my interpretation throughout. For example, by virtue of the poetic conventions used in presenting it—conventions now all but forgotten—the garden or arbor in the *Pearl* would simultaneously suggest to the poet's immediate audience a garden, a bower of love, and a graveyard, and it would become, as the poem progresses, a symbol of Nature itself, the fallen garden. (This is not to say that all medieval gardens in all medieval poems must suggest to all medieval audiences the contrast between Nature and Paradise. The contrast is one carefully introduced and developed as the poem progresses.) To get the necessary hints of this multeity into the translation, I have introduced new but consistent imagery, for instance the gates in stanza 4, aimed at enforcing the idea of the garden as graveyard. Elsewhere, particularly in *Purity* and *Patience*, I have consistently narrowed the connotations of some of the poet's words for the sake of preserving the unity and coherence of the poems. In all of the poems of the *Gawain*-poet, the setting is the world of chivalry: the Old Testament figure Lot is a knight, a bold baron, a sturdy duke; the prophet Jonah is a vassal of God; Jerusalem is a fortified medieval city with towers and battlements and bridges spanning a moat. If we see the Old Testament world as the world of King Arthur, and its heroes as models of chivalric courtesy, there is nothing very startling in the poet's treatment of the Beatitudes as allegorical ladies—in *Patience*, for instance:

> These, all eight, are the honors that await us
> If we will but love these ladies and live in their service—
> Dame Poverty, Dame Pity, Dame Penance, the third,
> Dame Meekness and Dame Mercy, and merry Dame Cleanness. . . .
>
> [Prologue, st. 8, ll. 29–32]

But if we lose our sense of the milieu, such passages are jarring. And so in translating words which can have either a strictly medieval sense or a more general sense, for example the word *douþe*, which can mean "band of retainers" or simply "people," I have generally selected the more medieval meaning.

The translations necessarily neglect many of the poet's intricate prosodic devices. The poem which has suffered most from this is the *Pearl*, which is in the original the poet's most highly ornamented work. For the sake of preserving the imagery, the larger symbolic structure, and the dramatic force of the poem, I have substituted half rhyme (and sometimes not even that) for true rhyme, and a pervasive suggestion of alliteration for the poet's regular alliteration. Abandoning true rhyme and alliteration has certain advantages: at least to some extent it reduces the pressure pushing one toward awkward inversion, archaic or "poetic" diction, and padding. At the same time, however, to let rhyme go is to abandon much of the music.

The remaining translations follow the poet somewhat more closely. When I began, my general principle was to follow the poet's own rules of alliterative versification exactly, but without attempting to match in translation the rhythm or alliterative structure of corresponding lines; in the end I found it necessary to abandon that principle about as often as I followed it, for it betrayed me into writing self-conscious verse. The poet plays ingenious games with alliteration, flourishing it with a master's frank delight in mastery. I have decided it would be vulgar to follow a master's flourishes when one cannot really match the plain competence and good taste of the poetic foundation.

Whatever their shortcomings, these translations ought to be of some interest, particularly to readers who do not have enough Middle English to read the poems in the original and would therefore be kept from them entirely. The translations here do, I hope, keep the poet's symbolic structures more or less intact, as earlier translations were not able to do, being grounded on a less advanced stage of *Gawain*-poet scholarship; they preserve at least some of the poet's puns and much of his play of wit; and they offer what is so far the closest approximation of the poet's rhythm and tone. The translations of *Purity* and *Patience* are the first verse translations to appear (indeed, these poems are at the moment difficult to obtain even in the original Middle English), and so I offer them with some pride. Both poems are, in the original, very good; *Patience*, in fact, is much the best homiletic poem in English. A further virtue of this group of translations is that it gives every reader a chance to examine the complete canon, until now available only to specialists. With all of the poems at hand, it becomes possible to study relationships between them and thus to interpret particular poems with a greater degree of certainty; it becomes possible to trace the poet's progress as an artist; and it becomes possible to apprehend the controlling vision which made the man the poet he was.

Since, as I have suggested already, the quality of these translations must depend heavily on the quality of my interpretation of the poems, and since at the moment there is considerable disagreement about how medieval literature ought to be interpreted, perhaps I will be excused for discussing briefly the principles by which I work out interpretation. I do not approach medieval poetry with any prejudgment whatever about how medieval poetry works: I do not assume with such New Exegetes as Professor D. W. Robertson, Jr., that all major medieval poems are constructed to suit the method of scriptural interpretation practiced by medieval patristic exegetes such as Augustine; I do not assume that courtly love must always and everywhere have the same meaning; I do not assume with Professor Kemp Malone that most medieval poetry is loosely constructed, and neither do I assume at the outset that all or any medieval poetry is tight. I assume only that one must not dismiss a line or passage as pointless or arbitrary until one has attempted to account for it without conscious wrenching. Behind this assumption lies another: that a modern reader's intellectual and emotional responses are close enough to those of a medieval reader to enable him to work out, through careful study of the poem as a whole, what responses the poet intended to evoke. If I find that a given detail is best accounted for by the New Exegetes, whose assumptions happen to be unconvincing to me but whose identification of symbols and stock phrases often do seem to me convincing, then I accept their findings; if I find that the anthropological interpretation of a critic like Jessie L. Weston explains the presence of a detail which cannot be better accounted for in some other way, I accept that point of view. One good statement of the position I am advocating is that of E. Talbot Donaldson (in his "Patristic Exegesis: The Opposition," *Critical Approaches to Medieval Literature*, pp. 24–25):

> I believe that great poetic art offers something very close to an ultimate reality. In order to read it well one has to put oneself into the impossible position of having all one's wits and faculties about one, ready to spring into activity at the first summons; yet, like hunting dogs, they must not spring before they are summoned; and only those that are summoned must spring; and the summons must come from the poem.

Whether, on one hand, the summons cries out from the page for the reader's response or, on the other hand, lies muted by time, discoverable only by the evidence of some detail or group of details which at first glance seems completely arbitrary or pointless, a proper response to the summons seems to me any response which adequately accounts for the detail in its immediate context and which is also supported by the appearance of similar details involving similar techniques and attitudes elsewhere in the given poem and within the total body of the poet's work.

This approach has, admittedly, one serious limitation. From the point of view of strictly scientific scholarship, nothing can be said about a poem until the statement can be proved valid by a carefully reasoned, fully documented argument which logically answers every logical objection that might be raised against it. What is sought is "scholarly agreement." If it were possible to demonstrate scientifically that, say, Chaucer intended his "Tale of Melibeus" as Virginia Woolf believes he intended it, the scientific point of view would be unassailable. But the truth is that no such demonstration is possible. The man concerned with matters specifically literary cannot afford to disregard completely the findings of scientific scholarship, but finally his only choice is to transfer to the sphere of literature Hobbes's famous remark on the study of Man: "When I have set down my own reading orderly, and perspicuously, the pains left another, will be onely to consider, if he also find not the same in himself. For this kind of Doctrine, admitteth no other Demonstration."

In examining these translations, no reader, I hope, will accuse me of rewriting the poems to suit a presumptive critical theory. As for my critical comments in the Introduction, it should go without saying that they follow from my reading of the poems. They are not prima facie judgments but, instead, generalizations which follow my firm conviction, derived from emotional and intellectual experience of the poetry, that the poet was a certain kind of medieval man and a certain kind of Christian who wrote in a certain way. If my generalizations are wrong, I hope the translations themselves will indict me, for I have tried to follow the poet even where, as Kafka says, "in the dark woods, on the sodden ground, I found my way only by the whiteness of his collar."

For permission to incorporate into the Introduction to this book material earlier presented in article form, I am indebted to the editors of the *Journal of English and Germanic Philology*. I should like to acknowledge my debt to Donald Finkel and William Dickey, who, in innumerable ways, have helped me with the rudiments of translation. Needless to say, mistakes or aesthetic deformities here are my own. I am also greatly indebted to Burton Weber, whose work on John Milton led me to important insights into a very different Christian vision, and whose conversation has always been of enormous value to me. I must thank, too, my wife and children, who make life and work worthwhile.

CONTENTS

INTRODUCTION
AND COMMENTARY

1.

THE POET

The fourteenth century produced two great English poets, Geoffrey Chaucer and the anonymous poet who wrote the *Pearl, Purity, Patience, Sir Gawain and the Green Knight*, and *St. Erkenwald*. The two poets quite obviously differ in depth and scope; whereas Chaucer's art is matched by that of no English poet but Shakespeare, the art of the *Gawain*-poet, like that of George Herbert, for instance, is minor. The *Gawain*-poet lacks Chaucer's moral complexity, lacks Chaucer's fascination with men unlike himself and the psychological insight that goes with that fascination, and lacks Chaucer's philosophical and artistic eclecticism. But granting the fundamental difference between them, that is to say the difference in poetic stature of a certain kind, one is nevertheless increasingly struck by similarities as one studies the themes, techniques, and attitudes of the *Gawain*-poet and Chaucer. It may be simply that they wrote from approximately the same medieval Christian vision, or it may be, as I am at times inclined to believe, that some more direct relationship exists between the poetry of the two men. At all events, one good way of introducing the *Gawain*-poet is to compare him more or less systematically with his greater contemporary.

We know a good deal about Chaucer considering our distance from him in time, but about the *Gawain*-poet we know virtually

3

nothing. For some scholars it is not even absolutely certain that the five poems we commonly ascribe to him are all his.[1] More important, whereas we read and enjoy Chaucer's poetry, much of the *Gawain*-poet's work, despite its excellence, is still hard to appreciate as literature. One reason for this is the difficulty we have with his language—a difficulty which inhibits not only reading but also translation. We read Chaucer in the original with relative ease, for the London dialect in which he wrote evolved in time into modern English; but the *Gawain*-poet is accessible only to specialists, and not fully accessible even to them, for his northwest Midlands tongue, never adopted in linguistically influential cities, has remained the curious, runish language it probably was to the average Londoner of the poet's own time. The dialect survives, drastically altered, here and there in rural England; in America, traces of it appear among backwoods or mountain people—in rural Missouri, for example, where the expression "I hope" can still mean "I understand, I believe."

The *Gawain*-poet's dialect is not all that gets in the way of our reading his poetry, for not all of the fourteenth-century poems composed in the northwest Midlands are as difficult as his. Part of our trouble is the temperament of the man. He knows and uses the technical language of hunting, hawking, cooking, chess, and the special terms of the furrier, the architect, the musician, the lawyer, the courtly lover, the priest; he knows the names of the parts of a shield, the adornments of a horse, the zones of a knight's bejeweled helmet; he knows too the names of the parts of a ship, the parts of a coffin, the accouterments of farming; knows the Bible and its commentary (probably even commentary in Hebrew), the chronicles, old legends, the ecclesiastical traditions of London. His knowledge rivals that of Chaucer, but it is in some respects knowledge of a very different kind. Chaucer's technical language comes mainly from books—on astrology, on alchemy, on medicine, and so forth. The *Gawain*-poet's technical language seems to come less from books than from medieval occupations. One suspects that he was, like Chaucer, gregarious, but what emerges from Chaucer's talk with people, at least in the *Canterbury Tales*, is less what they do than what they are, have been, and hope to become. The *Gawain*-poet

THE GAWAIN-POET

does not seem much interested in the individualizing traits of people; he gets from them a knowledge of "all trades, their gear and tackle and trim." More than a difference of temperament is involved. In his implicit theory of identity, as in everything else, Chaucer looks forward to the Renaissance. The *Gawain*-poet is far more a man of the Middle Ages, less influenced by the humanistic strain in classical thought, and he is therefore harder for the modern reader to approach.

Biography might help here, if we knew it. Chaucer—a Londoner, a high-ranking servant of the crown, and a fashionable poet in his day—left the marks of his existence not only in his poetry but also in civil registers, in account books of noble families, among passport records, in court documents, and in the tributes of poetical friends. The *Gawain*-poet seems to have left no such marks. Dunbar, writing in the next generation, lists by name all but one of the poets he admires, and the one exception is, of course, the man who wrote *Sir Gawain*. The *Gawain*-poet probably lived a good distance from London, in Yorkshire or Lancashire most likely, for his language marks him no southern man and everything in his poetry marks him a man who loved the country. He may have visited the city, may conceivably have lived there for a time, since he shows familiarity with obscure old London traditions,[2] but when he speaks of the city or its general environs, as he does in *St. Erkenwald* and in the *Gawain*, he speaks as though "beautiful London," or the "New Troy," were far away. What has greatest immediacy in his work is the country: cliffs, rivers, forests, moors, gardens, fields, barns, sleeping towns on a winter's night, animals, birds, storms, seacoasts. Perhaps one's strongest sense of the poet's sensitivity to rural life comes in *Purity*. When God, in the form of three aristocratic strangers, comes down the road that runs past old Sir Abraham's farm, the knight leaves the shade of the oak in his front yard and goes to meet the three. The weather is unbearably hot, and Abraham invites the strangers to rest under his tree for a while, away from the sun. He tells them he will fix them dinner, and the strangers accept and sit down on a huge surface root of the oak. (The detail is symbolic as well as literal.) Sir Abraham calls instructions to his wife, telling her to move quickly "this once," and then with some servants hurries out to the cowbarn to catch a calf, which he orders skinned and broiled. When he returns to his guests, he finds them sitting in the shade where he left them, and this detail crowns all the rest—they have taken off their sweaty hats.

The poet's metaphors, too, are those of a country man. Throughout his work, men are like wild animals or birds, and emotions and ideas find expression in images of places, animals, weather, plants. Thawed after his deadly winter ride, flushed with wine now and wearing fine robes, Gawain looks and feels like Spring. (Admittedly, Chaucer uses the same device for a similar symbolic purpose in the *Troilus*, but the effect there seems far more clearly literary and conventional.) Later in the *Gawain*, when the young knight is waiting for the Green Knight's blow, Gawain stands rooted to the ground like a tree. In the *Pearl*, when the narrator first sees his daughter on the far side of the river, both his sense that he must not move a muscle and his fear that if he does the vision will shatter take the form of hawking images:

> More than I liked my dread arose;
> I stood dead still and dared not call—
> My eyes wide open, mouth drawn close—
> I stood as still as the hawk in the hall;
> Ghostly I knew that vision was,
> And I feared any moment the dark might fall,
> Feared she might yet fly up from the place
> Before I had brought her to reach or call.
>
> [st. 16, ll. 181–88]

Even theological argument may find expression through natural images in the *Gawain*-poet's work. In the *Pearl*, the child-queen tells her father:

> Then make instead the sign of the cross
> And love God well, in weal or woe,
> For anger will gain you never a cress:
> Who needs to be bent He'll bend. Be now
> Less proud, for though you dance like a doe
> And brandish and bray with all your rage,
> When you make no headway to or fro,
> Then you'll abide what He will judge.
>
> [st. 29, ll. 341–48]

None of the *Gawain*-poet's work survives in more than one manuscript. The likelihood is that his poetry was by no means as well known as Chaucer's even in his own day.[3] The reason may be simply that the poet's isolation from London restricted his reputation; but it may also be because he was temperamentally a country man, fully satisfied with the old native meter and uninterested in most of the new poetic genres of Europe, that the *Gawain*-poet's work was less fashionable than Chaucer's. Some scholars have thought that the poet was relatively unknown in his time because, unlike Chaucer, he was an inconspicuous figure, a private chaplain to a nobleman, or a priest. The theory that the poet was a priest has very little to recommend it. It is true, as Professor Gollancz has observed, that all of his poems except the *Gawain* are explicitly religious and show a general knowledge of exegetical typology and Scholastic philosophy, and that even the *Gawain* explores a religious theme;[4] and it may be true that the fact that the poet had a daughter need not work against an identification of the poet as a priest.[5] But as Osgood argued long ago, it seems unlikely that a man who was a priest himself would speak of "God who, in the form of bread and wine, / The priest reveals to us every day"; and the poet's intimate knowledge of—and obvious interest in—courtly flirtation, among other things, may also argue against his identification as a priest.[6]

Others have suggested that the poet may have been a lawyer, possibly (as Gollancz first argued) Chaucer's neighbor "philosophical Strode," Thomist philosopher at Merton College, later well-known London lawyer, and also, as old documents suggest, a poet.[7] Most scholars now agree that, though the poet may indeed have been a lawyer, the claim for Strode is no longer worth serious consideration. Professor René Wellek has summed up the difficulties: "There was, it is true, a poet Ralph Strode who wrote a 'Fantasma Radulphi' before 1360, but there is not the slightest evidence that this Fellow of Merton College, Oxford, was a Northerner or that he even wrote in English or that 'Ralph's Spectre' is in any way identical with the *Pearl*. Moreover, it has been shown that this Strode was probably not identical with the logician Strode, who played some part in the history of scholastics."[8]

Other attempts to identify the poet have been equally unsuccessful.

At the suggestion that our poet is the author of the mediocre "Pistill of the Swete Susane," Huchown, the literary mind must boggle, and there are also strong philological arguments against it. The more recent theory of Oscar Cargill and Margaret Schlauch which seizes on a "minstrel" named John Prat, or else a John Donne, "valet of the king's kitchen,"[9] is at best whimsical.

It may be true, however, that the *Gawain*-poet was a ranking vassal of some powerful western baron, and that, like Chaucer, he hunted with gentlemen, traveled on diplomatic missions, and sometimes wrote poetry for the court he served. There are, in my opinion, indications that *Sir Gawain and the Green Knight* is a poem written for a Christmas festival of some sort,[10] and the descriptions of hunting, feasting, and arming in the poem all sound authentic enough to be the work of a man with firsthand experience in these things. As Gollancz pointed out, the sea descriptions in *Patience* and *Purity* sound authentic, even granting that some of them have literary sources; and the poet's knowledge of words like "hurrack" may point to experience on shipboard. In the light of all this, one is inclined to believe that the poet may be speaking literally as well as figuratively when he says in *Patience:*

> If unto this destiny I am duly appointed,
> What good can indignation do, or outrage?
> For lo, if my liege lord likes, in this life, to command me
> Either to ride or to run or to roam on his errand,
>
> What good is my grumbling except to get greater griefs?
> And if he commands me to talk, though my tongue be raw,
> I must do what his power impels, despite displeasure,
> And bow myself to his bidding, be worthy my hire.
>
> [Prologue, sts. 13–14, ll. 49–56]

Whoever the poet may have been, there are certain interesting parallels between his poetry and that of Chaucer which are worth pointing out as indications of the extent to which the two men shared common techniques and concerns.

In the "Squire's Tale," Chaucer writes:

> And so bifel that after the thridde cours,
> Whil that this kyng sit thus in his nobleye,
> Herknynge his mynstralles hir thynges pleye

THE GAWAIN-POET

> Biforn hym at the bord deliciously,
> In at the halle dore al sodeynly
> Ther cam a knyght upon a steede of bras,
> And in his hand a brood mirour of glas.
> Upon his thombe he hadde of gold a ryng,
> And by his syde a naked swerd hangyng;
> And up he rideth to the heighe bord.
> In al the halle ne was ther spoken a word
> For merveille of this knyght; hym to biholde
> Ful bisily they wayten, yonge and olde.
>   This strange knyght, that cam thus sodeynly,
> Al armed, save his heed, ful richely,
> Saleweth kyng and queene and lordes alle,
> By ordre, as they seten in the halle,
> With so heigh reverence and obeisaunce,
> As wel in speche as in his contenaunce,
> That Gawayn, with his olde curteisye,
> Though he were comen ayeyn out of Fairye,
> Ne koude hym nat amende with a word.

["Squire's Tale," Fragment V (F), ll. 76–97]

Coolidge O. Chapman has pointed out that the pattern of details closely parallels the pattern in *Gawain*. In both poems the stranger hales in suddenly on a remarkable horse while dinner music is playing; the stranger rides directly to the dais where he is met by absolute silence; the ranked order of the court is noted (hardly a remarkable feature in Chaucer's poem, but quite unusual, given the traditional significance of the Round Table, in the *Gawain*); in the *Gawain* we are told that the stranger greets no one, while here a point is made of his greeting all the assembly; and finally Gawain himself is mentioned.

It seems to me that there are also similarities between the *Pearl* and the *Book of the Duchess*.[11] In both, the Virgin is identified as the *Phoenix of Araby;* in both poems de Lorris' religious service of the birds is put to specifically Christian use; in both poems the contrast of grace and works comes up (in the *Pearl* it is a central argument; in the *Book of the Duchess* it serves as the basis of a serious joke [ll. 1112–14]). Two or three of the shared features are not conventional and would suggest at the very least a peculiarly English treatment of French poetic material. Both poems are personal elegies, the first in

English, and both represent departures from accepted conventions of the dream-vision in that they incorporate to an unusual degree elements of realistic dream psychology—the *Pearl* in a highly stylized fashion, the *Book of the Duchess* in more fluid, distinctly realistic terms.[12] Equally interesting is the appearance in both elegies of a vision of that eternal bliss which contrasts with the temporary joy of human love. The narrator in the *Pearl* is unable to resign himself to the death of his beloved and sees, toward the end of his dream, the New Jerusalem standing on Zion "as it was seen by the Apostle John"; and much the same sort of thing happens in the *Book of the Duchess*. If we accept (with whatever reservations) B. F. Huppé's reading of the poem, the Black Knight in the *Book of the Duchess* is unable realistically to accept the death of his lady and is unable to see the parallel between devotion to her and devotion to a love which is immutable. The parallel is indicated by such passages as this one:

> As helpe me God, I was as blyve
> Reysed [by the lady], as fro deth to lyve,
> Of al happes the alderbeste,
> The gladdest, and the moste at reste.
>
> [*Book of the Duchess*, ll. 1277–80]

What the Knight fails to see, according to this reading of the poem, is that Christ's still more puissant love raises man from actual death to life which is eternal. At the end of the *Book of the Duchess*, when the Knight has finally opened his heart to the narrator—that is, has faced reality by saying, "She is dead"—Chaucer tells us:

> With that me thoghte that this kyng
> Gan homwardes for to ryde
> Unto a place, was there besyde,
> Which was from us but a lyte,
> A long castel with walles white,
> By seynt Johan! on a rych hil. . . .
>
> [*Book of the Duchess*, ll. 1314–19]

Chaucer does not ordinarily choose saints' names at random, and, as Huppé has shown, there are throughout the poem strong Christian overtones: "seynt Johan" is the apostle by whom the revelation of the New Jerusalem was recorded. And if "this kyng" is, on one level, a dream-symbol for Christ, "the hunter of the heart," and identified in patristic exegesis with the number eight (we are told earlier of the king *Octovyan*), then the white-walled castle is more than a pun on the name "Lancaster," as critics have thought it, and the hill is more than a pun on "Richmond." According to this view, the castle is, on one level, that same white castle to which the jeweler and Sir Gawain come. The bell in Chaucer's castle rings twelve times. Twelve, in patristic exegesis, is the number of the Church Universal, or salvation (cf. the use of *twelve* in the *Pearl*), and the narrator of the *Book of the Duchess* is expelled from his joyful dream, much as the narrator is expelled from Heaven in the *Pearl*.

Between the *Gawain* and the *Troilus* there are also curious, though much more general, parallels.[13] The two poems have one important theme in common— the courtesy of the cosmos (see my discussion of *Sir Gawain* below); both make symbolic use of the turning of the seasons; both symbolically identify characters, particularly the central knight in each poem, with particular times of the year; both are to some extent associated with the Fall of Man;[14] both make symbolic and dramatic use of the medieval concept of the tripartite human soul and associate this with the larger concept of feudal interdependence; and both contrast the tenure of mortal kingdoms (beginning with Troy) with the everlasting kingdom.

Unlike Chaucer, the brilliant genial egotist who figures as the central character in many of his own poems, the *Gawain*-poet, though sometimes equally brilliant and genial, maintains his detachment. His narrators are more or less conventional personae. Even in the *Pearl*, for all the emotional force of the poem, the narrator is as restrained and impersonally refined as the Black Knight in the *Book of the Duchess*. The *Gawain*-poet never mentioned himself by name, as Chaucer did again and again, and at the end of his life he left no retraction listing his major works. There was no need for retraction; his poems were in every case religious. And there, of course, lies the real reason that the poet is difficult to identify: he was indeed medieval, as Chaucer was not.

For Chaucer, this world of ours—though "lyte" in comparison to "the Galaxie," though a ludicrous little speck when viewed as Troilus views it from the eighth sphere—was glorious and good and wholly to be affirmed, a parliament of singing, a place where even before Christ's law there were good women who died for ideals just as saints die for theirs. For the *Gawain*-poet, this world was Plotinus' passing shadow, one's own life in the world included. Chaucer affirms and celebrates Nature without ever forgetting his Christian commitment to the larger order, but the *Gawain*-poet, though he loves Nature and knows it far more intimately than Chaucer does, insists upon the subservience of Nature to Spirit. Whereas Chaucer is, as Thomas Usk put it, a "noble philosophical poet," the *Gawain*-poet is a medieval Christian apologist—the best of them all—and a modern humanist only in the sense that he loves life and scrutinizes experience, and knowing himself an otherworldly Christian at the same time, can laugh at himself and at all who share his predicament. The poet believes that man is an animal who must try to become Godlike; on the chaos of his nature man must impose order, Platonic "form." Crafts, arts, occupations, impose form. A carpenter is not a mutable beast but the mutable embodiment of an immutable idea, carpentry. Read allegorically, as the *Gawain*-poet explicitly reads it in *Purity*, courtly love imposes form; feudalism or "courtesy" imposes form; and, above all, the teachings of Christ as interpreted by Scholastic philosophy—the laws of love and devotion to duty as opposed to the laws of power and obedience out of fear—impose form. Wholly rejecting Nature for Christian idealism, in this profoundly medieval view, man becomes worthy of salvation. That is almost but not quite the whole message of the *Gawain*-poet. The rest, and what finally elevates the *Gawain*-poet above most of his contemporaries, is the emotion which informs the conventional message—the humor, compassion, irony, dread, joy. Sir Gawain's soul is safe at the end of the poem, but the poet does not leave it at that—as Lydgate or Langland would. Having failed to be perfect, as all men must fail, Gawain is ashamed. But as far as Arthur's sensible, well-adjusted court is concerned, a man who regrets an unavoidable failure is, however noble, comic.

2.

CONVENTIONS AND
TRADITIONS IN THE POEMS

In their selection of poetic forms, Chaucer and the *Gawain*-poet differ. Chaucer's parson disparages the ancient English "rum, ram, ruf" school of poetry, and whether or not Chaucer agrees with his parson, his poems are not alliterative. The *Gawain*-poet, on the other hand, announces at once in *Sir Gawain and the Green Knight* that he intends to tell his story

> Rightly, as it is written,
> A story swift and strong
> With letters locked and linking,
> As scōps have always sung.
>
> [part I, st. 2, ll. 33–36]

And whereas Chaucer explores numerous poetic genres and more often than not completely transforms them, the *Gawain*-poet for the most part holds to the old conventions, within them writing homilies, a courtly dream-vision, a saint's legend, and, surprisingly, a most unconventional Arthurian romance. In both his choice of form and his choice of subject, the *Gawain*-poet is mainly, though not entirely, a conscious traditionalist.

To call a poet a traditionalist is not to call him unoriginal. The questions to be asked concerning such a poet are: Where was the tradition when he found it? How did he reinterpret or extend the tradition? For the most part we can only speculate, drawing inferences from the poems and from the practice of other poets of the day. The chief hindrance is our lack of information concerning the courts where the provincial poets wrote. It must be understood that, generally speaking, a poet of the fourteenth century wrote for an audience, not primarily for himself or posterity. To allude to books or build symbols from philosophical systems his immediate audience could not possibly know might suggest overweening pride. In practice poets frequently put together extremely familiar materials in new ways to achieve new effects, at best a new vision of reality. Thus in the *Troilus*, for instance, Chaucer combines Dante, Boethius, a story from Boccaccio, and possibly the story of the Fall of Man, among other things, to create something strikingly new.

All the surviving west and northwest Midlands alliterative poetry shows a similar manipulation of conventional materials. A stock May morning passage—shining leaves, birds singing like angels, fields full of flowers—enters the *Morte Arthure* as an ironic contrast to Arthur's warlike deeds; in *The Parliament of the Three Ages* the same materials comment on the narrator's poaching of a deer; in *Winner and Waster* the stock passage, slightly modified, establishes the parallel between winning and wasting in Nature, on one hand, and winning and wasting in human society, on the other; in *Piers Plowman* the same convention, treated more realistically and localized at Malvern Hills, becomes the foundation for a series of allegorical dreams. Many of these alliterative poems present arming scenes like those in *Sir Gawain*, and *The Parliament of the Three Ages* presents a hunt which seems designed to contrast with legal and noble hunts like those in *Sir Gawain*. The description of Youth in the *Parliament* may or may not be conventional but certainly calls to mind the *Gawain*-poet's description of the Green Knight. The *Parliament*-poet says of Youth (ll. 109–23):

> The first was a fierce man, fairer than the others,
> A bold knight on a steed and dressed to ride,
> A knight on a noble horse, a hawk on his wrist.
> He was big in the chest and broad in the shoulders,
> And his arms, likewise, were large and long,
> And his waist was handsomely shaped as a maiden's;
> His legs were long and sturdy, handsome to see.
> He straightened up in his stirrups and stood aloft,
> And he had neither hood nor hat to hide his hair,

> But a garland on his head, a glorious one
> Arrayed with bright red roses, richest of flowers,
> With trefoils and true-love knots and delicate pearls,
> And there in the center a splendid carbuncle.
> He was outfitted in green interwoven with gold,
> Adorned with golden coins and beautiful beryl. . . .

Other parts of the description of Youth recall the *Pearl*. Like the child in the *Pearl*, Youth's garments are sewn all around with gems, but the gems are, instead of pearls, the chalcedonies, sapphires, emeralds, amethysts, and so forth which are associated in the *Pearl* with the New Jerusalem. Two of the alliterative poems, *Morte Arthure* and "Summer Sunday," present elaborate descriptions of Lady Fortune spinning her wheel. And a host of poems in Middle English, from *The Owl and the Nightingale* to *Winner and Waster*, make use of the formal debate. In short, the new use of old materials is a central feature of the medieval poet's practice.

But though some literary sources of the provincial poetry have been identified, we still know relatively little about what books poets had at hand in the provincial centers or what the audiences there were like. This much is certain: the works which emanated from them demonstrate a high culture. All of the great poems from the provincial centers reveal a common interest in the gentleman's pursuits—hunting, hawking, music, chess, law, the old code of chivalry, theoretical discussion of heaven and earth. It is now generally agreed that the poems also reveal something more: the technical mastery of Old English meter in the many alliterative poems from the various sections of rural England in the thirteenth and fourteenth centuries argues not so much an "alliterative revival" as a fourteenth-century renaissance within a continuous poetic tradition from Anglo-Saxon to late medieval times.

Continuous or not, it is clear that the tradition did not come down to the *Gawain*-poet in its tenth-century form. Between the Anglo-Saxon era of "wide gabled halls" and the High Middle Ages with its "chalk-white chimneys," life in England changed drastically. Simple adornment of jewels and gold plate evolved to splendid ornamental shields, carved fretwork, gold-trammeled tapestry work from Toulouse and Tars; the plated boar's head helmet gave way to riveted steel and the Near Eastern helmet cover intricately wrought of crochet work, rubies, diamonds, and plumes; the simple scheme of protector and retainers became the elaborate feudal system emanating from God. Poetic theory reflected this efoliation. (One can see the change coming, perhaps, in the Old English poetry of Cynewulf, when he fashions a picture of the cross in the scheme of human relationships in *Elene*, when he weaves a runic signature into his verse, or when he shifts, in his comments on art, into rhyme.) By the late fourteenth century, especially in the northwest and in Scotland, elaborate prosodic devices are the fashion. *Gawain* is only one of many poems which play classic Old English alliterative long lines against French rhyme in a bob and wheel. The *Pearl* is only one of many poems in which stanzas are interlinked by verbal repetition. Consider the extreme ingenuity of "Summer Sunday," a poem the *Gawain*-poet may have known:

SUMMER SUNDAY

[?*A Lament for Edward II, 1327*]

—Anonymous

On a summer Sunday I saw the sun
　　Rising up early on the rim of the east:
Day dawned on the dunes, dark lay the town;
　　I caught up my clothes, I would go to the groves in haste;
With the keenest of kennel-dogs, crafty and quick to sing,
　　And with huntsmen, worthies, I went at once to the woods.
So rife on the ridge the deer and dogs would run
　　That I liked to loll under limbs in the cool glades
　　　　　　And lie down.
　　　　　The kennel-dogs quested the kill
　　　　　With barking bright as a bell;
　　　　　Disheartened the deer in the dell
　　　　　And made the ridge resound.

Ridge and rill resounded with the rush of the roes in terror
　　And the boisterous barking the brilliant bugle bade.
I stood, stretched up, saw dogs and deer together
　　Where they slipped under shrubs or scattered away in the shade.
There lords and ladies with lead-leashes loitered
　　With fleet-footed greyhounds that frolicked about and played.
And I came to the ground where grooms began to cry orders,
　　And walked by wild water and saw on the other side
　　　　　　Deep grass.

I sauntered by the stream, on the strand,
And there by the flood found
A boat lying on the land;
    And so I left the place.

So I left the place, more pleased with my own way,
    And wandered away in the woods to find who I'd find.
I lounged a long while and listened—on a slope I lay—
    Where I heard not a hound or a hunter or hart or hind.
So far I'd walked I'd grown weary of the way;
    Then I left my little game and leaned on a limb
And standing there I saw then, clear as day,
    A woman with a wonderful wheel wound by the wind.
            I waited then.
        Around that wheel were gathered
        Merry men and maids together;
        Most willingly I went there
            To try my fortune.

Fortune, friend and foe, fairest of the dear,
    Was fearful, false, and little of faith, I found.
She spins the wheel to weal and from weal to woe
    In the running ring like a roebuck running round.
At a look from that lovely lady there,
    I gladly got into the game, cast my goods to the ground.
Ah, could I recount, count up, cunning and clear,
    The virtues of that beauty who in bitterness bound
            Me tight!
        Still, some little I'll stay
        To tell before turning away—
        All my reasons in array
            I'll readily write.

Readily I'll write dark runes to read:
    No lady alive is more lovely in all this land;
I'd go anywhere with that woman and think myself glad,
    So strangely fair her face; at her waist, I found,
The gold of her kirtle like embers gleamed and glowed.
    But in bitter despair that gentle beauty soon bound
Me close, when her laughing heart I had given heed.
    Wildly that wonderful wheel that woman wound
            With a will.
        A woman of so much might,
        So wicked a wheel-wright,
        Had never struck my sight,
            Truth to tell.

Truth to tell, sitting on the turf I saw then
   A gentleman looking on, in a gaming mood, gay,
Bright as the blossoms, his brows bent
   To the wheel the woman whirred on its way.
It was clear that with him all was well as the wheel went,
   For he laughed, leaned back, and seemed at ease as he lay.
A friendly look toward me that lord sent,
   And I could imagine no man more merry than he
          In his mind.
        I gave the knight greeting.
        He said, "You see, my sweeting,
        The crown of that handsome king?
         I claim it as mine!

      "As mine to me it will come:
      As King I claim the kingdom,
      The kingdom is mine.
      To me the wheel will wind.
      Wind well, worthy dame;
      Come fortune, friendly game;
      Be game now, and set
      Myself on that selfsame seat!"

I saw him seated then at splendid height,
   Right over against the rim of the running ring;
He cast knee over knee as a great king might,
   Handsomely clothed in a cloak and crowned as a king.
Then high of heart he grew in his gambling heat;
   Laid one leg on the other leg and sat lounging;
Unlikely it looked that his lordship would fall in the bet·
   All the world, it seemed, was at his wielding
          By right.
        On my knees I kissed that king.
        He said, "You see, my sweeting,
        How I reign by the ring,
         Most high in might?

      "Most high in might, queen and knight
      Come at my call.
      Foremost in might,
      Fair lords at my foot fall.
      Lordly the life I lead,
      No lord my like is living,
      No duke living need I dread,
      For I reign by right as King."

                                          THE GAWAIN-POET

Of kings it seems most sad to speak and set down
  How they sit on that seemly seat awhile, then in wastes are in sorrow
    sought.
I beheld a man with hair like the leaves of the horehound,
  All black were his veins, his brow to bitterness brought;
His diadem with diamonds dripped down
  But his robes hung wild, though beautifully wrought;
Torn away was his treasure—tent, tower, town—
  Needful and needing, naked; and nought
          His name.
          Kindly I kissed that prince.
          He spoke words, wept tears;
          Now he, pulled down from his place,
            A captive had become.

          "Become a captive outcast,
          Once mighty kings would call
          Me king. From friends I fall,
          Long time from all love, now little, lo! at the last.
          Fickle is fortune, now far from me;
          Now weal, now woe,
          Now knight, now king, now captive."
A captive he had become, his life a care;
  Many joys he had lost and all his mastery.
Then I saw him sorrier still and hurt still more:
  A bare body in a bed, on a bier they bore him past me,
A duke driven down into death, hidden in the dark.

The ornamental devices in "Summer Sunday" are unusually intricate. Lines both alliterate and rhyme, and in certain sections the last word of a line is the same as the first word of the next line in the same stanza; stanzas are linked by verbal repetition; separate episodes are linked by the image of the circle; and the shape of the stanzas in the poem comes to be reversed, reflecting the thematic reversal of Fortune. But though this poem is, like the work of the *Gawain*-poet, intricate, many of the same devices are to be found, in isolation or together, in even the most slipshod popular poetry of the day. And since they appear frequently, rhyme linking, combined alliteration and rhyme, and other entirely ornamental devices can doubtless be considered conventional. Thus, to the extent that it is merely ornamental, we probably ought to consider conventional even the *Gawain*-poet's "signature," his characteristic use of a particular phrase or stylistic device at the beginning and end of each of his poems. (The same device appears in some Scottish poetry.)

The real significance of the *Gawain*-poet's devices is not simply that he uses them, but rather that his use of them is meticulous—his alliterative rules are unusually rigorous—and that his devices normally embody a direct fusion of form and content. Take, for example, the *Pearl*. Gollancz pointed out that the twelve-line stanzas of the *Pearl* are perhaps best viewed as primitive sonnets. (His view has for some reason not been widely accepted, but he is right that sonnets of roughly the same type appear in Italy before Dante.) If we accept Gollancz' suggestion, or at any rate if we are able to see each stanza as, at least much of the time, more or less a unit in itself, developing a single dramatic tension, image, or philosophical idea, then the linked ring of one hundred (or, surely by accident, one hundred and one)[15] stanzas in the *Pearl* has symbolic relationship to the transmutation within the poem of flower imagery into jewel imagery (Nature into Art), reflecting the contrast between mortal life and eternal life. Thus the circular poem becomes the artistic reflection of the "garland" of the blessed (a circle of artificial flowers) about the throne of God.[16]

If we believe that the poet had some reason for linking stanzas and organizing other material as he did, we are, I think, forced to conclude that number symbolism of an ingenious sort is also used in the poem. *Three* is the mystical number of the Trinity, complement of the tripartite soul in man, and it may also suggest unity and completion, the Pythagorean "beginning, middle, and end." This Pythagorean (and Christian) use of three appears as an element in the five-part structure of the poem. The first and last five-stanza sections frame a dream that comes in three parts which, as we shall see later, may be interpreted as presenting together the whole of Christian illumination. *Five*, the number of linked stanzas in each section, has various associations as we learn in the *Gawain*, but most commonly suggests the five joys of Mary and the five wounds of Christ, both of which associations are appropriate in the *Pearl*, where the Virgin is both emblem and road of man's salvation and where the blood of Christ functions throughout as a controlling symbol. In the first of the three sections of the dream the central image is a stream, a detail

THE GAWAIN-POET

borrowed from courtly French and Italian poetry but explicitly identified here as the river in Paradise, which for the patristic exegetes is a "sign" or foreshadowing of the "well-spring," Christ (cf. John 7:38). The second section of the dream focuses first on the parable of the vineyard, hence, symbolically—and this too is made explicit in the poem—the "wine" or blood by which man is redeemed, and then (starting at stanza 51) on grace, which comes to be identified with "Water and blood of the wide wound." The third section of the dream identifies blood, grace, light, and music. *Ten* is in a different way a number of completion. (Ten times ten is the number of stanzas probably intended.) St. Augustine writes:

> Again, the number ten signifies a knowledge of the Creator and the creature; for the trinity is the Creator and the septenary indicates the creature by reason of his life and body. For with reference to life there are three, whence we should love God with all our hearts, with all our souls, and with all our minds; and with reference to the body there are very obviously four elements of which it is made.[17]

Four, or the square, is traditionally associated with world-wide extension (four winds, four evangelists), and for Augustine it is also emblematic of time (four seasons, four parts of the day). Thus at the end of time, on the day of the Last Judgment, Christ reads from a book with square pages. (This image is not found in the Apocalypse but is introduced by the poet.) *Twelve*—a number repeatedly mentioned in the final section of the *Pearl*—is the number of the Mystical Body, the Church Universal, and is thus also the number of salvation. In addition to the relevance of specific symbolic numbers to the theme of the *Pearl*, number symbolism has a general relevance in that mathematical relationships, unlike human beings or roses, are immutable. Boethius writes that mathematics deals with the *intelligible* and finds that

> it itself includes the first or *intellectible* part in virtue of its own thought and understanding, directed as these are to the celestial works of supernal divinity and to whatever sublunary beings enjoy more blessed mind and purer substance, and, finally, to human souls. All of these things, though they once consisted of that primary intellectible substance, have since, by contact with bodies, degenerated from the level of intellectibles to that of intelligibles; as a result, they are less objects of under-

standing than active agents of it, and they find greater happiness by the purity of their understanding whenever they apply themselves to the study of things intellectible.[18]

And Hugh of St. Victor, commenting on this passage, writes:

For the nature of spirits and souls, because it is incorporeal and simple, participates in intellectible substance; but because through the sense organs spirit or soul descends in different ways to the apprehension of physical objects and draws into itself a likeness of them through its imagination, it deserts its simplicity somehow by admitting a type of composition.[19]

Thus by the use of mystical numbers the poet reinforces the central contrast in the poem between the soul in Nature and the soul liberated from Nature.

The "signature" in the *Pearl* is equally functional. The contrast between the first and last lines of the poem focuses the conflict between unselfishness and selfishness, or in exegetical language, between a proper and reasonable view of earthly treasure, on one hand, and on the other, "concupiscence" in the theological sense, an undue regard for the things of this world.

Ornamental devices are less conspicuous in the *Gawain*, mainly because the symbolic extension of the surface action is more deeply embedded in the poem. The alliterative long lines are appropriate, though only in the most general way, reflecting the ancient English poetic mode in a poem purporting to deal with ancient native tradition. (The *Gawain*-stanza, sometimes modified in one way or another, is common in courtly provincial verse and may itself have been regarded as traditional.) The bob and wheel device found in this poem is sometimes merely decorative, but it does often have an important thematic or dramatic function. For instance, in the opening lines the poet writes:

Felix Brutus

On the slopes of many broad hills established Britain

with joy,

Where war and wrack and wonder

Have sometimes since held sway,

And now bliss, now blunder,

Turned like dark and day.

[part i, st. i, ll. 13–19]

Here all that follows the pivotal phrase "with joy" (the "bob") contrasts with the force of that phrase, setting up an irony which extends to the whole of the poem. (The four lines which follow the "bob" comprise the "wheel.") The "signature" in the *Gawain*, the opening and closing concern with the fall of Troy, is relevant to the central conflict in the poem between the vulnerability of mortal kingdoms and the permanence of the Kingdom of God.

In some respects the most interesting of the *Gawain*-poet's signatures—if we may rightly call it a full-blown signature—is that in *St. Erkenwald*. The signature here involves not verbal repetition but the repetition of a stylistic device. The poem opens:

> At London in England no long while since—
> Since when Christ suffered on the cross and Christendom was built—
> There was a bishop. . . .

The last two stanzas of the poem read:

> For as soon as that soul was established in bliss,
> That other creation that covered the bones corrupted;
> For the everlasting life, the life without end,
> Voids all that vanity that avails man nothing.

> Then was there praising of the Lord and the lifting of hymns:
> Mourning and joy in that moment came together.
> They passed forth in procession, and all the people followed,
> And all the bells of the city sang out at once.

The poet's repetition is stylistic: "since, since" in the opening lines has its echo in "all the people . . . all the bells" which appears in the closing lines. The echo calls attention to the relationship between the two passages. Both contrast London (a particular point in space) and the spatial concept of universal Christendom, earth and heaven; and both passages also contrast historical time and time as it exists in the mind of God. The opening lines set up a concept of time stretching backward out of sight. In terms of such a concept, St. Erkenwald lived not long ago and Christ not a very long while before that. The end of the poem, on the other hand, focuses on "the everlasting life, the life without end," introducing a concept of time stretching forward out of sight. The contrast of finite and infinite time and space is central to the organization of the poem, accounting not only for the historical material and the bishop's prayer for more than mortal wisdom, but also for specific images throughout—the runes on the coffin, undecipherable to mortal reason; the crowd which gathers like "all the world . . . in an instant"; the chess image in which, when the human mind is checkmated, God moves one pawn and recasts the whole game. At last this contrast between the finite and the infinite becomes the poet's artistic justification of the miracle. And so what might have been merely ornamental in the work of another medieval poet becomes in the hands of the *Gawain*-poet both the thing said and the way of saying it.

For the *Gawain*-poet, plots, images, and certain rhetorical devices were also largely a matter of convention. It has often been pointed out that the two most elaborately developed symbols in *Sir Gawain and the Green Knight*, the shield and the girdle, are standard devices for characterization in medieval poetry. In the alliterative *Morte Arthure* (almost certainly earlier than the *Gawain*) shields are the usual means of identifying a knight's particular virtues; and in *The Parliament of the Three Ages*, as in Chaucer and elsewhere, the girdle or waistband (on which one hangs one's moneybags) is the usual detail singled out to suggest a man's concern with possessions. But the *Gawain*-poet's use of the standard devices is ingenious. The emblem on Arthur's shield in the *Morte Arthure*, a picture of the Virgin, is transferred to the *inside* of Gawain's shield to show, as the poet explicitly tells us, the source of Gawain's inner strength; and for the usual gryphon on the outside of Gawain's shield the poet substitutes a pentangle indicative of his strength—that is, his virtues—as seen from outside. With the shield, as Donald R. Howard has pointed out, Gawain serves the world but stands aloof from it; with the girdle he serves himself.[20] No such ingenious use of the two images, and no such juxtaposition of the two, can be found outside *Sir Gawain and the Green Knight*.

Borrowing plots, descriptions, even especially elegant lines from the work of other poets was standard practice in the Middle Ages—as it has been among good poets of almost every age, for that matter. At its best this borrowing becomes imperatorial confiscation. Thus Chaucer seized Boccaccio's elegant and slight *Il Filostrato* and trans-

THE GAWAIN-POET

formed it into the greatest tragic poem in English; and thus Shakespeare transformed the curious tragedies of earlier poets into the world's most powerful modern drama.

The artistry in poetic borrowing can also lie in adapting borrowed material to its new context without obscuring its meaning in the original context, for here the poet's object is not to confiscate but rather to enrich meaning by playing one context against another. Only if the reader remembers that the revels of Arthur's court are usually licentious can he see the humor in the poet's pious celebration of the Christmas revels which open the *Gawain*.[21] It is as though the revels were being seen through the eyes of the innocent Sir Gawain himself. It is impossible, however, to know the extent to which the *Gawain*-poet's work is meant to operate in this way. Knowing virtually nothing of his audience, we cannot know how much knowledge the poet was able to assume; and knowing almost as little of his immediate sources, we cannot be perfectly sure how much of the given poem is the poet's own. Scholarship on the *Gawain*-poet has veered between two extremes: the tendency to attribute nearly everything to the poet himself and the tendency to trace all virtues to a hypothetical source.

Undoubtedly our best clue to the poet's method is provided, as Professor Mabel Day has sensibly suggested, by the homiletic *Purity*, for here we do know most, if not all, of the poet's sources. We find in *Purity* the clear influence of the *Roman de la Rose*, Mandeville's *Travels* (in the French version), *Cursor Mundi*, *The Knight of La Tour-Landry* (probably in French), and the Vulgate Bible. In a complicated plot made up of three linked biblical episodes the poet brings these materials together, associating each episode with the other two by means of puns and verbal repetitions, and at the end of the poem he tells us that he has preached "in three ways" the same moral lesson. Since puns and verbal repetitions of the same sort appear in the other poems, we may safely suppose that he combined other materials with equal freedom and ingenuity in *Gawain*, *Patience*, the *Pearl*, and *St. Erkenwald*.

If we make this supposition, we can make guesses concerning the extent to which the poet extended or modified tradition in such poems as the *Gawain*, even though the exact sources are unknown.

In the *Gawain* two old motifs appear, the Beheading Game (parts 1 and 4) and the Temptation (part 3).[22] Both the general outline of the Green Knight's challenge and the general outline of the Temptation are common, the first deriving from a Cuchulain legend of about the ninth century, the second perhaps deriving from the thirteenth-century French *Yder*. The parallels are slight between the *Gawain* and known versions of the two motifs, especially with regard to the Temptation, and many details in the *Gawain*-poet's treatment of the two motifs come from sources which have nothing to do with either. Given the poet's combination of diverse materials in *Purity* and given the obvious coherence of the *Gawain*, we have every reason to suppose that the combination of diverse materials here is the poet's own work and not, as Kittredge suggested in 1916, work done in a lost French original. Certain details are unquestionably of English origin (the legendary founding of Britain and the arming of Gawain); and a few details are clearly peculiar to our poet (for instance, the stanzas on the turning of the seasons at the beginning of part 2). And to the extent that all elements in the poem are interrelated to form a coherent and balanced whole—both literal and symbolic—from which no part can be removed without serious damage to the poem on both levels, we can be absolutely certain that the interrelationship, together with the resulting aesthetic effect, is to be credited to the *Gawain*-poet himself. Once the structure of the poem has been understood, once it has been recognized that we are dealing here not with borrowing but with total transformation of old material, the search outside the poem for the poem's meaning becomes pure pedantry. But internal analysis does have a limitation, nevertheless. What it cannot show, and what must therefore be left to the scholarship of the future, is the straight or ironic play of text against source. Reading the *Gawain* may be roughly equivalent to reading "The Waste Land" without knowledge of Eliot's sources.

Perhaps the single most important set of poetic conventions open to the medieval poet came from the poetry of courtly love. The central metaphor in the *Divine Comedy*, the identification of Beatrice as the Neoplatonic Christian image of the ideal—Truth, Beauty, Goodness—derives from this poetry. Chaucer's dream-visions, *Troilus*, and much of the *Canterbury Tales* all draw from the same well. A good deal of the *Gawain*-poet's meaning will escape us if we are not familiar with the common devices used in the poetry of courtly love. Take, for example, the conventional love bower or garden. In the *Book of the Duchess*, the dreamer comes upon a "floury grene" which is

> Ful thikke of gras, ful softe and swete,
> With floures fele, faire under fete,
> And litel used, hyt semed thus;
> For both Flora and Zephirus,
> They two that make floures growe,
> Had mad her dwellynge ther, I trowe;
> For hit was, on to beholde
> As thogh the erthe envye wolde
> To be gayer than the heven,
> To have moo floures, swiche seven
> As in the welken sterres bee.
> Hyt had forgete the povertee
> That wynter, thorgh hys colde morwes,
> Had mad hyt suffre, and his sorwes,
> All was forgeten, and that was sene.
> For al the woode was waxen grene. . . .
>
> [*Book of the Duchess*, ll. 399–414]

The same sort of garden is to be found in the *Roman de la Rose*, in Dante, and in a hundred other places. It is a garden from which mutability has been banished—or rather, one is usually given to understand, a garden from which mutability *appears* to have been banished. The garden looks back to the unfallen Paradise, a poetic subject at least as old as the *Ave Phoenice*, source of the Old English *Phoenix*.[23] It represents Nature at her best, and so it contrasts both with Nature as we usually see her and with the immutable idea of which Nature is a corporeal embodiment. If we are familiar with this conventional garden, there is a beautiful irony for us in that passage in *Patience* where Jonah, sheltered from the burning sun by a lovely green bower of woodbine which God has erected around him, thinks of his arbor as a lover's bower. God is indeed Jonah's lover—a point poor Jonah misses—and this bower, like every lover's paradise, is a mutable thing which can be thrown to the ground in an instant. Looking at the bower in worldly terms, Jonah puts his hopes on false felicity. In the *Pearl* the idea of the earthly paradise is explored in quite different terms. The poem opens in a garden which is the conventional love garden in all respects but one: it is a real arbor, where mutability has *not* been banished. The tension between the actuality of the garden and the idealism of the convention suggested by its description is moving in itself, and it also prepares for the narrator's vision of the true Paradise in his dream. But the poet's most complex treatment of the conventional garden comes in *Sir Gawain and the Green Knight*. The white castle Gawain comes upon, surprisingly, in the center of a grim, dark forest, is a paradise of ambiguous meaning as are most such paradises, but ambiguous in unusually ominous ways. It is at once an unfallen Paradise, a factitious heaven, a garden of Venus, the land of Faery, Asgaard, and the haunt of Druids.

The garden is only one of many conventional devices from courtly-love poetry used in old or new ways in the work of the *Gawain*-poet. Another is the formal paradox familiar to every reader through Renaissance Petrarchan poetry or through Chaucer. Chaucer's Black Knight says:

> My song ys turned to pleynynge,
> And al my laughtre to wepynge,
> My glade thoghtes to hevynesse;
> In travayle ys myn ydelnesse
> And eke my reste; my wele is woo,
> My good ys harm, and evermoo
> In wrathe ys turned my pleynge
> And my delyt into sorwynge. . . .

[*Book of the Duchess*, ll. 599–606]

This formal balance of opposing concepts is used by the *Gawain*-poet when Sir Abraham bargains with God to save Sodom; it is transformed into a vehicle for strong emotion in the dreamer's plea for the compassion of his pearl; and it becomes rich comedy in Sir Gawain's sophistical attempts to fend off the amorous lady of the castle. Still another conventional element is, of course, the device of the dream-vision itself. The device is obviously central in the *Pearl*, and combining with traditions of fairy magic it becomes the basis of the mystery and uncertainty which pervade the *Gawain*. When the Green Knight enters King Arthur's court all sounds die out as if everyone in the hall had suddenly slipped off into sleep, and the

THE GAWAIN-POET

green man seems a magical phantom or an illusion. By means of a pun, Middle English *prayere*, the *Gawain*-poet leaves a trace of doubt whether the castle in the forest is "pitched on a prairie" or pitched "on a prayer." That trace of doubt is perhaps strengthened by our recollection that dream paradises so often come after pathless wandering in great, dark forests; and for the poet's immediate audience that hint may have been further reinforced by the recognition that whereas the general area of Gawain's search and the Green Chapel to which he comes in the end were real and recognizable places, there had never in the memory of man been a castle or any sign of one in the area.[24] On the other hand, the castle does not go up in smoke as Morgan's phantom castles ordinarily do. Nothing is certain. That is an important part of the meaning of the poem.

As all we have said thus far should suggest, another very important aspect of medieval poetic convention is what we may call the idea of symbolic equation. The idea is rooted in the medieval view of the cosmos. Scholastic thinkers speak of two "books" by which man may learn his road to salvation. One is Nature; the other, Scripture. Before the Fall, man could perceive God's revelation of Himself directly, by looking at His created works. But, as Bonaventura puts it, "turning himself away from the true light to mutable goods, he was bent over by his own sin, and the whole human race by original sin, which doubly infected human nature, ignorance infecting man's mind and concupiscence his flesh."[25] Now Nature carries, for man, only "vestiges" or "traces" of the divine hand, and to be saved he needs a clearer text, one which, incidentally, helps him to understand that first text, Nature, which has become hopelessly obscured. The clearer text is Scripture, God's new revelation not only of Himself but also of what he wished man to see, in allegorical and moral terms, when he looked at the oak tree, the serpent, the rose. As elements of God's self-revelation, all superficially similar things in Nature may be seen as types of one another and of something higher; thus (as the earlier exegetes had it) all Nature is a vast array of emblems.

The literary importance of patristic exegesis may easily be exaggerated or misunderstood, but exegetical symbolism can by no means be dismissed as a possibility within any given poem by anyone seriously concerned with the meaning of medieval poetry to its immediate audience. Indeed, the basic technique has come down to us practically unchanged in the work of, for instance, Melville and Faulkner. Petrarch, Boccaccio, and Dante—poets of enormous influence in their day—all subscribed to a theory of criticism developed roughly in terms of the three-fold system of the exegetes. They would all differ profoundly, however, with the New Exegetes. Boccaccio, for instance, denies that any good poet would ever intentionally introduce obscurities for the purpose of withholding his meaning from any reader,[26] and neither in his criticism (in the *Genealogy of the Gods*) nor in his own poetry does he apply this system or any other system rigidly. But the early Italian poets were unanimous in their opinion that good poetry was inspired and that the method of poetry was the method of the Holy Ghost. Indeed, the theory that poetry comes from God was still vital enough in Sidney's day to provide the first argument in his *Defence*, though Sidney was not much interested in what was earlier supposed to be the exact method of divine inspiration.

It is a commonplace that the Middle Ages saw the world as ordered, but in a practical way we might as easily characterize the medieval world as one of celestial disturbances, terrestrial plagues, witch-hunts, slums, devastating fires, crop failures, earthquakes, physical and mental sickness, bloodletting, peasant revolts, corruption in church and state, wolves and boars a mile outside London, and, above all, endless, apparently hopeless, thoroughly wasteful war. Men have always known that what *is* is not necessarily what ought to be, and disorder seen on every hand heightens man's need for a conceptual scheme of order. On the basis of divine revelation and the essential, though not always evident, order in Nature—the regular succession of generation, corruption, and regeneration—the Middle Ages worked out its schemes. The best minds of the period went into the work, drawing hints wherever they might be found—from Aristotle, from fragmentary third-hand accounts of Plato's thought, from Vergil, Ovid, Statius, old mythologies, and, above all, of course, from the Bible.

That the Bible was directly inspired by God went without saying; and since the Bible, the work of perfect wisdom, had obvious obscurities and seeming contradictions, it was clear that when speaking to man, God chose to speak in dark conceits. The whole truth, embracing infinite time and space, would doubtless be too much for mortal minds. Moreover, a man had to prove himself worthy of truth; it must not come to him easily but must follow from diligence.[27] Man's work, then, was to decipher as well as possible the dark conceits of God and thus to discover as much as he could of the total system. What medieval exegetes found, playing one scriptural text against another in accordance with the accepted principles of classical Greek literary criticism, was that, like ancient Greek poetry, the Bible worked on several levels—sometimes on one level at a time, sometimes on all levels at once. The levels were these:[28]

1. *The Literal or Historical Sense.* On the first and most obvious level, the intent of Scripture is that which the words signify in their natural and proper acceptation, as in John 10:30, "I and the Father are one," in which passage the deity of Christ and His equality with God the Father are distinctly asserted. The literal sense has also been called the grammatical sense, the term *grammatical* having the same reference to the Greek language as the term *literal* to the Latin, both referring to the elements of a word. When words are taken metaphorically or figuratively, diverted to a meaning they do not naturally carry but which they nevertheless intend, as when the properties of one person or thing are attributed to another, they operate not on the literal level but on some other. Thus the adjective "hardness" applies literally to stone, figuratively to the heart. On the literal level, those narratives which purport to be true accounts of historical events are to be read as certain history; but this is not to say that they may not operate on other levels as well. When the Jews are said to "possess" or "inherit the land"— phrases of frequent occurrence in the Old Testament—the literal meaning is that the Jews are to hold secure and undisturbed possession of their promised land; but the phrases have figurative meaning as well, having reference to the Christian's possession of the life everlasting.

2. *The Allegorical Sense* (sometimes treated as merely a mode of the anagogical and tropological senses). On a second level, Scripture signifies, besides or instead of the literal meaning, things having to do

with faith or spiritual doctrine. It is this level that is most likely to embarrass the modern reader, for it frequently does violence to obvious surface meaning. And it is their insistence upon reading medieval poetry as though it worked in this way and in no other that is most troublesome in the interpretations of the New Exegetes, Robertson and Huppé, for instance.[29] Bonaventura's comments upon Christ's cry on the cross, "I thirst," will serve to illustrate. Bonaventura writes:

> Earlier, as the hour of His passion was approaching, the most sweet Jesus *fell prostrate and prayed, saying: "Father, if it is possible, let this cup pass away from Me."* He said this not once but a second and a third time; and by the cup He was to drink He meant the passion He was to suffer. Now, having emptied this same cup of the passion, He says: "*I thirst.*" What does He mean?
>
> Before tasting the cup, O good Jesus, You prayed that it might be taken away from You; but now, after emptying it, You thirst. How wonderful this appears! Was Your cup perhaps filled with the wine of delight, instead of humiliation and the worst bitterness? Emphatically not! It was filled with the most withering shame. This should not produce thirst, but rather aversion to drink.
>
> When, before You suffered, You prayed that the cup be removed from You, we must believe it was not a refusal of the passion itself. You had come for this very suffering, without which mankind would not have been saved. But it might have been said that, true man though You are, since You are also one with God, the bitterness of the passion did not really affect You. That is why You prayed once, twice, and even three times that the cup be removed from You: to prove to the doubters how supremely bitter was Your suffering. . . . By praying before You suffered that this cup might be taken away from You, and by saying, after it was emptied: "I thirst," You showed us how immeasurable is Your love. For this seemed to mean: Although My passion was so dreadful that, because of My human sensibility, I prayed to be saved from it, My love for you, O man, triumphed even over the torments of the cross, making Me thirst for more and greater tortures, if need be. . . .[30]

It is important to resist the temptation to dismiss commentary of this sort as lunacy, childishness, or pernicious sophistry. The practice of contemporary writers of prose fiction leads us closer, perhaps, than some generations have been to the symbolic mode of thought common in the Middle Ages, but we are nevertheless sufficiently committed to the literal or realistic to be made uncomfortable by such insistent allegorical reading. If we were in the habit of finding "signs" or "figures" all around us as some medieval people clearly were, or if, like James Joyce, we were accustomed to seeing profound philosophical significance, not mere linguistic accident, in puns, we would probably find interpretation like Bonaventura's somewhat less farfetched than we do. If he can avoid pursuing the principle intemperately, the student of medieval literature will do well to bear in mind Augustine's warning that

> when that which is said figuratively is taken as though it were literal, it is understood carnally. Nor can anything more appropriately be called the death of the soul than that condition in which the thing which distinguishes us from beasts, which is the understanding, is subjected to the flesh in the pursuit of the letter. He who follows the letter takes figurative expressions as though they were literal and does not refer the things signified to anything else.[31]

The corollary to this is, "Every analysis *begins* from things which are finite, or defined, and *proceeds* in the direction of things which are infinite, or undefined."[32] (The italics are mine.) One must watch for signs, particularly where no other explanation will account for details within the poem, but one should not abandon the literal level until forced to do so by the text.

3. *The Anagogical or "Typical" Sense.* On a third level, objects, actions, or prophetic visions secretly represent things present or future; more particularly, events recorded in the Old Testament presignify or adumbrate events related in the New Testament. The exegetes declare that, rightly understood, Moses' story is parallel to the stories of Adam, Noah, Joseph, Christ. The water which gushes from the rock Moses strikes is a "type" or presignification of the blood and water which gush from Christ's side; it is obversely analogous to the flood of Noah's time and symbolically analogous to the flood of sin in which man was drowned with the fall of Adam (the fiery lake in *St. Erkenwald*); and it is analogous to the flood of grace from the throne of God (first seen in the visions of Ezekiel), introduced on earth by the Holy Ghost (cf. light and water imagery in the *Pearl*). The job of patristic exegesis was to determine the exact nature of the relationships, and the result of exegesis was an elaborate symbology (or "typology") in which, for instance, grapes,

wine, blood, wheat, bread, the lamb, the lily, the rose, the pearl, the lion, the falcon, the temple, the number *eight*, and so forth, become emblematic of Christ or attributes of Christ. Appearing in paintings, church windows, fretwork, sermons, and popular songs, this system of relationships comes to be—at least potentially—the shared tradition of all medieval men and thus material for poetry. Within the framework of typology the poet has two alternatives. He may retell biblical stories, introducing new typic images or situations which further elaborate or extend an orthodox typic interpretation; or he may introduce into a non-biblical story images or situations which establish a biblical parallel or group of parallels and which thus encourage an allegorical reading of the otherwise realistic or literal story.

4. *The Moral or Tropological Sense.* On the final level, Scripture tells us of the progress of the soul: the nature of man before and after the Fall, the conditions of his salvation, and the terms and impediments of redemption. The parable of the talents, for example, shows on the tropological level (according to one account) that the duties which men are called to perform are suited to their situations and the talents which they have received, that whatever a good man possesses he has received from God, together with the ability to improve that good, and that the grace and temporal mercies of God are suited to the power a man has of improving his talents.

But there is more to medieval symbolism than the system of the exegetes. Classical philosophy and feudalism introduce complications. Aristotle's basically Platonic notion of order extending from a Prime Mover through various natures or, to use the English word, kinds, became in the Middle Ages "plenitude," the scheme founded on the view that everything that could be created had been created, completing the whole range of the possible from best (the angels) to worst (the basest form of earth). The whole scheme of plenitude can be divided into discrete categories, the links of the so-called great chain of being, and within each category of Nature can be found another hierarchy from best to worst: the angels, carefully ranked from the Virtues of Heaven down, are higher than men, who are also carefully ranked from king to serf; eagles are higher than ducks; lions are higher than cows; roses are higher than brambles;

gold is higher than lead. Given such hierarchies, it becomes possible to identify a station in one hierarchy in terms of the corresponding station of some other. A king might be emblematically represented by an eagle or by gold; God, or some attribute of God, might be represented by a crown or, as in Dante and Chaucer, an eagle.

Luckily for poets, the idea of equation was not altogether rigid. Certain emblems—particularly those having Scripture as their basis—tended to be of fixed significance; but whereas Chaucer's eagles in the *Parliament of Fowls* had to be eagles, to his goose and turtle-dove, for instance, he could assign meanings of his own, based on his private intuition of what geese and turtledoves would be if they were people.

Medieval symbolism is further complicated by heraldry with all its monsters, lions, deer, boars, birds, fish, reptiles, insects, plants, flowers, rocks, each with its specific meaning, and complicated also by the "language and sentiment of flowers," whereby the soldier or lover might send quite complicated messages in a simple bouquet. Still another complication comes through courtly love, a system developed by analogy to feudalism and Scholastic Neoplatonism. If the mistress is identified, in jest or in earnest, with God or the Supreme Good, and if Love is treated as a feudal lord, all symbols applicable to Christianity or feudalism may be transferred to the scheme of love.

The modern reader may well inquire how he is to make sense of poetry written for an audience which took all this symbolism for granted. For the most part he probably cannot without the help of scholars. But great poetry operates on the literal as well as on symbolic levels. One need not know heraldry to understand the importance and even, in a general way, the nature of the lady's temptation of Sir Gawain, and one need not know about jewel symbolism to sense the power of the vision which concludes the *Pearl*. The discovery of symbolic reinforcement and enrichment of the poet's literal narrative is not a starting point but a time for refining interpretation.

Finally, though, one does want to know what the *Gawain*-poet's symbols mean and the extent to which his handling of symbols is merely conventional. Where scholars can offer no sure explanations, the meanings of symbols—indeed, the extent to which the poems are symbolic—must be a matter of personal conjecture. As for the poet's contribution to tradition, we know at least this: most of the identifiable symbolism to be found in the *Pearl*, *Purity*, *Patience*, and *St. Erkenwald* can be found outside the work of the *Gawain*-poet; but the transitions from one symbolic identification to another and the personal emotion which charges the symbolic identifications are certainly the poet's own contributions. The symbolism in the *Gawain* gives more trouble. Structure points to possible symbolic identifications, but just what the identifications may mean no one has so far shown convincingly. The armor and appearance of the Green Knight are described in detail in part 1; in part 2, the arming of Gawain is developed in a parallel way; in part 3, Gawain is dressed up for Christmas festivities; and in part 4, the arming of Gawain is described once again. So far we have little idea what, if anything, the ritualistic armings mean. Critics have had just as much trouble with the Green Knight himself. How close was the poet to his ultimate mythical source (Gawain as sun-god)?[33] Did he intend a direct identification of the Green Knight as the "green man"? What is the meaning of the poet's consistent characterization of the Green Knight as a sophisticated adult with a keen sense of humor, a man thoroughly unlike those overly earnest "beardless babes," King Arthur and his court? Is there any significance in the fact that the huge knight's colors are green, gold, and red? And what is the significance of his hunting trips? It is possible to work out by internal analysis convincing answers to many of these questions, but the answers remain conjectural.

3.

THE GĀWĀIN=POET'S
VISION OF REĀLITY

In his religion, as in his choice of genres, the *Gawain*-poet was a traditionalist.[34] The central concerns in all his poems are the characteristic concerns of Scholastic philosophy, particularly, as various critics have shown, the philosophy of Augustine (a source in the *Pearl* and elsewhere). That he also draws indirectly at least from Bonaventura has not yet been demonstrated but seems likely in the light of some of his imagery and, perhaps, his structural devices (see my discussion of the *Pearl* and *Gawain* below).

A related influence on the poet's vision of reality is his apparently deep emotional commitment to feudalism, a system already on the wane in the fourteenth century. Professor Henry Savage has pointed out that such a commitment is not unnatural in a Yorkshire or Lancashire poet, for whereas in London the middle class was already able to urge its importance, for the man who lived in the northwest Midlands all benefits depended upon the "grace" of a feudal lord.[35] If, like Chaucer, the *Gawain*-poet was born into the middle class, as he probably was, his welfare must have depended upon some such lord. If that judgment was wise, and if, furthermore, the alternative to feudalism was anarchy, as it certainly was in most of rural England in the poet's day, then the poet's emotional commitment to the feudal scheme must have been all but inevitable. This commitment was no doubt as much religious as social. Scholastic writers frequently speak of Christ as a king and of Christians as his soldiers or knights; and since terrestrial kings are, in this view, the direct vassals of God, loyalty to one's king in this world is one with loyalty to God.

Another influence, mentioned already in another connection, is the scheme of courtly love. This influence is clear in all of the poet's work, but in the *Pearl* and the *Gawain* it is especially marked. The Virgin in the *Pearl* is the "Queen of Courtesy," and the narrator's first complaint is that he is "fordolked of luf-daungere" or cheated (symbolically by Christ the Bridegroom) of his love-right. Gawain's main problem is that of maintaining his Christian and chivalric codes without insulting or failing in his service to a lady. Whereas the poet takes Christian dogma as unimpeachable, he views feudalism and courtly love and also the chivalric code (which has reference to both feudalism and courtly love) more critically, recognizing them as noble but nonetheless human constructions which may or may not perfectly interpret the order of the cosmos.

A further element in the poet's view of reality is Nature. We have said that the poet's emotional response to Nature is everywhere evident in his work. We must add that theories as well as emotions are involved in that response. He sees Nature at least partly in the orthodox Christian way, as a test of the human soul, and medieval theology and psychology establish the terms of the test. As we learn in the *Pearl*, *Purity*, and *Gawain* (and the view is standard in Scholastic thought), man lost in the Fall the purity of his soul. In terms of medieval psychology, the soul is in fact three souls, the *rational* (loosely, "reason"), the *irascible* (loosely, "mettle" or "spirit"), and the *concupiscent* (loosely, "desire"). Before the Fall all three elements in the tripartite soul were noble; after the Fall all three were corrupted, weighted by what Plotinus in his system called the "indeterminate"—in Christian dualistic terms the non-spiritual quality, Nature. This corruption exists partly in fact, partly in potential. The Fall dimmed the mind so that we now cannot see God; but though we are made gross by Nature, we are still born virtually innocent. Original sin makes necessary God's extension of grace, but the child who has been baptized, that is, granted grace, goes directly to heaven if it dies before sinning on its own. Thus the Fall is re-enacted in every individual life.[36] Every man comes sooner or later to his Eden—as Gawain does in the forest and as the pearl would have done had she not died young. Given the fallen condition of man, the best defense one has in the test which is life on earth, the time of trial in Nature, is the careful ordering of one's dimmed soul in order to direct one's rational part, one's irascible part, and one's concupiscent part as nobly as possible.

But though the *Gawain*-poet accepts the view that Nature is a test, his view is not quite dualistic, like the view of the earlier exegetes or that of the later hermetic philosophers. Like Chaucer, but perhaps with less conviction, the *Gawain*-poet sees Nature as the vicegerent of God. Like Bonaventura, Hugh of St. Victor, and others, he sees in fallen Nature traces or *vestigia* of the divine. Unluckily, all this cannot be proved as certainly for the *Gawain*-poet as it can for Chaucer. The *Gawain*-poet nowhere introduces an explicit Dame Nature on a hill of flowers, nowhere presents in allegorical fashion the neo-Aristotelian concern with generation and corruption. For the older allegorical mode he substitutes, as Chaucer does in his later work, a symbolistic technique. Thus in the graveyard garden in the *Pearl*:

> Well might that spot with spices spread
> Where to rot such splendid riches run,
> And blossoms yellow, blue, and red
> Bloom there bright against the sun;
> Flower and fruit can feel no blight
> Where she drove down in the dark ground:
> Each grassblade wakes in a withering seed
> Or corn were never brought to bin.
> In the good is every good begun;
> So splendid a seed, then, cannot be brought
> To nothing: Branching spices spring
> From that prized pearl without a spot.
>
> [st. 3, ll. 25–36]

And thus in *Gawain* we find the stanzas on the turning of the seasons and that fusion of Dame Nature and the ancient green man, the Green Knight himself. J. A. W. Bennett's observations on the place of Nature in Chaucer's *Parliament* are relevant here. In that poem, Bennett points out, Nature "stands in counterpoise to the austere other-worldliness that characterizes African's preaching in the

Proem. . . . The greatest achievement of the twelfth and thirteenth centuries was to make better-balanced and catholic pronouncements on the relation of man to society as well as to the physical world."[37] Poetic expression of that better balance is as much the concern of the *Gawain*-poet as it is of Chaucer, though it cannot be said that the *Gawain*-poet ever quite reached the balance of Chaucer.

Christian Neoplatonism and feudalism, and courtly love, which is analogous to both, imply modes of behavior; and the codification of those implicit modes of behavior is that splendid ideal, Christian chivalry. To the extent that this ideal code has anything at all to do with Nature as it is, it urges that Nature either withdraw to its lair or adapt itself to the ideal. As a country man the *Gawain*-poet knows that ordinarily Nature, human nature included, will never withdraw for long and will not adapt. Moreover, he sees very clearly the possible though not inevitable limitation of merely human concepts. The "courtesy" of chivalric love, which contrasts sharply with those vulgar or common kinds of love that have no rules, indeed no manners, may contrast just as sharply with the ideal of love in heaven. Thus total reality for the poet embraces extremes: one extreme is Nature, which is beautiful and noble but also, because of its mutability, physically and spiritually dangerous; the other extreme is the perfect order of heaven, which man, fallen from perfection, perceives through a glass darkly, if at all. Because he longs for the true order, and because he wants to escape as well as he can the physical and spiritual danger in Nature, man rejects or tries to overcome Nature entirely, that is, tries to affirm the heavenly ideal by adapting his behavior and molding his nature to civilized codes or patterns, forms, the immutable containers (like mathematical relationships) of the mutable. The attempt is noble, but when man presumes to judge absolutely by his code, as the narrator does in the *Pearl* or as Arthur's court does in the *Gawain*, forgetting that he himself is a part of Nature and therefore ignorant and imperfect, man becomes at once pathetic and comic. In all his poems the poet explores the tragic or comic implications of a modified Neoplatonic scheme, in which Nature stands in opposition to the Ideal, and man's rejection of Nature for an Ideal imperfectly conceived stands midway between the two.

In his best moments the poet presents erring man as simultaneously tragic and comic. The *Pearl* is a moving elegy, but it is also sometimes funny and meant to be so. The same balance of emotions informs *Patience*, and the balance finds its highest expression in *Sir Gawain and the Green Knight*, the story of one of the most noble and comic of all the earnest young idealists to be met with in books. Courtly lover par excellence, known far and wide for his mastery of the art of "love talking," poor Gawain seems never to have reflected that he might someday meet a lady who has set her heart on something more than talk. An ideal vassal, with absolute faith in the feudal courtesy of Arthur's court, where every knight has the welfare of every other at heart, Gawain seems never to have anticipated that his own judgment and that of all the court might someday be fogged by wine. The beauty of the poem is that it dramatizes a real paradox in the human condition: Gawain's ideal is contrary to Nature and therefore makes him ridiculous; but it also dignifies and, indeed, saves his life.

4.

THE POET'S DRAMATIC SENSE

English poets of the late Middle Ages are not notable for their ability
to involve the reader in the emotions of their characters. Gower
tells a workmanlike story and may sometimes stir the reader by a
pretty line, but nowhere in his work do we find an event of overwhelming dramatic immediacy. What is interesting in Gower is
the symmetry and complexity of the grand design, the way part
plays against part and theme balances theme. His poetry passes
before us like a grand procession, and what is troublesome about it
is that it seems to take forever to pass. Lydgate, though a much
better poet than he has sometimes been considered, can recount even
the legend of St. George without rousing any emotional response
whatever. Action, in Lydgate, is ritualistic, not real; that is its
charm. The encounter of St. George and the dragon is stylized to
the point of ballet. With great pomp and circumstance, the dragon
elevates its head as

> Hooly Saint George his hors smote on þe syde
> Whane he þe dragoun sawe lyfft vp his hede,
> And towardes him he proudely gan to ryde
> Ful lyche a knight with outen fere or dreede;
> Avysyly of witt he tooke goode heed,
> With his spere sharp and kene egrounde
> Thorough þe body he gaf þe feonde a wownde.[38]

Langland is more exciting, but the excitement is all in the rant,
the power of bold images; it is by no means personal involvement in
the emotions of the characters that excites us.

Professor D. W. Robertson, Jr., has commented on the peculiarly undramatic quality of medieval literature, and despite some oversights, his discussion is useful:

> The concept of vicarious experience as a valid aesthetic process, or, rather, the spontaneous inclination to indulge in it now ingrained by the massive techniques of the cinema, affects our ideas of narrative structure as well as those of characterization. A narrative in which we follow the struggling will of the protagonist, as it overcomes obstacles, tends to fall into a pattern. Romantic criticism demanded, in the first place, that a dramatic presentation include "a compendium of whatever is moving and progressive in human life," omitting the trivial and uninteresting events that clutter up most lives in actual fact. The "progressive" or dynamic aspect of the narrative demands first that we become involved in a problem that "moves" us, and second that the problem be resolved. Hence the classic modern pattern of dramatically effective narrative consists of a "rising" action in which the conflict is developed, a "high point," a "falling action," and a catastrophe. . . . But if a narrative is not designed to introduce only "moving and progressive" elements, if its appeal is intellectual rather than emotional, if it is not intended to induce vicarious emotions at all, there is no reason why it should have a plot structure of this kind. We shall find medieval narratives less unsatisfactory if we deliberately suspend our romantic expectations concerning what a good plot should be. Moreover, we shall find them less crude if we abandon the assumption that they were written "for their own sakes," or, in other words, to stimulate and relieve our emotions—for this is the true aim of a story which is "just a story." Medieval comments on the classics characteristically disregard the emotional appeal we find in them, so that we say that they "disregard the poetry." We allege further that they destroy the poetry by introducing sequential ideas. But they saw in classical narrative exactly what they expected in their own narratives.[39]

Robertson tells us a little further on that medieval art "has a life and vigor and that sureness of touch which modern critics very naturally call 'tension,' but these qualities are not dependent on the creation and manipulation of fictional emotions." And he adds that

> . . . the medieval world was innocent of our profound concern for tension. We have come to view ourselves as bundles of polarities and tensions in which, to use one formulation, the ego is caught between the omnivorous demands of the id on the one hand, and the more or less irrational restraints of the super-ego on the other. Romantic synthesis has in our day become "adjustment" or "equilibrium." . . . But the

medieval world with its quiet hierarchies knew nothing of these things. Its aesthetic, at once a continuation of classical philosophy and a product of Christian teaching, developed artistic and literary styles consistent with a world without dynamically interacting polarities.[40]

We must object to Professor Robertson's sharp distinction between intellect and emotion. It will not work even for Scholastic philosophers, much less poets. (Bonaventura speaks frequently of how "moved" he is by ideas and events, and much of the energy of medieval writers of meditations, sermons, and religious manuals goes to giving emotional vitality to accepted religious ideas.) The notion that poets ever at any time wrote wholly for our profit is unconvincing, though it may be true that on extremely rare occasions they have written entirely for our pleasure and not at all to affirm or to instruct. (I can think of no examples.) But there is an element of truth in Robertson's assertion that the medieval world was not concerned, as we are, with tension. It is difficult to miss the "polarity" in *Sir Gawain and the Green Knight* between Nature and the Code; but if Gawain is pulled in two directions we are not invited to share his anguish. We are to look on with partial detachment. If we feel no concern for Gawain, then we are for all practical purposes dead men; but the concern we feel is not his concern. When the knight comes to the Green Chapel and hears the monster honing his terrible ax, his emotion is terror, but ours is something more complicated. We sympathize with Gawain, but we also see that the situation is comic. Sir Gawain's mistakes are the mistakes of an idealist, and even as we recognize them we affirm that a man who makes them is better than the ordinary man, who would not.

The dramatic interest in medieval poetry then is not "sentimental" (in the non-pejorative sense); it does not involve us in the feelings of characters, but, instead, in the development of the action and in the meaning of that action. This is not at all something we need to suspend our modern sensibility to understand. We view the plays of Ben Jonson or Samuel Beckett with the same detachment, responding to what happens, but retaining our separate identity, our judgment. And in presenting an action to be viewed in this way (here Professor Robertson is entirely right) a poet may or may not construct his plot according to the formula of rising and falling action. Those medieval English poets who concerned themselves with action—notably Chaucer, the *Gawain*-poet, and Malory—very often chose not to construct their actions according to that formula. The *Gawain*-poet, in fact, uses what Professor Robertson has rightly labeled a "hierarchal" structure in all of his poems. The *Pearl* falls neatly into five sections, and within the three sections of the dream proper the relationship between sections is not one of cause and effect but one of a more abstract and contrived sort (as is the relationship of the four books of *Gulliver's Travels*). *Purity* falls into four distinct parts, an introduction of the theme followed by three illustrations. *Patience*, after a short Proem, falls into three balanced parts, thematically repetitive but causally progressive. And though the plot of the *Gawain*, like that of *Patience*, superficially resembles a romantic plot, the relationship between the four parts and between the subdivisions within each part is thematic and symbolic, not intrinsically causal.

Within the non-sentimental limits in which medieval poetry usually operates, the *Gawain*-poet is surpassed by no one in his sense of the dramatic. No reader can miss the dramatic power of *Sir Gawain and the Green Knight*: the at once comic and nightmarish quality of the Green Knight's arrival at Camelot; the horror and remorse of the Round Table when it realizes just what sort of game it has taken on for Gawain; the terrible winter ride of Sir Gawain, a journey in which the poet brilliantly combines, on one hand, the vague, dreamlike quality of pathless wandering in the night and, on the other, sharply visualized detail—the frozen waterfall, the shivering birds. Nor can the reader very well miss the beautifully balanced comedy and horror of Gawain's test at Hautdesert Castle (the castle of high reward) or the comically macabre quality of the scene in which the young knight, riding staunchly to the Green Chapel, hears from the well-meaning but cowardly servant the grisly habits of the creature he must meet. No one can miss the dramatic force of *Purity* either, though the doctrine there may require some defending. And surely no one can miss the power of *Patience*.

Perhaps the *Pearl*, which the nineteenth century praised so highly, stands most in need of defense on dramatic grounds. We are less interested in theological debate than were readers of the poet's own day, and to the careless reader the poem may seem little more than that. Indeed, some readers of the poem have insisted that it is not to be taken as anything but theological argument. W. H. Schofield argued that the poem is not an elegy at all, but an allegory in which the pearl functions throughout as an emblem of virginity.[41] Professor R. M. Garret offered another view, that the pearl represents the Elevated Host and that the whole experience of the narrator takes place, arbor or no arbor, inside a church.[42] Other allegorical interpretations identify the pearl as the Virgin Mary[43] and as "the sensible sweetness of God," which at the outset the narrator has lost.[44] But such narrow interpretations of the poem are unnecessary; and as Professor J. B. Fletcher pointed out when advancing his reading, which is allegorical only in part, narrow interpretations are dangerous in that they prune from the poem its emotional content. Professor René Wellek hits the point exactly, showing that although the poem certainly is a theological debate, it is a debate with a clear and urgent dramatic purpose, that of bringing relief to a grieving parent.[45] Properly speaking, the poet's mode is symbolic, not allegorical. He explores a real situation by means of images which have, quite obviously, shifting and accumulating significance. At the outset the pearl is simply a metaphor for treasure: the father's treasure, the child, is lost. Later the pearl is associated (sts. 2 and 3) with a seed; next, by a species of rapid association of thought, with the Neoplatonic good (traditionally associated with the sphere, emblem of unity and completion), the "seed" or "root" from which all goods come; and at other points in the poem the pearl is identified with immutability, art, virginity, the soul in bliss, Christ, heaven itself, the wages of the Christian (which may or may not be related on the imagistic level to the Elevated Host), and the total order of the cosmos, the pearl being an indispensable part of the whole.

Other images in the poem shift in the same way. The child is a queen, hence elevated; she is also, as queen, an emblem of courtesy; an emblem, or at any rate a reflection, of the Virgin Mary; a bride of King Christ; and a relatively important chesspiece in the game of earth against heaven. The fact that she is both queen and counselor (the latter in both the common and the legal sense) may perhaps be significant for the chess imagery in that the medieval chesspiece

46   THE GAWAIN-POET

which corresponds to our modern queen was the "fers" (cf. Chaucer's *Book of the Duchess*), which was simultaneously considered both counselor and queen.[46] The basis of the imagistic and symbolic shifts is as much emotional as intellectual—to rule out either would be a mistake. Thus, in its way, the poem is dramatic from first to last.

The opening stanzas concentrate not on the abstract idea of mutability and human imperfection but on the grief and outrage of a man whose daughter has died. Incapable of resigning himself—in fact, impatient with the whole idea of Christian resignation—the central character returns compulsively day after day to the graveyard plot where his daughter lies buried. Every detail in this opening scene has symbolic implications; for instance, it is significant that the time is August, when the harvest begins, for the detail calls up the suggestion, to be made explicit later, that the child's death may be viewed as God's harvesting of the first fruits. This detail also prepares for the parable of the vineyard and for the view of man as humble laborer on God's estate, the view which is to resolve the narrator's conflict and close the poem. But though details are symbolic, nothing here is wooden allegory. The poet scrutinizes human emotion and evokes a sympathetic though detached response through organic imagery. The cloying overripeness of August comes to be identified with the soul sick on sorrow; spices come to be identified with the sensation of spiritual suffocation; strong emotions become a rush of music, smells merge with thought, distinctions between self and the external world vanish, and the narrator faints. The dreamer finds himself now in a world where mutability is replaced by perfection, where joy leads him to "more and more"; but even as his joy mounts he comes upon a river that bars his further progress toward finer things beyond. He follows the river, searching for a fording place, and he begins to hurry, to stumble. The farther he goes, the greater the gulf between him and what he desires. Like many dreams of wish fulfillment (like many a *somnium animale* in medieval terms), the dream subtly leads the dreamer home to his nightmare. Hope enters again with the appearance of the child—a child whose identity is at first, as so often happens in dreams, uncertain—and when the dreamer little by little perceives the child's identity, when she lifts her face, the narrator says:

> It made heart sting, struck all astray,
> And ever the longer, more and more.
>
> [st. 15, ll. 179–80]

They speak across the chasm, and everything the dreamer says, with his merely human notion of things, is wrong and infuriating to the child. She answers him sharply, and at last the narrator cries out:

> "When we parted, child, we two were one;
> God forbid that we now be cross;
> We meet so seldom by tree or stone!"
>
> [st. 32, ll. 378–80]

And so the poem continues, vividly realized, to the partly painful, wholly inevitable conclusion.

St. Erkenwald is not dramatic in the way that all the other poems are, for the forces in opposition are not human; but the poem has dramatic power of a kind. Consider characteristic passages. Take, for example, St. Erkenwald's first night in London after the news has reached him concerning the miraculously preserved corpse which has all the city in an uproar:

> When he reached the cathedral known far and wide as St. Paul's,
> Many men met him on his mare with a mighty clamor;
> He commanded silence, and he did not go straight to the grave
> But calmly passed into his palace and closed the door.
>
> The dark of night drove in, and the day-bell rang,
> And St. Erkenwald was up in the early morning hours,
> Who well-nigh all night long had knelt in prayer
> Beseeching his Sovereign Lord, by His holy grace,
> To vouchsafe to him some vision, some revelation:
>
> "Unworthy as I am," said the bishop, imploring
> In honest humility, "hear my request, O Lord;
> Confirm now the faith of all Christians: Allow me to grasp
> The full depth of this mystery no mortal mind fathoms."
>
> And so long did he call out for grace that at last it was given,
> An answer from the Holy Ghost. And then came dawn.
>
> [sts. 29–32, ll. 113–27]

Or consider Erkenwald's entrance into the burial vault, which all the city fears as something monstrous, dating from the ancient days when it was thought the Devil reigned supreme in England:

THE GAWAIN-POET

The bishop crossed the flagstones—lords bowed low—
And, dressed in his gleaming vestments, he visited the tomb.
They unlocked the cloistered crypt with a clatter of keys,
And all who watched him enter were uneasy at heart.

He came to the burial place, bold barons beside him,
And the Mayor, with his guards and his mace-bearers before him;
And the guard of the ancient grave gave a full account
Of the finding of the freakish thing, then pointed with his finger:

"Behold, my lords," he said, "here lies a corpse
That has lain here locked in this place—how long, no one knows.
Yet the color of the flesh and the cloth are unblemished,
Both flesh and the finely-wrought catafalque where he lies.

"We have learned of no man alive who has lived so long
That he can recall in his mind such a king as this,
No, neither his name nor what notable deeds he did;
Yet many a poorer man has been buried, and his grave
Set in our burial rolls and recorded forever.

"And we've searched all these seven long days among old books
And uncovered not one single chronicle of this king.
He has hardly lain long enough yet, from the looks of him,
To have melted so out of mind—save by monstrous power."

"So it seems," said the holy man, consecrated bishop,
"But a miracle among men amounts to little
Compared to that Providence that the Prince of Heaven
Wields when He cares to unlock but the least of His powers.

"When all man's might is mated, his mind played out,
And all man's plans blown apart and he stands with no move,
Then easily He lets loose, with a single finger,
What all the hands under Heaven might never hold up.
When the creature's pieces swerve away from wisdom,
The Creator can give him support and can cover the loss."

[sts. 35–41, ll. 138–68]

Or for simple medieval shock, take the description of what happens
when the bishop has baptized the corpse:

And then all sound ceased; he said no more;
And suddenly his sweet face sank in and was rotted,
And all the beauty of his body turned blacker than sod
And rotten as the rotted weeds that rise up in powder.

[st. 85, ll. 341–44]

Such moments are by no means rare in the *Gawain*-poet's work.

5.

THE PEARL GROUP: INTERPRETATION

The *Pearl*, *Purity*, *Patience*, and *Sir Gawain and the Green Knight* make up a single manuscript, the Cotton Nero A.x., in the British Museum.[47] For various reasons the first three poems have long been considered the work of a single poet. There has been scholarly debate, however, about whether or not *Sir Gawain and the Green Knight* is the work of the poet who composed the poems which precede it. Most scholars now agree on philological and stylistic grounds that it is.[48] Thematic considerations fully support that judgment. In a sense, the *Gawain* is to the *Pearl*, *Purity*, and *Patience* what "The Dead" is to the stories preceding it in *Dubliners*, a symbolic restatement and summation.

The poet's theme in the *Pearl* is the contrast between what I have called "the Ideal" and "the human conception of the Ideal"—that is, between "courtesy" as it is understood in heaven and the sort of courtesy ordinarily found on earth. To develop this theme the poet focuses on a man who, as a victim of the cruelty of Nature, loses all sense of order. In a dream, this central character learns the importance of order—both the imperfect order of this world's courtesy and the perfect order of heaven's courtesy, and learns that man, existing in Nature, must struggle for Christian submission, which results in order in the soul, before he can find his proper place in the social and metaphysical orders. The poet contrasts the narrator's state with the state of the pearl, a child who died pure and was

50

therefore raised directly to heaven. The salvation of the child is the result of her purity; the salvation of the father must come mainly from patience, that is, feudal loyalty. Whereas at the outset the narrator of the *Pearl* thinks his child a treasure worth as much as the pay of a prince or (taking Middle English "paye" in its more common sense) thinks himself a prince in that he owns this "delight" worthy of a prince, at the end of the poem he resigns himself to his vassalage:

> May He grant us our place as His serving men,
> Pearls pleasing to the Prince's pay.
>
> [st. 101, ll. 1211–12]

The interwoven themes in the *Pearl*, purity and patience, are further developed in the second poem, *Purity*, and in the third poem, *Patience*. The poet argues in *Purity* that although God punishes disloyalty, or impatience, this fault in man does not kindle His wrath; only impurity—physical or spiritual uncleanness—does that. The poet's stinging attack on impurity should not surprise us when we consider the relative places of impurity and of disloyalty in his scheme. (There is no reason to believe that the biography of the poet would explain his attack on impurity, as Gollancz suggested.) From disloyalty the narrator of the *Pearl* can be won back to God; but thoroughgoing impurity precludes the passing of Nature's test by so corrupting man's nature that reason can in no way affect him. Disloyalty, a sin against God rather than the self, leaves the soul disordered but intact. In the next poem, *Patience*, the poet argues first the futility of disloyalty to an omnipotent God, then the beauty of loyal service to a God whose omnipotence is wholly in the service of His love for and loyalty to His creature. Patience is not to be confounded with mere endurance of hardship. It is, rather, virtually unlimited endurance, either in a lord or in a vassal, because of devoted love. Chaucer writes in the "Franklin's Tale:"

> For o thyng, sires, saufly dar I seye,
> That freendes everych oother moot obeye,
> If they wol longe holden compaignye.
> Love wol nat been constreyned by maistrye.
> Whan maistrie cometh, the God of Love anon

Beteth his wynges, and farewel, he is gon!
Love is a thyng as any spirit free.
Wommen, of kynde, desiren libertee,
And nat to been constreyned as a thral;
And so doon men, if I sooth seyen shal.
Looke who that is moost pacient in love,
He is at his avantage al above.
Pacience is an heigh vertu, certeyn,
For it venguysseth, as thise clerkes seyn,
Thynges that rigour sholde nevere atteyne.
For every word men may nat chide or pleyne.
Lerneth to suffre, or elles, so moot I goon,
Ye shul it lerne, wher so ye wole or noon;
For in this world, certein, ther no wight is
That he ne dooth or seith somtyme amys.

["Franklin's Tale," Fragment V (F), ll. 761–80]

Chaucer's use of the feudal concept of patience is identical to that of the *Gawain*-poet. In these lines, in fact, Chaucer sums up the whole of the *Gawain*-poet's homily.

The first poem in the Pearl Group, then, presents the whole of the poet's scheme in the form of a philosophical debate, and in the second and third poems he further elaborates the central elements of his view. In the final poem, *Sir Gawain and the Green Knight*, the poet brings together every aspect and ramification of his total scheme in a symbolic dramatization of the whole.

Before turning to a close examination of the poems, let us consider in rather general terms the theme they have in common. The disparity between the imperfect and the perfect, earth and heaven, was a common fourteenth-century philosophical concern, as central to the eminently reasonable *Summa theologica* of Aquinas as it had been to the more passionate *Confessions* of Augustine. The terms in which the *Gawain*-poet treats this disparity were also common. In *Piers Plowman*, in the *Ancrene Wisse*, in numerous carols, and frequently in the poetry of Chaucer, Christian and chivalric systems of order fuse to form the single scheme of "cortaysye." But in the Pearl Group the fusion of the Christian and the chivalric is not merely a convenient metaphor or an ornamental device employed in the service of some larger subject; the poet makes courtesy his theme.

In its most usual medieval sense, courtesy describes the proper (not merely necessary) relationship of men to their superiors, their equals, and their inferiors on the social scale. Although the word originally had to do with specifically "courtly" manners, it had so broadened by the fourteenth century that it could be applied to the behavior of all classes. What E. V. Gordon says of the *Gawain*-poet's use of the word might equally well be said of Chaucer's use of it. Professor Gordon writes: "But *cortaysye* to the poet was more than a sophistication of behaviour in polite society: he sees it as a gentleness and sensitiveness of spirit pervading personal relationships."[49]

But for the *Gawain*-poet, as for some other medieval writers, courtesy metaphorically describes the proper relationship of all stations within the feudal order emanating from God. The pearl explains this proper relationship in its ideal form by an analogy from Scripture:

> "As head and arm and heart and leg
> Serve the body, true to trust,
> So every Christian soul is a limb
> Of Christ, and serves Him first and last.
> For listen: When has spite or spleen
> Made a man's arm lash at his chest?
> Your head grows neither crabbed or cross
> With your finger, though you wear fine rings.
> So we all live here in love and bliss
> By courtesy, as queens and kings."

[st. 39, ll. 459–68]

Since the Virgin, the Queen of Courtesy, "has all high Heaven's space / And all dim Earth and Hell in her sway," it seems clear that courtesy extends to all the universe the concept of feudal interdependence. Courtesy insists upon distinctions of rank and, at the same time, insists upon the absolute value of all stations within the scheme of plenitude.[50]

The poet consistently selects the metaphor of the cosmos as a feudal kingdom, and he consistently emphasizes, in this enlarged context, the feudal ideal. Consider the *Pearl*. The cosmos is a kingdom, both a royal court and the fief over which that court has suzerainty. God is king, Christ is prince, the Virgin, queen of queens. The souls of the blessed are at once field workers, that is, servants of Christ the Wine Lord, and wives of Christ.[51] Men on earth are God's humbler vassals. Early in the poem the narrator is presented as mortal jeweler to the court, one who owes fealty to God, for the pearl tells him that to think his Lord might tell a lie is "uncourteous";[52] and when in the end the narrator has learned his lesson, he asks that he and all of us may be God's "homly hyne" (loosely, household servants). Professor Savage does not take us far enough, then, when he observes that "Failure to abide by law or ignorance of its demands is the cause of sorrow and suffering in all of the poems."[53] For the conflict in the poems is not exactly the one Professor Savage sees: "Every poem which he is supposed to have written seems to have grown out of the conflict in his own mind between law (man-made or divine) and human frailty."[54] Law is the negative *thou-shalt-not*; courtesy is the affirmative *thou-shalt*. Lawbreaking is therefore dangerous not in itself but in its denial of the cosmic order which law is established to support.

For the *Gawain*-poet, order in the soul is as important as order in the cosmos. A central motif, particularly in the *Pearl* and in *Gawain*, is the proper functioning of the soul's three parts, the concupiscent, the irascible, and the rational. In the tripartite soul (a commonplace going back to Plato and available to the *Gawain*-poet through any of the Schoolmen),[55] each part of the soul is absolutely necessary and, if not perverted, good. The three parts are not of equal rank, just as roses, lions, and God are not. The irascible soul is of a higher order than the concupiscent soul, and the rational soul higher than the irascible. It is not possible to say even metaphorically, however, that the arrangement of parts is feudal in the sense that the highest faculty governs the lower faculties. In the medieval view, the parts of the soul function on an equal plane, the health of the whole depending upon the health or imperfection of the parts.[56] A relationship between the well-ordered soul and the well-ordered state does exist, however; in both, stations are interdependent.

The courtesy of the cosmos and the order of the soul are by no means easy for man to affirm. From within and from without, order is constantly threatened. The *Pearl*, *Purity*, and *Patience* deal with

THE GAWAIN-POET

disruptions from within; *Gawain* begins in disruption from without. Analysis of the poems will reveal the centrality of the courtesy theme.

Pearl

The dramatic tension in the *Pearl*, and the basis of profluence, is the conflict of human selfishness and the courtesy of heaven, a conflict rooted in the contrast between the mutability of this world and the immutability of the next. It seems clear that the poet accepts as a premise the common, derivatively Neoplatonic view that the phenomenal world is an imperfect copy or shadowy image of a higher world, and that the degrees of better and worse in it are essential to the order of the whole. The world in which the dreamer finds himself is our world idealized, or more precisely, as I have indicated already, a lost earthly paradise in the tradition of the *Ave Phoenice*, a world of flowers, trees, spices, mountains, clouds, birds —but no dullness, no ugliness, no mutability.[57] That the parts of the whole are related and valuable is not only implicit in the pearl's analogy from St. Paul, in which the human body and the Mystical Body are compared (st. 34, ll. 459–68), but is also fairly explicit here:

> Flower and fruit can feel no blight
> Where she drove down in the dark ground:
> Each grassblade wakes in a withering seed
> Or corn were never brought to bin.
> In the good is every good begun;
> So splendid a seed, then, cannot be brought
> To nothing: Branching spices spring
> From that prized pearl without a spot.
>
> [st. 3, ll. 29–36]

In the higher world, or in the unfallen world—after Bonaventura, we may treat the two as interchangeable, one being merely a phenomenal or sensitive projection of the other—unity and harmony prevail; but in the fallen, phenomenal world, unity and harmony are replaced by strife and discord, for this is the world of matter, the dark principle which Plotinus calls indeterminate, lacking in qualities, and which Christian thinkers describe as fallen from grace. The imperfect character of man, chiefly his strong attachment to the continually declining things of our world (in other words, the imperfection of the concupiscent soul), makes perfect courtesy virtually impossible on earth. Loving the things of this world, and in his overweening pride believing he owns them, man grows indignant (a perversion of the irascible soul) at having to relinquish to the cosmic general welfare what he considers his own (cf. st. 1 of the *Pearl*).

The psychological conflict informs the opening lines of the poem:

> Perle, plesaunte to prynces paye
> To clanly clos in golde so clere . . .

(in E. V. Gordon's literal translation, "Pearl, pleasing to a prince's delight to set fairly in gold so bright"). Professor Gordon has suggested that the prince is symbolically Christ, presumably on the assumption that the point of view in the opening stanza is retrospective and fully informed as a result of the process to be described in the rest of the poem. My own impression—and admittedly the disagreement is trifling—is that the opening lines set up an irony: *prynces* may suggest Christ to the reader, who is emotionally detached enough to discern proper order, but the narrator characterizes his earlier self as blinded by grief and by his sense that he has been robbed (*fordolked*). At the start of the poem, it seems to me, Christ is to be thought the farthest thing from his mind (cf. st. 5, ll. 55–56). The pricelessness of the pearl is important precisely because it does not belong to Christ or anyone else, as far as the narrator is concerned, but to himself. In the opening stanzas he repeatedly emphasizes his sense of possession. For instance, the pearl "raised [his] fortune and all [his] estate." And consider his words to the pearl later:

> "What matter then how my goods decline
> Or where I walk in the world's waste;
> When I have no part in my pearl, my own,
> What can men judge me but exiled, lost?"
>
> [st. 28, ll. 333–36]

But where true courtesy operates, exclusive ownership is outlawed: all one possesses must be at the service of the whole. One must resist, then, both the desire to possess (perverse concupiscence) and the passion which goes with that desire (perverse irascibility). It is this that the central character must learn. He must grow selfless, must bow at last to the will of his liege lord. The progress of the poem is the progress of the narrator's education.

The poet provides two schemes in terms of which we may observe the narrator's progress. One is a scheme which orders the main divisions of the action, the other a scheme which organizes the drama moment by moment. The first is an epistemological system which the poet might have come upon almost anywhere, since various Schoolmen developed it in similar ways. Bonaventura's account will do. Reinterpreting the Pseudo-Dionysian figure of the three eyes, Bonaventura argues that man may seek out God through the senses, which provide empirical knowledge of the actual and discern the vestiges of the divine in the world; through imagination or "intellect," which dispassionately studies the soul itself, the image of the divine Being; and through "pure intellect," which in a transcendent or mystical act grasps the Being of the divine cause.[58] The narrator's progress from the limited, merely human view to a larger view is a progress through three stages which seem to correspond to Bonaventura's three stages or grades of illumination. It seems to me that the opening of the dream (sts. 6–20, ll. 61–240) presents the first: the divine is revealed to the senses—sight, smell, hearing.[59] But the senses can take man only so far, as all the Schoolmen agreed. (Thus the pearl says, in effect, playing with the narrator's epithet, "jeweler": "What sort of jeweler would trust his naked eye?") The debate between the jeweler and his pearl (sts. 21–80, ll. 241–960) constitutes the second stage. The debate may, I think, be considered a dramatization of the soul's dialectic, for whereas the jeweler is passionate and materialistic, the pearl, who controls the debate, correcting and explaining to the narrator, is the human spirit purified to its essential quality, which partakes of the divine (cf. *Summa theologica*, Q. 12, A. 1). The jeweler at least means to be dispassionate, to speak "wythouten debate" in his attempt to learn the nature of heaven from the pearl, a liberated soul. And it seems clear that her liberation into essence interests him partly because it has implications for himself. The third stage of his progress (sts. 81–96, ll. 961–1150) corresponds to Bonaventura's apprehension through holy vision, the mystical leap. The jeweler sees God (the Lamb) and is filled with joy. The opening and closing sections of the poem frame this three-stage development and give it emotional force. The opening section establishes the emotionally charged conflict between human imperfection and human hunger for the perfect and immutable; the closing section effects the necessary compromise, only partly satisfying.

A psychological scheme, that of the tripartite soul, supports the epistemological scheme and governs the moment-by-moment drama of the narrator's progress. Quite regularly throughout the poem, successive impulsions of appetite, passion, and reason inform action. Cast into the splendid world of his dream, the jeweler is irresistibly drawn along by his desire for the "more and more" which opens up before him. With perverse irascibility he swears that nothing can stop him, and when at last he reaches a stream he cannot cross, his first response is anger ("anger gains you never a cress," the pearl tells him). Finally he is forced to reason: "At last I judged," for the most man has any right to ask is understanding of the perfection he cannot reach. The pearl's reprimand (sts. 22–23, ll. 257–76) also works in terms of the tripartite soul. Man's view of life is limited, she says. Since he cannot see the total scheme, he desires lower rather than higher good (an imperfection of the concupiscent part); and since man does not own what he thinks he owns or lose what he thinks he loses, his belligerent suit for his rights (an imperfection of the irascible part) is a "mad purpose" (an imperfection of the rational part). The pearl then comments on the threefold nature of man's limitation (sts. 25–27, ll. 290–324), saying, "Three strange things you've said at once, / And strangely confused, in truth, all three." The jeweler's three errors come about because: (1) his senses are dull, fit only to deal with material things (thus the fallen flesh degrades the concupiscent part); (2) his boldness does not suit his humble station (as vassal he must "first ask leave" to enter, hence the irascible part is imperfect); and (3) his reason is faulty (he needs better counsel). Next the jeweler learns that the ordinary human concept of station is inadequate because incompatible with that true courtesy which does not allow for exclusive possession (sts. 35–39, ll. 409–68); and he learns that the ordinary human concept of reward (that which one wins through the function of the irascible part) is also inadequate (sts. 41–60, ll. 481–720), for it ignores both the infinite wealth of God and the fallen state of the world. But the jeweler understands dimly. When he is reminded that the pearl is Christ's bride, he forgets his lesson and expresses wonder at the pearl's having won exclusive possession of the Lamb and amazement at her fortitude (she is "stout and styf"). The pearl corrects him rather irritably and the conversation turns to her home. The contrast central to the poem as a whole, the contrast between the mutable and discordant, on one hand, and the immutable and ordered, on the other, now takes emblematic form, becoming a contrast between the Old Jerusalem and the New. In the Old, Christ, though guilty of no crime, was murdered; in the New, Christ rules. The pearl's explanation prepares the jeweler for the vision itself, which seemingly should be sufficient for him. But he is even now a human being with human faults. What he sees he must possess. Stirred by perverse concupiscence, fortified by perverse irascibility, and directed by "madness," he decides to cross the river, starts violently, and awakens from his dream. Forced to recognize the limits of his power, he accepts his place in the total order, his station as humble servant of God.

The dramatic movement from disorder to order is reinforced by emblems and symbols derived from exegetical tradition and from Neoplatonism as it is reflected in the writings of the Schoolmen. Our imperfect world is the "world wet" with the wetness of decay and corruption, emblematically, the waves of sin in which Adam and all mankind are drowned; heaven, on the other hand, has grace, the eternally regenerative water of life, which on earth takes the form of the water of baptism and the blood of redemption (sts. 54–55, ll. 637–60).[60] A second traditional contrast is between the flawed and spotted condition of all things physical and the spotless condition of all things formed of the divine Spirit. Still another contrast in the *Pearl*, and one that becomes complex in its workings, is between Nature and Art. In the mortal world Nature and Art contrast in that one is mutable, the other immutable; in the earthly paradise, Nature is immutable, but even so it contrasts with the perfect Art of heaven. The poet introduces spices, birds, flowers—particularly the rose and the fleur-de-lys—repeatedly. Whereas the spices in the poet's garden at home become cloying and (by a shift to grain imagery) ripe for the harvest, the spices of the earthly paradise refresh the spirit and are ripe in all seasons, but do not suggest corruption. The music of the birds of the earthly paradise is superior not only to the music of mortal birds but also to the music of this world's citole players and citherners (imperfect Art); at the same time, as the harp is higher than the cithern and the angel higher than the bird, perfect Art is higher than perfect Nature. (Since the purity of the singing angels is emphasized—they are essences and, moreover, the poet makes a point of the fact that they never tell lies—one may speculate that in the poet's view angels are above birds [lower Nature] in that birds are not rational, and above men [higher on the Platonic Scale of Becoming] in that men are only sometimes rational.)

The Nature-Art contrast most fully developed in the poem is that between the flower in nature and the flower in art. The pearl tells the jeweler that she is changed from a "mortal rose" to a "pearl of price." The basis of the rapid association of flower and pearl comes from the medieval use of pearls to form artificial flowers such as those which in stanza 18 adorn the crown of the child. The artificial-flower image occurs throughout the poem, and at last the child becomes a part of heaven's "garland," the circle of the blessed, or perhaps the New Jerusalem—emblematically a crown—itself. The image of the blessed as figured pearls set in a garland or crown is consistent, of course, with the poet's view that Art perfects. In a metaphorical sense, one who closes the circle as an indispensable part of the priceless whole achieves fulfillment. It is obviously appropriate, then, that the poem itself be a garland, a ring of one hundred (or, by accident, one hundred and one) interlocked jewels coming full circle in the last line's echo of the first line.

Certain images in the poem call up the Neoplatonic strain in Scholastic tradition. The circle and the sphere, as we have seen, work throughout as emblems of unity and completion. Images of darkness and light and of the graduation from darkness to light also suggest the Neoplatonic world view—not that Neoplatonism as found, say, in Augustine, is the only possible source. The poet's Neoplatonism, however, is Christian and characteristically incomplete. Like Bonaventura, he knows that complete union is impossible for men of flesh and blood. Man can attain, at best, only the state of a "good Christian." Recognizing his limitations, he can take his lowly place in the scheme of the cosmos and thus contribute to the total order.

Other elements in the poem call up what D. W. Robertson, Jr., has called the scriptural tradition. As we observed earlier, number symbolism is important throughout, and the symbolic complexity of the poem depends upon the poet's use in a non-biblical context of biblical types and antitypes.

Purity

The second poem in the Pearl Group, *Purity*, deals with God's punishment of His celestial or terrestrial vassals guilty of either of the two possible forms of cosmic discourtesy. An essentially positive concept, and Neoplatonic in that it envisions the moral universe not in terms of good and evil in counterpoise but in terms of Supreme Good and a departure from good, courtesy would not at first glance seem to accommodate the idea of damnation. The recurrent courtroom metaphor in the *Pearl* does not show God actively condemning the defendant who stands before Him, but shows God withholding grace when the self-condemned man foolishly argues by rights he has forfeited. The Fall of Man is viewed in the *Pearl* as man's voluntary turning away from God toward death. To account for such occurrences as the destruction of Sodom and Gomorrah, one must shift from a passive concept of punishment to an active concept, the blow delivered in wrath.

If the reader understands the poet's treatment of wrath he is likely to find *Purity* a successful poem; but misunderstanding is easy. The poet identifies courtesy on every level—from table manners to the interdependence of heaven and earth—as one thing, and if the reader misses the exact terms of the identification he may find the whole poem impaired by an effect of "characteristic medieval brutality." One scarcely need balk at the poet's orthodox view that Noah's generation was punished for subverting Nature, for engendering monsters through grotesque forms of sexual perversion. Man's abnegation of his rightful position as lord of Nature, his defiance and mockery of his vassalage to God (who outlawed sexual perversion), his defilement of both external Nature and his own nature—thus, in a word, man's "discourtesy," his rude disregard for the total order of the cosmos—are dramatically sufficient grounds for the punishment he receives. But unless one is careful, one may unfairly condemn the poet for his treatment of the discourteous serf who comes to his baron's feast in stinking work clothes. The baron's outrage, which leads him to chain the serf in a dark, subterranean dungeon to gnash his teeth for the rest of his days, seems less the wrath of a courteous lord than the lunacy of a Tiberius. If God's punishment of the wicked is parallel to the baron's punishment of the serf, then God is wantonly cruel; good manners are not that important.

All this the *Gawain*-poet has anticipated. For him, as for medieval commentators and other medieval poets (the author of the *Southern Passion*, for instance), the parable of the wedding feast is first of all an allegory signifying what will happen to Jews (false vassals who renounce their lord), to true Christians, and to false Christians. The poet reinforces the allegory by introducing new imagery such as the underground dungeon "where sorrow dwells forever." But the *Gawain*-poet's version is not merely or even primarily allegory, and this may cause trouble. The realism is so pronounced that one critic has been led to suggest that the poet had some actual court in mind. What we need to perceive is that the focus of the realistic narrative is *not* on the justice but on the naturalness of the lord's wrath. The lord's behavior is to be seen from the outset as exceptional, for the poet presents the norm first and only then retells the parable. Any terrestrial baron would be indignant, the poet says, if some guest mocked his court by coming to it in grotesque attire. Imagine the scene:

> There the wretch in his rush comes running for the table
> In stockings ripped at the knees and in patchwork rags,
> His old shirt torn into shreds, and his shoes half gone!

[part I, ll. 39–41]

One can guess what would happen:

> They'd haul him away to the hall door and hurl the man out,
> And tell him in plain terms to come back there no more
> On pain of imprisonment or the pinch of the stocks.

[part I, ll. 44–46]

THE GAWAIN-POET

The difference between normal behavior, to which our attention is called here, and the behavior of the baron in the parable is that the baron is unusually angry. He has been insulted by his friends and now he is insulted by a stranger, a man who (as it seems to the baron at any rate) has not even bothered to make a pretense of cleaning himself up or dressing for the feast. (Many of the baron's guests are something less than spotless, the poet says, but they have apparently made at least some effort.) The baron's rage is underscored in the serf's reaction: confounded by his fear that he will be beaten, he cannot speak. The point of the parable is this: If it is to be expected that an earthly lord will be furious when his efforts to spread a pleasing feast are mocked and marred by discourtesy in the normal sense (bad manners), how much more it is to be expected that God will be stirred to wrath by discourtesy in the extended sense, which is superficially similar but much more dreadful in its effects, man's willful and scornful perversion of the order of the universe.

Other equations of cosmic courtesy and mere etiquette probably need no comment. Christ broke bread with His fingers, the poet says, because His fingers could cut more cleanly than the finest knife—an instrument He was much too well-bred to use. Gollancz has pointed out that this marvelous power of Christ's fingers was a common tradition,[61] and one is glad to hear it. To have invented the detail would have been to sink to triviality; to have included it in passing, as one more embellishment of the courtesy scheme, is something else.

The success of *Purity* is not restricted, as Professor Menner and others have thought, to good storytelling, bold imagery, and occasional stylistic vigor or lyricism. In the introduction to his edition of the poem, Professor Menner commented that

> in spite of the fact that the outline is clear and carefully worked out, the poem is not well proportioned. The story of the destruction of the cities need hardly have had so long a preamble as that which includes the announcement of an heir to Abraham. And the introduction to Belshazzar's Feast, which narrates the siege of Jesusalem and the seizure of the sacred vessels, both elaborated with much irrelevant detail, is also unnecessarily long. The poet apparently found such excellent material for story-telling in the events recorded that he could not refrain from in-

serting it. He becomes so engrossed in his narrative that he forgets that his stories are not being written for their own sake, but as illustrations of a particular theme.[62]

If we recognize that the theme of the poem is courtesy, and if we notice the typological connections which interrelate the episodes of the poem and identify them, moment by moment, with New Testament transactions and with the ultimate feudal reward or punishment which is to come on the Day of Judgment, we must see that the poem, though thin where discourse is substituted for action, has few if any irrelevant details and certainly no serious lack of proportion.

In *Purity*, as in the *Pearl*, two motifs are developed in counterpoint, purity and *trawþ* (which means "faithfulness" or, in a sense, "patience"; patience can be defined as *trawþ* in adverse circumstances). These two aspects of courtesy, together with the basic feudalism of the scheme, are set up at once in a comparison of the "court" of God and the courts of terrestrial barons.

The poet speaks first of priests, whom he carefully identifies as vassals of God. If they are pure and loyal, priests wield great power; if they are not, then because they defile themselves and because they in turn defile God's vessels (their feudal responsibility), God loathes them. It stands to reason, the poet says, that the King would want His vassals on earth to be as much as possible like His servants in heaven, and His heavenly servants are flawless, radiant angels. If an unwashed man were to come before God when He was sitting "above His dukes on the dais," that man would be thrown out at once. The same thing would happen on earth, as the poet shows in the story of the wedding feast.

False priests are found guilty on two counts: they are impure and they are disloyal. Unwashed intruders at the court of heaven or at earthly courts are guilty on the same two counts, for the unwashed, ill-dressed man's intrusion is an insult to the dignity of the court and is thus, in a vassal, an act of disloyalty. God punishes both disloyalty and impurity, the poet asserts, but only impurity rouses him to outrage. From this point forward the poem will consist of ingeniously balanced contrasts: God's responses to loyalty and disloyalty, purity and impurity; man's responses to the same things; righteous wrath and unrighteous wrath; the courtesy and discourtesy of angels, all mankind, kingdoms and cities, or individual men.

Once the general method is understood, *Purity* is not an enormously difficult poem, though it does require considerable familiarity with Scripture. Since the general method is simple, and since, moreover, much of one's pleasure as one reads the poem comes from catching the poet's use of types, verbal echoes, puns (some of them lost in the translation), and structural juxtapositions designed to release new anagogic identifications, it will be sufficient to present here only a brief and general account of the poem's design.

The poet begins with Lucifer and Adam, who were punished not for impurity but for disloyalty, and whose punishment therefore came as a blow of moderate wrath. The light and splendor lent by God to Lucifer and his legions were withdrawn, leaving the disloyal angels mere burnt-out coals, and their franchise to a place near God was annulled so that (prefiguring the rain of Noah's time) they fell for forty days. Similarly Adam, though ordained to bliss, allowed his eyes to rest on a nearer beauty (Eve), as Lucifer had done (overvaluing his own splendor),[63] and, persuaded by Eve, ate the poisonous apple against which God had warned him.

The poet tells next the story of Noah, loyal vassal of God and lord of Nature, a man who in loyalty and purity contrasts with those around him and who is therefore qualified to pilot his ship (with its many mansions) to the rocks of his salvation.[64] The contrast between the courteous Noah and the discourteous remainder of mankind is reflected in a contrast between the white, loyal dove and the black, rebellious raven. Verbal repetition and imagery suggest an identification of the raven and Lucifer, while the dove is identified, as one would expect, with the Holy Ghost. When the dove brings back the branch of olive, the poet says:

> Such was the sign of salvation sent them by the Lord,
> The settlement for themselves and the simple beasts.
> What bliss there was then in that boat so long a-building!
> What comfort in that chest sealed up with clay!
> And merrily one fair morn in the first month,
> First of all months of the year, and the first day,
> They laughed, who lived in that boat, and they rose and looked out
> And saw how the waters had waned, and the world was dry.
>
> [part 6, ll. 483–90]

The reader scarcely needs to be told that the "boat so long a-building" is typically Creation itself (cf. *Patience*, ll. 131–32), or that the "chest sealed up with clay" is both the ark and man, "that other creation that covered the bones," as the poet says in *St. Erkenwald* (st. 86). The significance of the date of Noah's release from the ark is that it looks back to the original Creation (which involved the separation of land and water) and that it looks forward to the Day of Judgment, when the just will rise to the place appointed for them.

In identifying as symbolically one the salvation of the soul by God, the salvation of man and Nature by Noah, and the salvation of the ark by the dove, the poet has brilliantly fused courtesy of three kinds, divine, human, and natural.

In his retelling of the story of the destruction of Sodom, the poet focuses first on the feast Abraham prepares for the Lord, then on Lot's feast for the two angels, and finally on the destruction of the cities and the preservation of Lot and all but one of his household. The green oak in Abraham's yard is a traditional presignification of the cross, and by emphasizing the surface root running out from the tree, the poet underscores this association. (Church writers frequently speak of Christ as the "root"; compare also Chaucer's "Canon's Yeoman's Tale," ll. 1461 ff.) Abraham's courteous feast for God, then, is a complement of the feast God prepares for man through the crucifixion (cf. the feast imagery in the *Pearl*) and also recalls the parable of the wedding feast at the start of the poem. Lot's feast for the two angels parallels Abraham's feast for God and similarly recalls the parable of the wedding feast.[65] The one striking contrast is between the behavior of Sarah and the behavior of Lot's wife. Sarah is by no means nimble in obedience—Abraham has to tell her to move quickly "for once"—and she is by no means perfectly courteous to God; in fact, she laughs at Him. But she does prepare the cakes as Abraham asks, and when God catches her laughing, she swears "*by hir trawþe*" that she never laughed—a pardonable lie. Lot's wife disobeys Lot's command that she use no salt or yeast (impurities) and later disobeys both Lot and God by looking back (with impure desire). And so she is punished.

The juxtaposed Abraham and Lot episodes also contain other, less striking, contrasts. Abraham's clumsy but successful attempt to bargain with God and later his plea that Lot be spared (his real purpose from the start) contrast with Lot's reasonable but unsuccessful attempt to quiet the wrath of the Sodomites and his plea that the two young men be spared. There is also the contrast between the barrenness of Sarah, which God will turn into an antitype of Noah's flood (the heirs who "fall" from Abraham shall "flood" all the world), and the situation of Lot's wife, who bears two daughters and then becomes, like the hills around Sodom, sterile stone and salt forever.

Like Noah's flood, the destruction of Sodom presignifies the Day of Judgment. When Abraham first sees the three strangers, the poet says

> If þay wer farande and fre and fayre to beholde,
> Hit is eþe to leve by þe last ende.
>
> [part 8, ll. 607–8]

"If they were handsome and noble and fair to behold, it is easy to believe, by what followed *or* by the Last End." Inferno imagery is everywhere in the destruction scene; and, in contrast, Lot's flight with his two "lily-white" daughters is to a "hill" where, as Abraham learns later, "*he is on lofte wonnen*," he dwells aloft. The episode concludes with the poet's comment, both realistic and allegorical, on the Dead Sea. Once Sodom seemed the sweetest region on earth, a paradise planted by God; now it is a poisonous waste, or, on the level of allegory, eternal damnation. Having betrayed both Nature and God (as the poet tells us, part 9, l. 709), the Sodomites, like Noah's generation, are destroyed by both Nature and God. Order will not be violated.

The third episode in the poem concerns the fall of Jerusalem and later the fall of Belshazzar. Once again the poet dramatizes the interrelationship of God, man, and Nature, and once again he comments on both disloyalty (the sin of Zedekiah) and impurity (the sin of Belshazzar). Anagogic symbolism here is particularly interesting because of its relationship to symbolism in the *Pearl* and *Gawain*. Belshazzar's feast is an antitype of the heavenly feast allegorically described in the parable which opens the poem: the jewels mentioned in connection with Belshazzar's feast—the jewels on the holy vessels—recall the apocalyptic vision of heaven "as seen by the Apostle John"; Belshazzar's castle surrounded by water recalls Noah's ark, type of heaven; like the heavenly castle in the *Pearl*, Belshazzar's castle is "square," but whereas the true castle of heaven is built of twelves, Belshazzar's castle, an *earthly* paradise, is built of sevens (seven is, as we noticed earlier, a number of Nature or man-in-Nature: four elements and three parts of the soul); and Belshazzar's castle is called "that rock" (cf. the Rock), a hall where, moreover, the drinking of wine is accompanied by the ringing of bells (that is, the cup covers thrown to the floor). The extremely close resemblance of Belshazzar's feast in *Purity* and King Arthur's feast in *Sir Gawain and the Green Knight* is almost sufficient in itself to identify Camelot as another earthly paradise, with the one important difference that Arthur's paradise has—at the start of the poem—not yet fallen.

Having reached the third episode in *Purity*, we are able to see the progression of the poem as a whole. The most obvious element of profluence is the gradual narrowing of focus from all mankind, in the Noah story, to a particular kingdom, in the story of Lot, to particular men—Zedekiah, Nebuchadnezzar, Belshazzar. But within the purity motif another progression is equally important. Noah's generation engenders monsters, deforming Nature in general; the homosexual Sodomites defile themselves and other men, but the rest of Nature only incidentally, if at all; and the emphasis in the third episode is individual self-defilement, though again all Nature may be tainted incidentally. The opening exhortation is against slipping from purity after shrift; Zedekiah and Nebuchadnezzar sin through disloyalty; Belshazzar through disloyalty and impurity, which is worse. Thus the ordinary Christian and Belshazzar are identified, for as the Christian must remain pure in order properly to keep what is God's (himself), Belshazzar ought to have avoided lechery and drink, the causes of his scornful use of God's vessels. And so the poem comes full circle—as the poems of the *Gawain*-poet invariably do: Belshazzar is a type of the false priest mentioned in the opening lines. As a temporal king he represents discourteous secular as well as discourteous ecclesiastical power. And born into God's law through his father's conversion, he is also himself a defiled vassal and vessel of God. His discourtesy is absolute, recapitulating every discourtesy in the poem.

Patience

The dominant theme in *Purity* is, of course, purity; and the subdominant is loyalty or patience. In *Patience* the emphasis is reversed. Both poems work by tropological and anagogical extension of a literal narrative, but *Patience* is a far simpler poem. On the literal level the impatience of Jonah contrasts with the patience of God the Father, and on the level of allegory Jonah's impatience contrasts with the patience of Christ and, at the same time, parallels the impatience of Satan. The typic identifications scarcely need pointing out: Jonah fears that the Ninevites might strip him to the skin and hang him on a cross in the company of thieves; the belly of the whale, where Jonah stays for three days and nights (the amount of time Christ spent in hell), is explicitly compared to Sheol, and the stink there (a common medieval association with hell)[66] is explicitly the stench of hell. On the tropological level, Jonah is the ordinary Christian; he is disloyal out of fear but repents his disloyalty, and in all situations—even in the belly of the whale—remains as pure as possible. Needless to say, he is unable to remain perfectly spotless. When the whale vomits Jonah up onto land—his salvation—the poet comments, "And well it might be that the robe he wore needed washing," a quibble on being washed in Christ's blood upon entering heaven, as mentioned in the *Pearl*.

The plot too is extremely simple. In the first episode Jonah's impatience takes the form of flight from the Lord; in the second it takes the form of petulant disapproval of God's ways. Jonah tells the Ninevites they will be destroyed; but when they repent, God forgives them and Jonah flees to the hills, embarrassed and sullen. There God teaches him the value of patience.

Such simplicity of structure is unusual in the work of the *Gawain*-poet. It may well be, as various critics have suggested, that *Patience* was the earliest of the poems. Nonetheless, it is a fine poem and in one respect second only to *Sir Gawain and the Green Knight*. Like Gawain, Jonah emerges as a character, a man at once comic and pathetic, foolish and admirable. One is struck throughout by the rather engaging willfulness of the man; and what makes the poem so moving is one's increasing sense as the story unfolds of the absurdity of such willfulness, given the extreme gentleness in God. It is not that one discounts *Purity* as one reads *Patience;* indeed, the more one studies the poems the more one is inclined to believe that the poet ultimately intended that they be read as a unified group. The force of *Patience* is partly an effect of *Purity:* God punishes those who would destroy His creation, but God's creation of the world and His preservation of order in the world are acts of love.

Sir Gawain and the Green Knight

If *Patience* is the story of a man made "uncourteous," first by fear and then by shame, *Sir Gawain and the Green Knight* is the story of a man known far and wide as a "courteous knight." If Jonah must rediscover his proper condition (like the narrator in the *Pearl*), the knight must try to maintain it. *Gawain* has links with all of the Pearl Group: Sir Gawain is, as one critic puts it, the "pearl" of knighthood, and both his purity and his loyalty (the two motifs first established in the *Pearl*) are tested by the Green Knight; the description of Belshazzar's feast in *Purity* closely parallels the description of the more courteous feast in the *Gawain;* and like Jonah in *Patience,* Gawain is symbolically linked with Christ. Since the basic world view is the same in all the poems, and since any systematic comparison of the *Gawain* with all three of the poems preceding it would require more space than we can afford, it will be practical to limit the present discussion to comparison of the *Gawain* and the poem most strikingly similar to it, the *Pearl.*

The dramatic tension in *Gawain*—identical to that in the *Pearl*—is the conflict between human selfishness and the ideal of selfless courtesy; and here, as in the *Pearl,* the conflict is rooted in mutability, the implications of man's existence within Nature. The poet sets up the conflict at once, focusing in his opening lines (as he will do in his closing lines) on the vanity of mortal kingdoms. He begins and ends with the fall of Troy. In our world the forces of darkness are everywhere: traitors in the court, monsters in the woods.

The poet establishes this central contrast between the actual and the ideal in various ways, among them the form of the poem itself.

On the level of "ready and obvious meaning," *Gawain* is a fairy tale (more precisely, a Christmas story of the supernatural); its appeal is to the universal human concern for the young and untested in a hostile universe.[67] So read, *Gawain* is the story of the age-old triumph of youth over age, good over evil; but unlike that of the typical fairy-tale hero, Gawain's success, both physical and moral, is not unblemished. The poet plays the milieu of the fairy tale against the conditions of life and thus ironically contrasts life as it ought to be and life as it is.

A more basic contrast in the poem is between the idealism of Gawain, as man and as servant of Arthur, and the nature of this fallen, traitor- and monster-ridden world. The sign painted on Gawain's shield is the pentangle, a very old symbol of perfection, and the poet's own comment on the symbol makes clear its importance to him.[68] And Gawain lives by the courteous code his emblem proclaims. His piety suggests his concern with maintaining the harmonious relationship of God and man (the metaphysical order); his acceptance of the challenge of the Green Knight, his opposition to Morgan le Fay, and again his pentangle suggest his affirmation of natural order (white magic as opposed to black) and of man's lordship over Nature; his scrupulously decorous behavior to Arthur, Guinevere, his fellow knights, and later to his host and hostess at Hautdesert, indicates his affirmation of the social order; and his concern for maintaining the harmonious relationship and healthy function of the concupiscent, irascible, and rational parts of his soul indicates his dedication to the ideal of Christian purity. Gawain's life affirms the ideal in yet another way: he bears on his shield an image of the Virgin, and much of the comedy in the poem comes from the fact that Gawain is—and desperately wants to remain—a virgin himself (cf. part 3, st. 26, ll. 1779–91). We have no reason for doubting Gawain's statement to the lady that he is not plighted to anyone and does not intend to plight himself to a lady "for a while." The fact that as he answers "*smeþely con he smyle*" (he smiled "smoothly"), and the fact that he swears "by St. John," strongly suggest that his answer is an understatement, that in fact he is sworn to chastity. Admittedly, Gawain is known for *luftalkyng*, but that is only to say that he knows backwards and forwards the French rhetoric of love. It might perhaps be added that courtly lovers are not, as a rule, promiscuous. They are characteristically initiated into love for a particular lady by Youth and Idleness, both of which are harmless, meaning "Noon harm ne slight in hir entente, / But only lust [not in the modern sense] and Iolitee."[69] One of the reasons lovers are tested for a year or two is to find out whether they are true lovers or merely men interested in sex, the horrid Venus of Chaucer's *Parliament*, a creature from whose domination we are preserved by observance of proper form.[70] Gawain's virginity is consonant with his innocence, and consonant too with the poet's identification of Gawain (at Hautdesert) as Spring (part 2, st. 15, ll. 866), the conventional time of initiation into courtly love (and not-so-courtly love as well). As a virgin, Gawain would be in the main tradition of Virgin-serving knights and that of knights enthralled by an elf-queen, both of which are possibly satirized in Chaucer's lines:

> "An elf-queen wol I love, ywis,
> For in this world no womman is
> Worthy to be my make
> In towne;
> Alle othere wommen I forsake,
> And to an elf-queen I me take
> Be dale and eek by downe!"[71]
>
> ["Sir Thopas," Fragment VII, ll. 790–96
> (B, ll. 1980–86)]

In medieval Christian thought virginity has a special significance. In the opinion of all the ancient writers of the Church up to Augustine, maintaining the virginity of heart and flesh is to live "the crucified life" in imitation of the Virgin Christ.[72] Indeed, through virginity one might transcend mutability, achieving, in Bonaventura's phrase, "in carne corruptibili incorruptionem." Gawain, then, is at the outset a man who comes as close as any man can to being Christlike. He seems the perfect courtier in the perfect court. But both the man and the court are yet to be tested.

As he sets up the action of the poem, the poet focuses carefully on the order which prevails (or seems to prevail) at Arthur's court, an order which in its pattern, its decorum, and its splendor reflects the order of a higher court, the court of God. The comparison is explicit: Arthur's court consists of the "Most renowned of knights, next to Christ himself." There is shouting and merrymaking, but the shouts are praise of Noel, the merrymaking that which accompanies gay dancing of the formal carole and gift-giving according to definite rules. Though the poet refers to the brotherhood of the Round Table, he does not seat his knights at the round table of Arthurian legend, but seats them at higher and lower tables according to rank (cf. *Purity*, part 1, ll. 49–160). When the meal is served, it is with due ceremony, the courses coming in proper order, properly announced. Almost certainly, for the poet's immediate audience, this treatment of Arthur's court as an emblem of physical and spiritual order must have been ironic—ingenuous (or *dis*ingenuous) praise of the sort we find in Chaucer—for traditionally Arthur's court was by no means known for its spirituality. If we knew the poet's direct sources we would probably know the basis of the effect E. Talbot Donaldson points out when he writes:

> The court of King Arthur is presented, in the most grandiose and laudatory of language, as the place where the ideal of chivalry has reached its zenith, where all is courtesy and martial prowess in defense of the right. The praise bestowed by the poet upon this court may seem excessive, and indeed the sequel suggests that the author made it so intentionally. For when the court is invaded by the Green Knight, arrogant, monstrous, and yet exasperatingly reasonable, it suddenly seems to become slightly unreal, as if, the Green Knight insultingly implies, its reputation were founded more on fiction than on fact—as if the poets that celebrated it had been working harder to enhance its glory than the knights themselves.[73]

Whatever the court may pretend to, the fact is that it is made up of human beings with human weaknesses. The knights themselves recognize, too late, that they would not have responded to the Green Knight's challenge as they did if they had taken the challenge as seriously as they should have (see part 2, st. 8), and the poet himself hints that the root of the trouble is the young King Arthur's pride (see, for instance, part 2, st. 1).

Nevertheless, the court pretends to excellence, and at least one knight believes in that excellence. For Sir Gawain, if for no one else, the Green Knight's challenge is a test of Arthur's court and of the chivalric concept of order itself. With proper fealty Gawain takes the challenge from Arthur, and the test becomes the test of the courteous knight.

Two tests are involved, one physical, one spiritual. Gawain's winter trip north, which occupies much of part 2, is a test of the knight's physical endurance. That, I think, is the point of the stanzas which open this section of the poem, for the description of the turning of the seasons presents the age-old cycle which, though everlastingly the same, never leaves man as it found him. The dust that must at last fly to heaven, the sun that must struggle against wind and darkness, the grass and all that now flourishes, now rots, share the condition of man. All that is physical must decline. If Gawain is not killed outright by his winter trip and his struggles with bad men, animals, and monsters, we may be sure that he will at any rate be left exhausted. Indeed, the trip is a kind of excursion into fallen and dangerous Nature, a journey from the known, the ordered, to the unknown; from the company of the court and Christendom to isolation and danger, where "few loved God." If we remember the poet's consistent treatment of Nature as the world "moist" with the wetness of corruption in the *Pearl*, I think we may legitimately argue that there is significance in his constant emphasis here on rivers, lakes, tarns, ice, and snow. At last, as every mortal must be, Gawain is physically beaten; for I think the lines

> And many small sorrowing birds upon bare twigs
> Piteously piped there for pain of the cold

[part 2, st. 11, ll. 746–47]

are not intended, as Mr. John Speirs thinks, to "restore a whole range of human feeling"[74] but to trigger Gawain's horrified recognition that if all this goes on much longer it may well kill him. Physically beaten but still spiritually true to his quest, Gawain prays.

Important as the test of physical prowess may seem to Gawain, for the sophisticated Christian poet the bulk of it is "too tedious to tell." But the poet develops the second test in great detail. The host's little game, the daily exchange of winnings, is in effect a series of temptations designed to try the order of Sir Gawain's soul.

The scene is, on one level, Eden, an Eden as lovely and dangerous as that first Eden; it is also a factitious heaven and a garden of Venus. The castle calls up the lost, walled-off earthly paradises to be discovered throughout medieval poetry, but the *Gawain*-poet's technique is symbolic, not allegorical. Whereas in the twenty-eighth canto, Dante enters "la divina foresta spessa e viva / ch'agli occhi temperava il nuovo giorno," and whereas Chaucer's park in the *Parliament* is green with leaves that "ay shal laste," the *Gawain*-poet contrasts the bare branches outside Hautdesert with Gawain himself:

> He looked like Spring itself, as indeed it seemed
> To all who gazed at him: a glory of color
> Shining and lovely, and not a bare limb showing.
> Christ never had made a more handsome knight than he,
>> they thought.
>
> [part 2, st. 15, ll. 866–70]

The wintry forest also contrasts with the plenty to be found in the castle and in the park surrounding. (The suggestion in the lines just quoted that Gawain himself is a kind of paradise is one to which we will return.) J. A. W. Bennett's comments, cited earlier, on the park of paradise and the garden of love throw light on numerous details in the description of Hautdesert. The moat surrounding the castle corresponds to the conventional river guarding Paradise (as in the *Pearl* a river guards heaven); the oaks in the park correspond to the huge, spaced trees (often of various kinds) always to be found in dream-visions of Paradise; the wall around the park is the wall surrounding all such parks (in fact, Bennett cites this wall among others). The castle is a rich and shifting symbol, however, as was the pearl. The oak, we recall, is traditionally associated with the crucifixion of the second Adam, Christ; the castle is, as I've mentioned before, "Pyched on a prayere" (*prayere* having been used a few lines earlier in the sense of "prayer"); the porter greets Gawain in the name of Peter (Keeper of the Keys); Gawain is given new robes and a splendid chair (cf. the robe of the pearl and her station as queen); on "a clean cloth that showed clear white" a feast is laid for the knight (cf. the feast imagery in the *Pearl* and *Purity*); the knight washes, then eats *fish, bread, wine*, all flavored with *spices;* and the meal is laughingly (and ironically) described as Gawain's penance. Bertilak, lord of the castle, is then a kind of Christ-figure, or rather a kind of false Christ.[75] But he may also be associated with "Cupide, oure lord"—the mighty medieval Cupid who is also (in the *Roman de la Rose*, *Paradys d'Amours*, etc.) a hunter. And so in this castle Gawain meets a lady who is to be the instrument of a test in which, in a sense recapitulating the fall of Adam, Gawain will fall from perfect grace.

Critics have given considerable attention to the relationship between Bertilak's three hunting excursions and Gawain's dalliance with the lady. Professor Savage has pointed out the heraldic significance of the hart (" 'representing the Hearing,' " and " 'a Man that is wise and politick, and well foreseeth his Times and Opportunities, a Man unwilling to assail the Enemy rashly, but rather desirous to stand his own Guard honestly, than to annoy another wrongfully' "),[76] the boar (" 'a Man of bold Spirit, skilful, politick in warlike Feats, and One of that high Resolution, that he will rather die valorously in the Field, than he will secure himself by ignominious Flight' "),[77] and the fox (crafty and deceitful, " 'seldom met in British Heraldry' ").[78] Savage more or less convincingly urges that these heraldic identifications suit the behavior of Gawain on, respectively, the first, second, and third days. Professor F. L. Utley has suggested another interpretation which might, as he says, "co-exist with" that of Savage:

> . . . the deer, being mere venison and a common source of food, is the minimal goal for a hunter; the boar, being both food and a test for martial valor, is much better; but best still, vermin or not, is the fox, who leads one on a merry chase to no purpose at all except the sheer sport of it.[79]

Savage's interpretation provides the key to corresponding details in the hunting scenes and the bedroom scenes; but it does not provide, as Utley's interpretation does, an explanation of the order of the related hunts or tests. On the other hand, though Utley's interpretation accounts for the dramatic progression, it coexists with Savage's interpretation in a very uncertain fashion. If the hunts establish a progression, in what sense do the scenes in the bedroom progress? In the light of our examination of the *Pearl*, one possible answer seems obvious: Gawain may be tested not simply by sexual temptation on three different days but by temptations of three different kinds.

While the host hunts deer, "a common source of food," Gawain endures a test of concupiscence: the lady tempts him sexually. Accepting Savage's heraldic interpretation, we observe that *deer* functions as a double symbol. Keen in his senses, able to foresee "Times and Opportunities," Gawain evades the temptation of the senses (seat of the baser appetites and perverter of healthy concupiscence). On the second day, while the host hunts the boar, Utley's "test of martial valor," Gawain endures first sexual temptation, as on the first day, then a test of his irascible soul. The lady tries to get Gawain to take a kiss by force (part 3, st. 14, ll. 1496–97), and when the knight replies that in his country force is not approved, she tries to get him to boast about his conquests in love and war (part 3, st. 15, ll. 1508–34); but Gawain remains courteous. In this scene, *boar* functions as a double symbol, for as Savage has shown, by boarlike frontal attacks and by keeping his boarlike mettle up, Gawain resists the temptation toward perversion of his irascible soul. On the third day, while the host hunts the fox, who because of his cunning "leads one on a merry chase" (note the poet's emphasis throughout this hunting scene on the cunning of the fox), Gawain endures first a third test of appetite, then a second test of his irascible part, and finally a test of the rational part, or his reason. The third day's test of appetite (part 3, st. 25, ll. 1755–69) is presented quickly and briefly; then comes the test of the irascible part. The lady asks Gawain for a love token, a sign that she is the object of his loyalty (part 3, st. 27, ll. 1799), and when she learns that Gawain has nothing to give her, she asks him to accept a rich ring, significant both as a sign of conquest and as property, source of power; but this Gawain courteously rejects. Finally the lady tempts Gawain to forsake reason for a perversion of reason, cunning: she offers a magic girdle which will protect him from all harm. This test Gawain fails. His own comment on his failure is interesting:

> "Cursed be cowardice and covetousness both,
> Villainy and vice that destroy all virtue!"

[part 4, st. 16, ll. 2374–75]

And a moment later:

> "Foolish cowardice taught me, from fear of your stroke,
> To bargain, covetous, and abandon my kind,
> The selflessness and loyalty suitable in knights."

[part 4, st. 16, ll. 2379–81]

All three parts of the soul fall with the fall of the rational part: healthy irascibility turns to cowardice; healthy concupiscence turns to "couetyse" (for the desire to possess life itself is the desire for a lower end). Thus the knight has forsaken his kind, which is characterized by *larges* (selflessness, which implies right desires and a concern with what Chaucer would call the common profit) and *lewte* (loyalty, which implies a right function of the irascible part). In accepting the girdle, Gawain lacks a little as servant of God (he no longer puts all his faith in Christ and the Virgin), lacks a little as knight, and lacks a little as Christlike man. When Gawain arms himself for the trip to the Green Chapel, his gear is tarnished (part 4, st. 1, ll. 2017–18).

At the Green Chapel, however, order is re-established. When the Green Knight's second and third feints come, Gawain does not flinch; he resigns himself. And whereas in saving one's life one loses it (in the traditional Christian view), in resigning one's life one wins it. (Gawain stands rooted to the ground like a tree, or, the Tree.) The bargain made at Camelot has been fulfilled; the Kingdom of God, the order of Nature, and the order of Arthur's court are vindicated. And through confession (to Bertilak as priest, part 4, st. 17, ll. 2391–95), and through contrition, repentance, and penance (the wearing of the baldric), order is re-established in Gawain's soul.

The return to order has a special significance in this poem, for as I have suggested already (as have others before me), *Sir Gawain and the Green Knight* is a Christmas poem, an early work in the same tradition as Dickens' *Christmas Carol* or James's *Turn of the Screw*. Most of the action in *Gawain* takes place during Christmastide; exchanges and gift-giving are important motifs; and whatever else the Green Knight's colors may mean emblematically, surely green, red, and gold carry here some part of their traditional Christmas burden. But the poem is not only a tale to be told around the yule log; it is also an exploration of the meaning of Christmas.

As virgin, Gawain is an imitator of Christ; as courteous knight, he is Christlike. Gawain's temptations in the forest directly parallel the temptations of Christ in the wilderness (Luke 4:3–12). Gawain's failure, then, glorifies Christ's success and underscores man's need for grace. It has often been pointed out that Gawain's tempter in some ways seems an agent of the Devil,[80] but as far as I know no one has examined closely the significance of Hautdesert Castle and the "goddess" Morgan le Fay in this connection.

The order which reigns at Hautdesert is a false and discourteous order. At the head of the table in Arthur's court sits Bishop Baldwin, God's religious emissary; at the head of the table in Bertilak's court sits Morgan le Fay, who serves the Devil. To understand that Morgan le Fay is the demonic center of the false court is to understand more clearly the predicament of Gawain and, in effect, all men. Gawain is the nephew of both Morgan and Arthur. He carries in his blood a dual heritage, both evil and good, disorder and order. Morgan perverts order on all levels: as goddess she is the embodiment of perverted metaphysical order; as sorceress—counterpart to Merlin, whom she has tricked out of his secrets through the dalliance of love—she perverts the natural order; as ruler (a woman) she is an emblem of perverted social order; and as unmarried woman she is perhaps emblematic of the perverted soul.

The deeper significance of Gawain's discourse on the wickedness of women now begins to be apparent:

> "Thus one of them fooled Adam, here on earth,
> And several of them Solomon, and Samson,
> Delilah dealt him his death, and later David
> Was blinded by Bathsheba, and bitterly suffered.
> All these were wrecked by their wiles. What bliss it would be
> To love them but never believe them—if only one could!"
>
> [part 4, st. 18, ll. 2416–21]

Gawain is the victim not only of a lady's tricks but also of the feminine principle in himself. He is womanly not only in that he has allowed himself to be ruled, like Eve,[81] by perverse appetite and irascibility, but also in that he has fallen from the proper male role (in terms of both the chivalric and Christian schemes), a role which calls for an awareness of male and female interdependence (hence chivalrous behavior), into the dependent female role. One should "love them but never believe them" because that is the courteous arrangement—to recognize the proper and necessary value of womanhood but not to become subservient to women.

For some medieval writers, the "feminine principle" in man would be more specific than I have thus far suggested. D. W. Robertson, Jr., has assembled three tropological descriptions of the Fall of Man, and these, as we might expect, have some relevance to the fall of Sir Gawain. For our purposes the three accounts are similar in all important respects, and so it will be sufficient to consider only John Scotus' account as Robertson reports it:

> Scotus envisages Paradise as human nature, which includes in a Pauline sense two regions: interior and exterior. The first of these is the man, called νοῦς, who represents the spirit, and in it dwells truth and all good, which is the Word of God—"veritas et omne bonum, quod est Verbum Dei." Hence, this is the habitat of reason. It contains the Tree of Life, called πᾶν, which was placed there by God, and the *fons vitae*, the Fountain of Life, from which flow the four streams of the cardinal virtues. This interior region should be "married" to the exterior region in a manner prefigured by the marriage of Christ and the Church. The exterior region, or the woman, is called αἴσθησις, since it is the region of the corporal senses, and it is a region of falsity and vain phantasies—"falsitatis et vanarum phantasiarum." It contains the Tree of Knowledge of Good and Evil, called γνωστόν, and the serpent, which is illicit delight, *illicita delectatio*. These details should give us no trouble if we remember the convention in accordance with which the spirit is "married" to the flesh and also recall the Augustinian attitude toward phantasies. The allegorical machinery is simply the conventional machinery of spiritual exegesis. To continue with the figure, it is obvious that in a garden of this kind, true beauty and delight are to be found in the inner region, and that whatever impresses the outer region as being beautiful should be referred to the inner region for judgment.[82]

(Illicit delight as used here may signify any illicit delight, including excessive love of life itself.) The failure of Gawain's reason, in the third test, is a failure of the male principle. Having perceived the beauty of life, he fails to refer that beauty to its source.[83]

The chivalric ideal of courtesy may directly reflect the ideal order of God, but it discounts Nature. No man of flesh and blood since Christ can be perfectly chivalrous, for at last the desire to save one's own neck is overwhelming. And so it is not surprising that the knights and ladies of the Round Table adopt the green baldric, not solemnly, from Christian compassion, not out of an anguished sense that they share Gawain's spiritual weakness, but joyfully, granting glory to the girdle; for Gawain, who in his own view has sinned through lack of faith, is from the court's point of view a great hero, and from that point of view his wish to be more than almost perfect is indeed laughable. No child of Adam is capable of perfection. One does the best one can, one finds that one has "lacked a little," one repents and receives forgiveness, and the cycle starts over again. That is, after all, the point of Christmas. The poet has good reason, then, for opening and closing with the fall of Troy: only one kingdom lasts forever, the kingdom of Him "þat bere þe croun of þorne" ("who bore the crown of thorns"). Exchanges, bargains, gifts are a necessary part of life on earth, but one can never be sure one will be able to keep one's bargain. Only God's Christmas bargain, ironically inverted in the Green Knight's challenge, is certain: a life for a life.

Symbolism in *Gawain* supports the reading I have offered. In the light of the Christian symbolism in the *Pearl*, it is interesting to observe that Gawain's trip is from light to dark, from the chivalric order into Nature, and that Gawain, most Christlike of men, and Gringolet, best of all possible horses, are associated here (as in earlier Gawain tradition) with the sun. Conceivably elements of the old sun-god myth enter the poem as Christian reinterpretation of the myth.

The symbolic significance of the Green Knight may also perhaps work in terms of the Christian world view. Coming from outside Arthur's realm of order, Bertilak is a tester; thus he may conceivably represent, though not in any strict allegorical fashion, Nature itself, that phantom or illusion into which every man is introduced at birth and which, to save himself, man must interpret and deal with correctly. Such a reading must begin with the usual Christian interpretation of the Green Knight but must carry that reading further than it is usually carried. It seems true (as Gawain himself thinks) that the Green Knight is the Devil's agent—and more: a symbolic summary of all that opposes the law of God, a fusion of elf-knight, druid, and fiend.[84] His castle is surrounded by oaks, the sacred tree of the druid; he is, like the fairy, like the druid, and like the Devil, a shape-shifter and a hunter; and like the fairy, the druid, and the Devil, he inhabits (or at any rate pretends to inhabit) a mound. But to view the Green Knight simply as an agent of the forces of darkness is to forget that the Green Knight serves God (as Gawain's priest-confessor) as readily as he serves the Devil.[85] It therefore seems more satisfactory to view the Green Knight as a symbolic representation of the force of Nature. Like Nature, Bertilak is a jubilantly vital, changeable, more or less perpetual force (cf. the traditional significance of the Christmas tree; consider again the decapitation and the opening of part 2 of the poem; and see also ll. 206–7). We have said that the corporeal world tests man; and clearly both the character and the effects of Nature are urged upon man's senses, seat of appetites, man's irascible part, and man's reason. This is perhaps because, rightly understood, Nature is a revelation of God—His *goodness* (which appeals to desire), His *power* (which merits loyal vassalage, that industrious service and devotion antithetical to sloth, hence a function of irascibility), and His *wisdom* (which appeals to man's reason). Bertilak's three colors—green, red, and gold—may conceivably represent specific aspects of the test. Green is traditionally associated with life, specifically with mortal flesh ("Flesh is grass"), and sometimes with sensation;[86] and in conventional Christmas symbolism green has the same association with life (as if miraculously, the holly and the evergreen tree are green even in winter). Hence green seems emblematic of Nature's test of the flesh, the basis of earthly appetites; or, conversely, it may be emblematic of God's goodness, demonstrated by His gift of life. Red is traditionally associated with emotional force (as in the expression "a red-blooded man"); and in conventional Christmas symbolism red represents Christ's passion (Latin *passio*, any powerful emotion).[87] Hence red seems emblematic of Nature's test of the irascible part; or, again, it may be emblematic of God's power. Finally, gold is traditionally associated with the excellent, the regal (an identification based on the alchemistical view that in its purest form earth is gold). Thus gold may emblematically suggest Nature's test of that highest of faculties, reason;[88] or it may represent God's wisdom. This view

82   THE GAWAIN-POET

of the significance of the Green Knight—a view I offer only as a partial explanation—makes sense in terms of the Christian world view we find in both *Gawain* and the *Pearl*.

Lest this interpretation seem unduly speculative, let me quote an interesting passage from Bonaventura, from the same book which presents the "three stages of illumination," for in this one passage an imaginative poet with a knowledge of folklore and romance might have found the whole religious scheme of the *Gawain:*

> For the *origen* of things, according to their creation, distinction, and beauty, in the work of the six days indicates the divine power producing all things from nothing, wisdom distinguishing all things clearly, and goodness adorning all things generously. *Magnitude* of things, either according to the measure of their length, width, and depth, or according to the excellence of power spreading itself in length, breadth, and depth, as appears in the diffusion of light, or again according to the efficacy of its inner, continuous, and diffused operation, as appears in the operation of fire—magnitude, I say, indicates manifestly the immensity of the power, wisdom, and goodness of the triune God, Who exists unlimited in all things through His power, presence, and essence. *Multitude* of things, according to the diversity of genus, species, and individuality, in substance, form, or figure, and efficacy beyond all human estimation, clearly indicates and shows the immensity of the aforesaid traits in God [wisdom, power, goodness]. *Beauty* of things, according to the variety of light, figure, and color in bodies simple and mixed and even composite, as in the celestial bodies, minerals, stones and metals, plants and animals, obviously proclaims the three mentioned traits. *Plenitude* of things —according to which matter is full of forms because of the seminal reasons; form is full of power because of its activity; power is full of effects because of its efficiency—declares the same manifestly. *Operation*, multiplex inasmuch as it is natural, artificial, and moral, by its very variety shows the immensity of that power, art, and goodness which indeed are in all things the cause of their being, the principle of their intelligibility, and the order of their living. *Order*, by reason of duration, situation, and influence, as prior and posterior, upper and lower, nobler and less noble, indicates clearly in the book of creation the primacy, sublimity, and dignity of the First Principle in relation to its infinite power. The order of the divine laws, precepts, and judgments in the Book of Scripture indicates the immensity of His wisdom. The order of the divine sacraments, rewards, and punishments in the body of the Church indicates the immensity of His goodness. Hence order leads us most obviously into the first and highest, most powerful, wisest, and best.

He, therefore, who is not illuminated by such great splendor of created things is blind; he who is not awakened by such great clamor is deaf; he who does not praise God because of all these effects is dumb; he who does not note the First Principle from such great signs is foolish. Open your eyes therefore, prick up your spiritual ears, open your lips, and apply your heart, that you may see your God in all creatures, may hear Him, praise Him, love and adore Him, magnify and honor Him, lest the whole world rise against you.[89]

Number symbolism also seems to play some part in *Gawain*, as it did in the *Pearl*. The main significance of the fact that the poem is in four parts may be that *four* is, for Augustine and others, the number of time and the number of Nature (earth, air, fire, water). Most of what J. E. Cirlot has to say of the number also seems appropriate:

Four. Symbolic of the earth, of terrestrial space, of the human situation, of the external, natural limits of the "minimum" awareness of totality, and, finally, of rational organization. It is equated with the square and the cube, and the cross representing the four seasons and the points of the compass. . . . It is the number associated with tangible achievement and with the Elements.[90]

The number *three* is equally important in the poem. Threes are everywhere, as no reader can fail to notice. This use of the number three throughout the *Gawain* is relevant to the poem's purpose if the poem is, as I believe, a Christmas celebration. From a medieval Christian point of view, in which the Three Persons are always separate but inseparable (so that God the Father may speak of hanging on the cross, or Christ may speak of having "wrought" man, as He does in the Wakefield *Resurrection*), Christ's birth represents a triple extension of grace: man's feeble rational part is made complete by an extension of Wisdom; his feeble irascible part is made complete by an extension of Power; his concupiscent part, by an extension of Goodness or Love. And man escapes the grave. This use of the number three in connection with Christmas can be found outside the work of the *Gawain*-poet. It occurs in carols, sermons, and, as I have shown elsewhere, in the *Second Shepherds' Play:* three shepherds, three dramatic movements (separated by music), three themes—law, love, and wonder—set up in the opening soliloquies, and three gifts to the Christ child, each gift appropriate to one of the three aspects of the Trinity. But nowhere do we find a more ingenious use of threes than in *Sir Gawain and the Green Knight*.

THE GAWAIN-POET

6.

VERSIFICÃTION ÃND FORM

In the *Pearl* the poet uses twelve-line tetrameter stanzas which have both alliteration and a complicated rhyme scheme: *ababababbcbc*. Usually at least three words in a given line alliterate; occasionally only two. The alliteration is not that of classical Old English verse, however, for two reasons: whereas in Old English verse the third stressed syllable or word is always one of the alliterative words, the third stressed syllable or word in the *Pearl* may or may not be one of the alliterative words; and whereas Old English alliterative lines allow for considerable variation in rhythm, the *Pearl* lines are quite regular, showing the influence of accentual or accentual-syllabic verse. Stanzas in the *Pearl* are linked by verbal repetition. A key word, either thematically or dramatically significant, appears as the third or fourth stressed word (usually the fourth) in the final line of one stanza and reappears as the first or second (usually the first) stressed word in the first line of the next. That the device is as much ornamental as anything else is evident from the poet's occasional use, not of true verbal repetition, but of quibble, or, in one case, only a faint echo of sound. The link at lines 612–13 (st. 51–52) is established by *inoghe-now* (pronounced *nu*). The poet changes his link word twenty times, dividing the poem into twenty sections, all but one of which contain five linked stanzas. Section XV contains six linked stanzas, one of which the poet may have intended to revise out.

The first two stanzas in the Middle English will serve to illustrate the alliteration, rhyme, and verbal linking:

Perle, plesaunte to prynces paye
To clanly clos in golde so clere,
Oute of oryent, I hardyly saye,
Ne proued I neuer her precios pere.
So rounde, so reken in vche araye,
So smal, so smoþe her sydeȝ were,
Quere-so-euer I jugged gemmeȝ gaye,
I sette hyr sengeley in synglere.
Allas! I leste hyr in on erbere;
þurȝ gresse to grounde hit fro me yot.
I dewyne, fordolked of luf-daungere
Of þat pryuy perle wythouten spot.

Syþen in þat spote hit fro me sprange,
Ofte haf I wayted, wyschande þat wele,
þat wont watȝ whyle deuoyde my wrange
And heuen my happe and al my hele.
þat dotȝ bot þrych my hert þrange,
My breste in bale bot bolne and bele;
ȝet þoȝt me neuer so swete a sange
As stylle stounde let to me stele.
For soþe þer fleten to me fele,
To þenke hir color so clad in clot.
O moul, þou marreȝ a myry iuele,
My priuy perle wythouten spotte.

In *Purity*, *Patience*, and *St. Erkenwald*, the versification is based
more closely on that found in classical Old English poetry, but the
poet modifies the older system in the direction of greater complexity
and does not always use alliteration as a signal of the stress pattern.
Critics agree that the *Gawain*-poet's lines have great vigor and flexi-
bility, but there has been disagreement about where the stresses are
supposed to fall. There are four common theories.[91] The first is that
the lines have four stresses and that each line naturally divides into
two two-stress half-lines, with stresses signaled by the alliteration
of one or more words in the first half-line and the first (or first and
second) of the important words in the second half-line. According to
this theory the poet's versification follows the Old English. The
opening lines of *St. Erkenwald*, then, might be analyzed this way:

In Lońdon in Engloǹde / not fulle lonǵe sythén,
Sythen Crı́st suffride on crosśe / and Crı́stendom stablyd.

The second theory finds eight stresses to a line; the third, seven; and the fourth, five and occasionally four.[92] The last of these theories allows much the most natural reading of the lines. If we accept this theory of the meter, the lines are simply pentameter, much like blank verse, but rhythmically more flexible than normal iambic pentameter, for the poet may use more unstressed syllables than the writer of blank verse would be able to use (cf. Hopkins' "riders"); or he may, on the other hand, drop out unstressed syllables we would normally expect, for the alliterative poet has a means of signaling his stress pattern when he wants to. Moreover, the tradition of alliterative poetry gives him the ability to shift, whenever he wishes to break the pentameter effect, to a classical four-stress line. Thus the opening of *Sir Gawain and the Green Knight* would read:

> Siþen þe sége and þe assaút watʒ sésed at Tróye,
> þe bórʒ bríttened and brént to bróndeʒ and áskeʒ,
> þe túlk þat þe trámmes of trésoun þer wróʒt
> Watʒ tríed for his trícheriè, þe tréwest on erthe. . . .

While alliterative signaling is available when the poet wants it, the reader's general expectation of pentameter allows the poet to play with alliteration when he chooses. Professor Menner's comments on alliteration in *Purity* will serve to illustrate.

> Alliteration is becoming less of a structural necessity and more of an ornament. This may be seen, in the first place, in the fact that unstressed words and prefixes may bear the alliteration, as in the following lines:
>
> 63 On hade *bo*ʒt hym a *bo*rʒ, he sayde, *by* hys trawþe.
> 114 Ay þe *best by*fore and *bry*ʒtest atyred.
>   (Cf. bifore, 918, 978)
> 127 And *re*hayte *re*kenly þe *ri*che and þe poveren.
> 197 *Bot* never ʒet in no *bo*ke *bre*ved I herde.
>
> Another indication that the alliteration is becoming mere ornament is the tendency to crowd as many alliterating words as possible in a single line. Lines with three alliterating words in the first half are very common, but many lines have even more. The author of *Purity* is especially fond of such superabundant alliteration, for example:

113 Wheþer þay wern worþy oþer wers, wel wern þay stowed.
661 þenne sayde oure Syre þer he sete: "Se, so Sare laȝes."
1681 His hert heldet unhole, he hoped non oþer. [Since the *h* is silent,
     every word but one alliterates.]

In *Purity*, as in most contemporary alliterative poems, double alliteration is not unusual. This is generally parallel—a a b b, as in

299 Sem *s*oþly þat *o*n, þat *o*þer hyȝt Cam.

Here, and in 345, 1304, 1573, 1622, it is essential in the structure of the
verse, since these lines would otherwise have to be considered defective;
but elsewhere it is added to the regular alliteration as additional ornamentation, as in

25   *M*e *m*ynez on *o*ne a*m*onge *o*þer, as *M*aþew recordez.
493 *M*yryly on a *f*ayr *m*orn, *m*onyth þe *f*yrst.

Transverse alliteration—a b a b—appears in

515 For I *s*e *w*el þat hit is *s*othe þat alle mannez *w*yttez,

and possibly in 228, 327, 1618. Inclusive alliteration—a b b a—appears in

608 Hit is *e*þe to *l*eve by þe *l*ast *e*nde,

and perhaps in 67, 735.[93]

In addition to the alliterative pattern, the poet sometimes uses the
larger organizing device of stanzaic division. The manuscript of
Patience is not divided into stanzas, but stanza divisions are marked
by dots, one before the first line of each new stanza. Stanza division
is sometimes clear and sometimes not clear in *Purity*, and editors
have printed the poem in various ways. The proper grouping of
lines in *St. Erkenwald* is also in doubt.

Sir Gawain and the Green Knight is in four parts. The average
stanza consists of twenty alliterative, unrhymed lines followed by a
bob and wheel:

> wyth wynne;
> Where werre & wrake & wonder
> Bi syþeȝ hatȝ wont þer-inne,
> & oft boþe blysse & blunder
> Ful skete hatȝ skyfted synne.

> [part i, st. i, ll. 15–19]

The *bob* is the short line ("wyth wynne"); the *wheel* consists of the
four alliterative trimeter lines which follow the bob. The bob and
wheel rhyme *ababa*.

THE GAWAIN-POET

To speak in this technical fashion of the *Gawain*-poet's versification is perhaps not to do full justice to his art. What is chiefly note-
worthy about his alliterative long lines is their infinite variety and
richness and their capability of handling any kind of subject with
appropriate sound. He can write:

> Bi a *mo*únte on þe *m*órne *m*érylỳ he rýdes
> Into a *f*órest *f*ul dep, þat *f*érly watȝ wýlde,
> Hiȝe hílleȝ on *v*́che a hálue, & hólt-wodeȝ *v́*nder
> Of hóre ókeȝ ful hóge a húndreth to-géder. . . .
>
> [part 2, st. 11, ll. 740–43]

(Initial *h*'s are not pronounced. The alliteration in the third and
fourth lines here is on the vowels. Final *e*'s are not pronounced
either.)

Here, within the basic pentameter pattern, the poet manages some
fine rhythmical effects. The first line moves slowly, held in check
not by the easy trick of absolute iambic or trochaic regularity but
by subtle rhythmical tensions. The first two feet (i.e., the compo-
nents of the first half-line) are anapaestic, but against the anapaestic
rush there is the use of *m*'s and long vowels. The second half-line
balances the first, moving slowly, almost hesitantly for an instant,
to accommodate the light stress on *-ly* and the long syllable *rydes*.
As the line moves, so Sir Gawain moves. The first word of the
second line would not ordinarily receive stress, being a preposition,
but the enjambment (*rydes / Into*) infects the word slightly. This
second line, then, begins in an uneasy light stress followed by two
unstressed syllables, then the heavily stressed *forest*. The line itself,
in other words, plunges into its central image. Of the two words
that follow next, ordinarily only *dep* would be stressed. But the
alliteration of *forest* and *ful* (and this would be true even if the poet
were not working with a strong alliterative tradition) moves *ful* in
the direction of stress, forcing a hovering accent upon *ful dep*. After
its plunge and hovering moment, the line rights itself in the fairly
regular second half-line. The third line has superabundant alliteration—six initial vowel sounds. Within the over-all pentameter feeling, the hovering stress above or between *Hiȝe* and *hilleȝ* is obvious
and neatly underscores the image of high hills. The final line here

has the heaviness of the oaks represented: the vowels in *hore, okeȝ*, and *hoge*, forced into stress not only by alliteration but by rhyme or near-rhyme as well, have weight as relatively long vowels, and a certain density because they occur close together, two of them without a separating unstressed syllable. The second half-line here, on the other hand, moves quickly because of its many unstressed syllables (*ă húndreťh tŏ-gédĕr*), sound once more reflecting sense.

The poet's line can accommodate much more bold demands when he wishes. "Springing" the verse by means of alliterative signaling, the poet can manage, for instance:

> For sućhe a bráwne of a bést, þe bolde búrne sáyde
>
> > [part 3, st. 20, ll. 1631]
>
> For þe cośtes þat Í haf knówen vpon þe, knyȝt, hére
>
> > [part 3, st. 6, ll. 1272]
>
> For boþe two heȟe I þe bede bot two bare myntes
>
> > [part 4, st. 15, ll. 2352]

(In this last example, alliteration, rhyme, verbal repetition, and sense combine to establish the springing of the verse. My phrase symbol and the number 2 are meant to suggest the presence of two stresses impossible to establish as hovering either in the pattern ∧ / or in the pattern / ∧. The use of conventional spondees in place of hovering stresses "clarifies" the problem by evading it: / / /.)

The boldest line in *Sir Gawain and the Green Knight*—the analysis of which must be left to the judgment of the reader—occurs when the host is hunting the boar:

> [þ]ise oþer halowed hyghe! ful hyȝe, & hay! hay! cryed.
>
> > [part 3, st. 12, ll. 1445]

Few poets in English, and for that matter few poets anywhere, can surpass the music of the *Gawain*-poet.

THE POEMS

PEARL

1

Pearl, pleasing as a prince's pay,
So chastely buckled in gold, so pure,
In all the East, I boldly say,
I never found her precious peer;
So light, so priceless her array,
So small her sides, so smooth they were,
Wherever I judged fine jewelry
I found her supreme and singular.
Alas! I lost that pearl in an arbor;
Through the grass to the ground she shot;
And robbed of what was mine, I mourned
My own prized pearl without a spot.

2

Since then, in that same spot I've lain
For hours, longing for longer sight
Of the gem that once made all griefs nothing
And raised my fortune and all my estate;
In grief my breast would swell and burn:
The shade closed stifling over my heart;
Yet I never heard a sweeter song
Than the music that still moment brought.
For in truth, rich music flooded my head
When I thought of her color locked in a clod;
O sod, you've spoiled a splendid thing,
My own prized pearl without a spot!

3

Well might that spot with spices spread
Where to rot such splendid riches run,
And blossoms yellow, blue, and red
Bloom there bright against the sun;
Flower and fruit can feel no blight
Where she drove down in the dark ground:
Each grassblade wakes in a withering seed
Or corn were never brought to bin.
In the good is every good begun;
So splendid a seed, then, cannot be brought
To nothing: Branching spices spring
From that prized pearl without a spot.

4

And so to that spot I came, as it happened,
Walked through the high gray gates of the garden,
In August, just at the height of the season
When corn is cut with sickles keen;
Came to the mound where my pearl had fallen,
A cool place shadowed by shrubs that shone
Where gilvers, ginger, and gromwell ripened,
And peonies powdered the ground between.
Lovely that place to look upon,
And fair the fragrance, heady, sweet,
Where in beauty dwelled that priceless gem,
My precious pearl without a spot.

5

Before that spot I wrung my hands,
My chest in the cold of anguish caught;
Wordless rage in my heart rang,
Fierce questionings that fiercely fought;
Though reason chided, "Child, be calm,"
I cursed my sorrow's prison-house;
No thought of Christ's calm suffering
Could ease my wild, rebellious heart.
And I fell down there on that flowering earth—
Such sweet scents through my brain shot—
And sank, struck down in a sleep like death
On that precious pearl without a spot.

6

My spirit soared from that spot to space;
Above the mound where body lay,
Ghost went forth, by God's grace,
Mounted, moved in mystery.
I knew not where in this world I was,
But cliffs all round me cleaved the sky;
And toward a forest I set my face
Where the richest of rocks rose awesomely.
The light of those rocks no man would believe—
The glint and glory that gleamed to the eye:
No tapestry might a mortal weave
Of half such rich resplendency!

Splendid those towering mountains shone
With crystal cliffs as clear as ice;
At the base, bright holtwoods covered the ground
Great apple trees with deep blue boles;
Like burnished silver the leafage turned
And shimmered, thick on all the trees;
As clouds and sky slid over them
They shrilled and shivered with changing gleams.
And the stones heaped high below the leaves
Were precious pearls from the Far East.
Mere sunlight would seem blue and grave
Compared to such resplendencies.

Seeing those splendid hills in air,
My ghost had soon forgotten grief;
The fragrance of the fruited air,
Like manna, gave my ghost relief.
And bright birds flew in the forest together
With plumes of fire, both small and great;
No citole string or citherner
Could touch their sweet triumphant note:
For as they beat their wings those birds
All choired in sweet chorale on high;
No finer prize might a mortal get
Than hear that song's resplendency!

9

How splendid all that forest was,
How lovely every lane, how fair,
No mortal word might rightly praise,
No poet's song come anywhere near;
And I walked on in the wildest of joys,
No hill so steep it could stop me there,
And the farther I walked, the finer each spice,
The fairer the bowed-down branches were;
Fair hedges, borders, a broad river—
Like bright gold thread the banks hung steep—
And I came where the water cut into the shore;
Dear God what rich resplendency!

10

There rose resplendent on the riverside
Beautiful banks of perfect beryl;
Slowly the water swung past me and eddied
With a whispered murmur, and rippled and turned;
And jewels lying on the river-bed
Glowed like glints through glass; they shone
Like clean white stars on a winter's night
When the candles are out in the valley town;
For every pebble placed in that stream,
Making the water flash merrily,
Was an emerald, a sapphire, or some other gem;
And great was that resplendency.

11

The splendor of every dune and dell,
Of woods and water and the wide green plain,
Brought sharper joy, made sorrow pale,
Drove distress out, deadened pain;
Beside that river's steady roll
I walked in peace, brim-full my brain;
And the farther I followed those flooded vales,
The stronger the joy inside me sang.
As Fortune flies on free-born wings,
Whether she sends him joy or care,
The man on whom her glance lands
Must mount or fall to more and more.

12

More marvels I saw below those skies
Than I'd tell, whatever time I had,
For the mortal mind might never rise
To the tenth dole of that keen delight;
For in truth, I thought then Paradise
Lay just beyond where the banks stretched wide,
And I thought that waterway a device
To lock off Heaven and the Liege Lord;
Beyond that brook, by slope or slide,
I thought the castle boundaries marked;
But the water was deep, I dared not wade;
And longing leaped in me more and more.

13

More and more and ever more
I longed to cross over and look beyond,
For if that bank where I stood was fair,
Far fairer lay that farther land.
I started to stumble about and stare,
Fiercely, frantically hoping to find
Some ford; but greater gulfs I saw
The farther I walked the water's strand.
Never, I swore, would I stop or turn
For fear where yet such wonders were;
Then a finer thing I found at hand
That stirred my spirit more and more.

14

O, more than marvel!—mind ran wild!—
I saw, ablaze beyond the water
A crystal cliff where splendor shrilled,
Shot forth ringing, royal, rare,
And there at the foot of that cliff—a child,
A maiden, noble, gentle her air,
Her little robe all gleaming white;
And I knew her—knew I had seen her before.
As gold gleams when men clip it bare,
So gleamed that beautiful child on the shore;
I looked then long at that fairest of fair,
And longer, and knew her more and more.

15

Still more I searched her sweet, fine face
And her figure when I found her there;
Such gladness hammered and hit in my chest
As seldom stirred my heart before.
I longed to call out to the child at once,
But my heart was hurt with the pain of wonder:
I saw her here in so strange a place,
No wonder if wonder numbed my heart!
And then she lifted her face as fair
And white as ivory, and more pure;
It made heart sting, struck all astray,
And ever the longer, more and more.

16

More than I liked my dread arose;
I stood dead still and dared not call—
My eyes wide open, mouth drawn close—
I stood as still as the hawk in the hall;
Ghostly I knew that vision was,
And I feared any moment the dark might fall,
Feared she might yet fly up from the place
Before I had brought her to reach or call.
Then, gentle child without a flaw,
So smooth, so delicate, so small,
She rose in her place and stood, all still,
A precious image set in pearl.

A setting of pearls of royal price
Men by God's grace might have seen
That day when, fair as the fleur-de-lys,
She came in her play to the brilliant bank.
Gleaming all in white her amice,
The sides open and splendidly sewn
With pearls, the brightest Marjories
That ever my eyes had looked upon.
Her sleeves were full and thickly adorned
With pearls in a double braid; her kirtle
All adorned with the same pure stone,
Set on all sides with precious pearl.

And a crown of pearls she wore on her head,
Bright Marjories, no other stone,
A pinnacle of purest white
Where perfect floral figures hung;
She wore no coif or cloth or hood,
And her hair, loose, swept softly down
As, solemn as duke or earl, she stood,
Her hue as white as whale's bone.
Yellow as gold her tresses shone
Where they lay on her shoulders, lovely, light;
Her innocence glowed clear and clean
With precious pearls embroidering it.

19

Set with pearls were sleeves and hem,
There at her hands, her sides, her throat,
Pure white spheres, no other gem,
And all her dress was dazzling white.
And the finest pearl, a blazing stone,
Above her heart shone heaven-bright.
Surely the mortal soul would swoon
Before it grasped the worth of it;
Surely no tongue of flesh and blood
Could find fit words to speak of it,
So clean and clear and pure that light,
That precious pearl where it was set.

20

Set in pearls, that gem of grace
Came down on the farther bank to the shore;
No gladder man from here to Greece
Than I when that wonder walked so near.
She was nearer to me than aunt or niece;
My joy was therefore much the more!
She spoke, my special pearl of price,
Inclining low in lordly manner;
Removing her crown, her gleaming treasure,
She hailed me with her hand. O, well
For me that ever I was born
To answer my sweetheart set in pearl!

21

"O pearl adorned in pearls," I cried,
"Are you the pearl that I have mourned,
  Grieving alone in my house at night?
  Much bitter loneliness I've borne
  From the day I lost you to grass and sod.
  Heartsick, broken I've been, forlorn,
  Yet you've landed here on a life of delight
  In Paradise, where pains are gone.
  What fate has taken away my gem
  And cast me down in this crevasse of care?
  Since we two, love, were torn in twain
  I've lived a joyless jeweler."

22

  My jewel adorned in jewels fair
  Lifted her face and eyes of gray,
  Replaced her crown of Orient pearl
  And spoke to me then solemnly:
"Sir, you have misread your tale
  To think your jewel taken away
  That is held in so handsome a chest as here
  Am I in this garden that cannot fade,
  To linger freely forever and play
  Where men's grim griefs come never near.
  You would think it a treasure chest indeed
  If you were in truth a jeweler!

"But gentle jeweler, if you would lose
  All joy for a gem that once was dear,
  Then surely you're set in a madman's purpose,
  And come into court with a careless brief.
  What have you lost but a mortal rose
  That flowered and failed like all Nature alive?
  By nature of the casket where it is cased
  It is changed to a pearl of price. In your grief
  You've foolishly called your fate a thief
  That has given you something for nothing. Sir,
  You cry against your care's relief!
  You seem no natural jeweler."

A jewel to me was that gentle guest,
  And jewels the words she cast to me;
"At last," I said, "dear heart's best,
  My dole of distress will be drawn away.
  I beg that my fault may be excused:
  I thought you gone from the light of day,
  But now that I've found you, my heart shall feast
  And dwell with you here in these groves forever
  And love the Lord and all His laws
  That have brought me at last to my happiness here.
  For when I am with you in Paradise
  I'll be a joyful jeweler."

25

"Jeweler," cried my jewel chaste,
"Are you joking or can it be lunacy?
  Three strange things you've said at once,
  And strangely confused, in truth, all three;
  You miss all the meaning in your mad words:
  Released from your wits, away they fly!
  You say that you've seen me here in this place:
  But mortal man sees merely with his eye;
  Again, you've said you will come to me
  And dwell with me here in delight forever;
  And you've said you will cross this boundary.
  Not yet, my joyful jeweler!

26

"I judge that jeweler worth no praise
  Who values all that his eye sees,
  And much to blame, and discourteous,
  Who thinks his Liege Lord tells him lies,
  Who leally swears that He will raise
  Your life when your feeble flesh dies.
  You read His words in strange ways
  To trust what you find in the flesh of your eyes.
  Such overweening pride as this
  Is an evil good men ought not know,
  To think no saying worthy of trust
  Unless mere reason judge it so.

27

"Judge for yourself whether you have spoken
    Fitting words for a man to heave
    To God. You say you'll enter Heaven.
    But might you not at least ask leave?
    —And even then you might not get in.
    And you say that you will cross these waves.
    First you must come to a crueller line:
    Corpse must cool in the cold of the grave;
    It was given up in the Paradise grove
    When our first father failed in his guard;
    Only the man dragged down by death
    Will God judge fit to cross this flood."

28

"Judge me less harshly, my love," I said.
"Must sorrow return and my soul sink down
    Now that I've found the fair one I lost?
    Must I even now lose all in the end?
    Why must I here both miss and meet?
    The pearl of my joy revives my pain!
    Is treasure good but to make men weep,
    For what men love they must lose again?
    What matter then how my goods decline
    Or where I walk in the world's waste;
    When I have no part in my pearl, my own,
    What can men judge me but exiled, lost?"

29

"You judge all life by your own distress,"
The child said then; "Why do you, though?
Pursuing his suits over little things
Many a man has forfeited more.
Then make instead the sign of the cross
And love God well, in weal or woe,
For anger will gain you never a cress:
Who needs to be bent He'll bend. Be now
Less proud, for though you dance like a doe
And brandish and bray with all your rage,
When you make no headway to or fro,
Then you'll abide what He will judge.

30

"Judge your God and loudly indict!
The Lord falls never a foot from His way;
Your recompense will rise not a mite
Though you for grief forswear all joy.
Then stop your struggling, give up spite;
Seek a settlement swift and sure.
Petition may win you mercy yet,
And kindness show her craft to you.
His comfort eases the heart's care,
For what griefs cannot your God assuage?
Rage, rave, or recoil and bear,
It lies with Him to order and judge."

At last I judged before that jewel:
"Let not my Lord be wroth with me;
If I rashly rave, if I stumble in a spell,
My heart was torn by misery.
As rising water flows from a well
I give up my spirit to God's great mercy.
Do not rebuke me in words so cruel,
Dear heart, even though I may go astray;
Have pity, and as you once did, give me
Comfort; for remember this:
Once you made peace between care and me,
For you were the ground of all my bliss.

"My bliss, my pain—love, you have been both;
But mainly you have brought me pain;
For you were vanished from every path
And I knew not where my pearl had gone;
Now that I see, I forget my grief.
When we parted, child, we two were one;
God forbid that we now be cross;
We meet so seldom by tree or stone!
You speak very well, my courtly one,
But I am mere dust and speak amiss;
And Christ's mercy—and Mary and John—
Those are my only grounds for bliss.

33

"I find you in bliss and one with God,
  But I am a man in mourning's mate;
  You take of that, love, little heed,
  Though I give way to gambits hot;
  But here where earth and heaven stand
  In truce, let us leave off argument;
  I beg you, tell me, fair little maid,
  What life you lead here morning and night.
  You know I am thankful that your estate
  Has turned to such wonderful wealth. It is
  For all my joy the high street,
  And building-ground of all my bliss."

34

"Bliss be with you, and all good,"
  My love said then, my fairest fair;
"You are welcome now to walk in our land,
  For now your voice is sweet to hear.
  Haughty mood and high-flown pride,
  I warn you, are not honored here;
  My Liege Lord does not like to chide:
  He signals none but the humble near.
  And when at last you must appear
  At His throne, then think with selflessness;
  My Lord the Lamb will grant you honor,
  Who is the ground of all my bliss.

35

"You've said that I dwell in bliss here
 And asked to hear more of how I live:
 As you know well, when I left the earth
 I was still a child of tender age;
 Nonetheless, the Lamb, in His power,
 Took me to Himself in marriage,
 Crowned me His queen to live in joy
 For all the length of Heaven's age;
 I share in all His heritage,
 His bride, His wife, and wholly His;
 His praise, His price, His high estate
 Are root and ground of all my bliss."

36

"Blissful," I said, "can this be true?
 Please, if I'm wrong, don't rise up in anger;
 But are you, then, the queen of the sky
 And she whom all the earth shall honor?
 We think Christ's mother supremely high,
 Who brought forth a child in virgin flower;
 Then who might steal her crown away
 Except that she excel in favor?
 Yet we speak of that Queen as supreme in splendor
 And call her 'the Phoenix of Araby,'
 Flawless creature conceived in fire
 And like to the Queen of Courtesy."

37

"Courtesy's Queen," my beloved cried,
  Genuflecting, lifting her face,
"Matchless mother and merriest maid,
  Blessed beginner of every grace!"
  She rose again, stood still in thought,
  Then spoke once more across the waves:
"Listen. Many find favor with God,
  But no usurper has power in this place.
  That Queen has all high Heaven's space
  And all dim Earth and Hell in her sway,
  Yet none will she drive from her heritage,
  For she is the Queen of Courtesy.

38

"The court of the great Lord God in the Highest
  Is not some flimsy mortal thing:
  All who arrive in Paradise
  Rule all the realm as queen or king
  Yet rob no other ruler's place
  But indeed exalt that other's throne
  And wish his crown worth five of such,
  If skill could fashion a finer crown.
  But my Lady from whose womb Christ sprung
  Still reigns supreme in royalty,
  And none would ask that throne pulled down,
  For she is the Queen of Courtesy.

39

"In courtesy, as Saint Paul said,
   All mortal men are the members of Christ:
   As head and arm and heart and leg
   Serve the body, true to trust,
   So every Christian soul is a limb
   Of Christ, and serves Him first and last.
   For listen: When has spite or spleen
   Made a man's arm lash at his chest?
   Your head grows neither crabbed nor cross
   With your finger, though you wear fine rings.
   So we all live here in love and bliss
   By courtesy, as queens and kings."

40

"Here courtesy," I answered then,
"And infinite charity abound;
   Still—if my speaking stirs no pain—
   Your words seem queer to me, and wrong;
   You're lifted, child, too high in Heaven:
   You, a queen, who died so young!
   What greater honor might one win
   Who suffered much in the world, held strong,
   And lived in penance his whole life long
   That the body's grief might get him joy?
   What greater glory might man gain
   Than the crown of a king in courtesy?

THE GAWAIN-POET

41

"Too free is that courtesy, indeed,
  If your state is truly what you say.
  Less than two years you lived in our land,
  Could neither please your God nor pray,
  No, nor knew either Pater or Creed—
  And yet, crowned queen on the first day!
  I cannot believe, as I love my God,
  That God would order all awry!
  As countess, child, I can easily see
  It might be fair that you hold estate,
  Or as lady of somewhat lower degree;
  But queen! It is an end too great!"

42

"No end can be marked to infinite bliss,"
  My loved one instantly replied;
"By nature, that which Truth is, God is,
  And all His acts are by nature right.
  So Matthew explains in the holy mass,
  In the true gospel of Almighty God,
  And there in a parable he gives
  An image and emblem of God's estate,
  For he says: 'The King of Heaven is like
  To a rich lord who had a vineyard:
  And there the time of year drew nigh
  For harvest, at the season's end.

" 'And seeing that it was the season's end,
　Early one morning the wine-lord rose
　To hire workers to clip and haul in
　The grapes. He found good men for his purpose
　And they entered into agreement soon
　On the wage; then away that wine-crew goes;
　They bend their backs in the blistering sun
　And prune and bind and bring in the grapes;
　And at noon that noble wine-lord goes
　To the market once more to find more men;
　"Why do you stand without work?" he asks,
　"Have you found no job worth the work in the end?"

" ' "By the end of cockcrow we'd reached this place,"
　So one of the men who stood there said,
　"And we've waited here since the hour of sunrise,
　And by heaven, we haven't been hired yet."
　He said: "Then go to my vineyard and harvest";
　So the lord spoke, and so he sealed it:
　"What hire is fair, when darkness falls
　I'll pay you, both in thought and deed."
　And so they went to the vines and worked;
　And so all day the lord of the land
　Went out among men to find workers and brought
　New men until daylight was near its end.

THE GAWAIN-POET

" 'Near end of day, at evensong,
   An hour before the sun went down,
   The lord found more men idle though strong;
   And he said, as he'd said to the other men,
  "Have you stood here idle all day long?"
   They told him that no one had work for them,
   And the lord said, "Hurry to my vineyard then,
   Young yeomen, and do there all you can."
   When bright green hills were burnished brown
   And the sun was setting, and daylight waned,
   The lord called all his men to him
   To take their wage at the day's end.

" 'The day was ended, the lord well knew;
   And he said to his reeve, "Sir, pay these men;
   Hand them over the hire I owe;
   And this: So none can make complaint,
   Set all the workers in one long row
   And settle with each at the same amount;
   Begin with the last, who worked least today,
   And move till you come to the men in front."
   At once the first of the crew complained,
   And said, "My lord, we've sweated sore!
   You could pour what these other men did in a pint!
   It seems to us you owe us more.

47

" ' "We ought to get more, it seems to us;
    We heaved and hacked in the noontime heat,
    And these men helped for a mere two hours—
    And you settle with all at one same rate!"
    Said the lord of the wine to one of those:
"Friend, I wish you no ill fate;
    Go now, and take with you all that is yours.
    I hired you here for a sum agreed;
    Why do you chafe at me now and chide?
    Have I not paid all that I promised before?
    More than one's bargain one must not bid.
    How is it, then, that you ask for more?

48

" ' "Moreover, man, is the money not mine
    To give or keep as seems good to me?
    Or is it perhaps that you're happiest feeling
    Wronged? Here there's no robbery."
    And Christ said: "Such is the Kingdom of Heaven.
First shall be last, be he never so swift,
    And he who comes last shall be first in his turn,
    For many are called but few are chosen." '
    Thus shall poor men take their portion,
    Late though they come and low though they are;
    Their little labor is soon spent,
    But the mercy of God is much the more.

49

"More heart's joy I've found in Heaven,
  Prouder place and brighter bloom
  Than any man in the world might gain
  Who asked for the fair wage owed to him.
  You know how late in the day I began;
  By vespers' light I came to the vine;
  Yet He thought at once of the wage that was mine
  And paid me at once of the total sum;
  And others there were who waited long,
  Who chopped and sweated long before
  I came, and yet He paid them nothing.
  Nor will He, perhaps, for a long while more."

50

I said more then; my mind grew bold:
"Child, your words are unreasonable!
  Like rock God's righteousness will hold,
  Or Holy Writ is a fool's fable.
  For are we not surely in the Psalter told,
  In words that are readily readable:
  'According to desert Thou wilt
  Requite, Thou Infinite and Eternal'?
  Others sweat long hours and labor,
  Yet here you come to your pay before;
  The less the work, the better the wages,
  And ever the longer, the less the more!"

51

"In God's great treasury, *more* and *less*,"
Said my gentle one, "are one word;
For here each man is paid alike,
Whether less or more his due reward;
Nor does that noble Lord hold back,
Whether He deals out less or more:
His gifts flow forth like floods from a ditch,
Or the whirlpool wheel that rolls afar.
Great is his franchise who shall dare
To come to Him for help. On such
Shall no expense or bliss be spared,
For the grace of God is great enough.

52

"And if you chide, for a checkmate,
That I am wrong to take wages here,
And cry that I who came so late
Do not deserve so high a hire,
Then I move this: Where yet have you met
With men, however holy in prayer,
Who never went out and forfeited
All claim and right at the Ruler's door?
And all the more often, the older they are,
Must men leave right in deed or thought;
Yet grace and mercy can lift them here:
The grace of God is great enough!

53

"But grace enough have innocents:
By law, as soon as a child is born,
In holy water he descends,
And so the child comes into the vine.
Then swiftly day and dark impinge;
The fist of dark Death bends him down
Who knew no wrong, kept innocence;
Then the rich Wine-Lord pays His men.
They did as He said: They served for Him.
Why should their labor be disallowed,
And why should the Lord not pay them soon?
For the grace of God is great enough.

54

"You know well enough how man was made
And first fashioned to flourish in light,
And how our first father forfeited
All ecstasy by an apple he bit;
The blood of man grew black on that meat,
To die in sorrow, far from His sight,
And after, to drag through Hell's dark heat
And writhe and wither without respite.
But soon men saw the antidote:
On the rough-hewn cross ran clean new blood
And purest water. That dark night
The grace of God was great enough!

55

"Enough flowed up from that rich well,
  Water and blood from the wide wound:
The blood bought us from Hell's bale,
  Delivered the ghost from the grim land;
And the water, the water of baptism, fell
  In a rush down the swordblade grimly ground
And washed away the waves of guilt
  Where Adam and all mankind were drowned.
Now there is nought in the whole world round
  Between us and bliss but what He withdrew;
In one fair hour was all restored,
  For the grace of God is great enough!

56

"Grace enough that man may get
  Who sins now, if he'll see and repent;
But with sorrows and sighs he must reach for it,
  And, heart stretched taut, he must put up with pain;
But reason, which cannot stray from right,
  Saves at once the innocent,
For Almighty God has never said
  That the guiltless need to be broken or shamed.
He who fails, falls, must find
  Contrition, and mercy must get him God;
But he who never once walked wrong,
  The innocent, is saved by right.

57

"And so it is right, as it comes to pass,
 That God will save two sorts by His skill:
 The righteous man shall see His face
 And also he who is spotless of soul.
 So the Psalter says, in a certain verse,
 'Lord, who shall climb Thy lofty hill
 Or rest within Thy holy place?'
 And God says straightway, neither is He slow:
 'He whose hand hath done no ill,
 Whose heart is pure and clean and bright,
 His foot shall neither falter nor fall.'
 The innocent is saved by right.

58

"The righteous, too, you may be certain,
 Shall stand safe in that strong-walled tower,
 Who has not wasted his works on nothing
 Or with craft and cunning robbed his neighbor.
 So Solomon says of the righteous man
 How the King of Wisdom welcomed him there
 And walked him down streets that were straight and
   gleaming
 And showed him a while His realm and power
 As if to say: 'Look, that lovely isle,
 If you hold to your way, you may well win yet.'
 But promptly, without either pain or peril,
 The innocent is saved by right.

59

"And as for the righteous, David says well
In the Psalter—no doubt you've seen it—'O God,
Let not Thy sentence on Thy servant fall,
For no man living is just in Thy sight.'
And so when you come to the time of that trial
Where all men's causes shall be cried,
Claim righteousness and your suit may fail
By these same words that I have said;
But He who shed bright blood on the rood,
Whose hands hard-hammered nails once bit,
Will signal past those cases tried
By innocence and not by right.

60

"And anyone who can read and write
Can easily study the Scripture and learn
How Christ walked once among mankind
And men made way to His place with their children
For blessing and the healing works He did
And implored Him to lay His hands on them:
The disciples said to them, 'Trouble Him not.'
And many gave way then and meant to be gone;
But Christ said, 'Suffer the little children
To come unto Me, and forbid them not,
For I say of such is the Kingdom of Heaven.'
The innocent are saved by right.

"To His right hand Christ called the mild
And He said, 'No man can hope to win
My riches unless he become like a child.'
No other man can enter in.
The honest, the harmless, the undefiled
Who show not a sign of stain or sin—
When those come knocking at the castle wall,
The great gate-latch is soon unpinned
And there lies the joy that gleams unfading,
Which the jeweler sought among gems of price,
And gave all his goods, both wool and linen,
To buy: the pearl supreme and flawless.

" 'For that pearl, flawless, priced most dear,
The jeweler gave up all his goods—
A gem as smooth as Heaven's sphere';
Thus spoke the Father of fields and floods;
That gem is unchipped and clean and clear
And endlessly round, the sign of all joys,
And that pearl will come to all who care
For right. At the center of my heart it glows,
For Christ who shed His blood on the cross
Has placed it there as an emblem of peace.
I beg you, sell off all earth's madness;
Buy that flawless pearl of price."

63

"O pearl, flawless, perfect, pure—"
I said, "—and bearing the pearl of price,
Who formed for you your figure fair?
Who wove your robe's rare artifice?
Your beauty never was born of Nature;
No mere Pygmalion painted your face;
Nor has Aristotle, for all his lore,
Yet named or counted your qualities!
Your beauty surpasses the fleur-de-lys,
My courteous one, my angel-child!
Tell me, brightest, what high office
Has set as its sign this flawless jewel?"

64

"My flawless Lamb, who can elevate
All things," she said, "dear Destiny,
Who made me His bride, though hardly right
Might once have seemed His choosing me.
When first I came from the world's wet
He called me to Him courteously:
'Come hither to Me, and be not afraid,
For I find no spot or stain in thee.'
Wisdom He gave to me then, and beauty;
In his fiery blood He washed my gown,
And He crowned me, clean in virginity,
And placed on my breast this flawless stone."

"O flawless bride as bright as flame,
Whose royalty runs so rich and rife,
What sort of wonder, love, is that Lamb
That He would wed you and make you His wife?
Behold how high over all you climb
To lead so grand a lady's life!
For many a fair one nobly born
Has suffered for Him in her dark of night;
Have you, then, driven all others off,
With pride and daring—all but yourself,
First and fairest, with flawless love?"

"Flawless, yes," said that gentle queen,
"Unblemished, clear, and without a spot;
That much I honestly maintain;
But *first* among queens I never said.
We who are brides of my Lord the Lamb
Are a hundred and forty-four thousand all told;
In the Apocalypse it is all set down:
Saint John, on Zion where they stood,
On the Mountain of God, saw the whole white crowd,
Saw all the host in his ghostly dream
Arrayed for their wedding on the world's crest,
The New City of Jerusalem.

67

"The New Jerusalem! fairest of all
  Fair cities, where that Majesty,
My Lamb, my Lord, my Priceless Jewel,
  My Love and my Groom reigns endlessly!
The prophet Isaiah has spoken well
  Of His gentleness, and movingly:
'That glorious, guiltless one men killed
  Without trial or proof of villainy;
As a lamb is led to the slaughter, so He
  Walked out; like a sheep at the shearer's hand,
He closed His mouth to their perjury,'
  When Christ was judged at Jerusalem.

68

"In Jerusalem my belovèd was slain,
  Racked and broken on the cross with bold
Thieves: He bore in our place our pain
  And martyred Himself to mortality cold.
His face was beaten and flayed and torn—
  My fair, my fairest of all to behold;
For our sins He suffered shame and pain
  Who sinned Himself not once in the world.
For us He let Himself break and fold
  And stretch out taut on a savage beam.
Meek as a Lamb, made no complaint—
  Died for us in Jerusalem.

"In Jerusalem, Jordan, and Galilee,
John the Baptist baptized men;
His words accorded with those of Isaiah,
For when my Lord came near to him
He spoke of Him this prophecy:
'Behold God's Lamb who, firm as stone,
Shall do away with all sin's weight
That all this world has labored on;
Himself He has laid on never a one,
And yet He will buy and balance them.'
All time and space were His generation,
Who died for us in Jerusalem.

"In Jerusalem my belovèd died,
And twice was He taken for the Lamb there,
By the true record of either prophet,
So mild was His mood and all His manner;
But the third time shall be ultimate,
As all the Apocalypse makes clear:
In the central throne where the saints sit
The Apostle John saw the Word laid bare,
Christ and the Book. And the pages were square,
And the seven seals were affixed to them!
At the sight, even those most courageous quaked
In Hell and Earth and Jerusalem.

71

"And the Lamb of Jerusalem bore no trace
  Of any hue but streaming white
  That neither flaw nor stain might touch,
  So splendid the wool, so immaculate.
  Thus every soul that shows no flaws
  Is locked to the Lamb as a worthy wife;
  And though each day that Lord brings others,
  There comes no hint or sign of strife;
  Each one He brings we would were five—
  The greater the court, the greater our bliss.
  In multitudes our love can thrive
  Increasing in honor and never grown less.

72

"What loss can any new love mean
  To one who bears this pearl on her breast?
  For how can they quarrel, queen and queen,
  Who walk arrayed in pricelessness?
  To crumbling earth the blood may cling,
  And mortals may stumble and find no rest,
  But for us, the unknown is the known,
  And out of one death we draw all trust.
  The Lamb, our joy and our Lord, can cast
  Out care, who serves our bountiful feast.
  Here each one's joy is richest and best,
  Yet no one's honor is less or least.

"And lest you doubt all I say, in your mind,
  The Apocalypse has it all there,
  For the Apostle says, 'I saw the Lamb
  High on Mount Zion, most rich and rare,
  With all the pure, a hundred thousand
  And four and forty thousand more;
  And written on all their foreheads I found
  The Lamb's own name and the name of His Father.
  And I heard a voice out of Heaven roar
  Like a flood full-laden and running in a rush;
  And as thunder tolls through dark, massed tors,
  That sound I heard was by no means less.

" 'Nonetheless, though it thundered, sharp,
  And loudly that deep voice rumbled there,
  I heard them forging a fair new note,
  And to hear it wake stirred all my awe;
  Harpers rang many a golden harp,
  And they sang out a new song full and clear,
  In resounding notes a noble score,
  A splendid argument in air;
  And right before the Almighty's chair
  And the four dread beasts that obey His laws
  And the gray elders, grave as they were,
  The angels sang out none the less.

75

" 'Nonetheless, no man begotten
For all his cunning or minstrel's skill
Could sing of that anthem so much as a stretta
Save only that heavenly host on their hill;
For the host was redeemed and lifted up
As the first fruits to pay Him well,
And those are unto the Lamb anointed,
And like to Himself in mien and color,
For never a lie or a half-true tale
Had touched their tongues for any distress.
Nor could that glorious company fall
From its matchless Master, or ever be less.' "

76

"Do not think less my thanks to you,
My pearl," I said, "though I still ask questions;
I would not debate against wits so high
As yours, to Christ's own chamber chosen;
I am but mingled mud and clay,
And you are a rich and royal rose
Abiding here among banks and sky
Where life and love can never be lost.
But lady graced with guilelessness,
There is one favor I long to ask,
And though I am wild as a wight of the woods,
I beg you to favor me nevertheless.

"Nevertheless, then, grant my will
    If in any way you can see it done;
    And as you are faithful and free of fault,
    Do not say no to this one last thing.
    Have you no homes in castle walls,
    No manor house for gathering in?
    You speak of Jerusalem of old,
    Where once King David held the throne;
    But here in these holtwoods it cannot be found;
    It stands in Judea, in the wet of the world.
    And as you are all moteless under the moon,
    So your mansions should be without mote or mold.

"This multitude remote from our plains,
    This throng of thousands, this vast host—
    Surely so mighty a multitude owns
    Some city on far-sweeping slopes and hills.
    So dazzling a mountain of precious stones
    Were ill-treated, left to grow dark among weeds;
    Yet here by this river, in fields and groves,
    I can see neither houses nor manors nor sheds.
    Perhaps you have walked from beyond the woods
    To stand by the stream and admire the spot;
    But if your great barony stands somewhere close,
    I beg you to show me the castle moat."

"You know of the moat in the Hebrews' land—"
 Thus my special jewel spoke,
"—For that was the city long sought by the Lamb
 To be harrowed in for humanity's sake;
You know of the Old Jerusalem,
 For there man's life was at last won back;
But the New, which descended at God's command,
 The Apostle John made the theme of his book.
The Lamb without stain or trace of black
Has gone to that place with his spotless flock,
And just as the flock has no fold or flake,
 So that city shows nowhere a speck or mote.

"To two moated cities my Lord has come,
 And Jerusalem is the name of both,
For in English the word has the meaning *Home
 Of God* and, also, *Vision of Peace*.
From one came our peace in a former time,
 For in that fair city the Savior chose
To die. And out of the other shall come
 The peace that shall outlast time and space:
That is the palace to which we press
When the flesh gives way and corrupts to rot;
There glory and bliss shall forever increase
 For that multitude without blain or mote."

"Moteless maiden, my lady mild,"
 I said eagerly then to that lovely flower,
"Lead me close to that castle wall,
 And let me look at your home for an hour."
My lady warned, "God never willed
 That mortal man might enter His tower;
I welcome you, though, with my Lord's good will
 To a view of the place, through special favor;
From without, you may look all you like at my cloister;
 Within, you shall move not so much as a foot;
Men sink here like lead, and lose all power
 Until they are clean without speck or mote.

"To come to the moteless city of God,
 Follow this stream till you reach its spring;
I'll walk with you here on the farther side
 At least till you come to the mountain's crown."
Then not one minute more would I wait
 But slipped under beautiful limbs that hung down
Until—stopping on a hill—I stood
 Looking at towers of dazzling stone
Beyond the brook where the slope swept down,
 Bright battlements shining like shafts of the sun
Just as the Apocalypse makes known,
 Where John the Apostle set it down.

83

And just as John the Apostle said,
I saw that city of splendid renown,
Jerusalem like a jewel, set
In shafts of light that shone out of Heaven.
The battlements were of burnished gold
And gleamed like crystal newly blown;
With priceless gems the floor was laid,
And twelve bright bantels rose from the ground
And twelve foundations with splendid tenons,
And each huge slab a precious stone,
As in the Apocalypse it is written,
Worked into words by the Apostle John.

84

And even as John reported by name
Each stone, I recognized them all:
Green jasper, I saw, was the first gem,
Spanning the first wide step of the hall
And glowing blue-green on the lowest hem;
And I saw that sapphire was second on the scale;
And frost-white quartz, uncracked and clean,
Shone on the third step, pure and pale;
And the fourth, awesome and still, was emerald;
Carnelian onyx was the fifth stone;
And the ruby was sixth, as men are told
In the Apocalypse of the Apostle John.

85

John joined to these the chrysolite,
The seventh gem in the great foundation;
And eighth the beryl of brilliant white;
Ninth the twin-hued topaz stone;
The elegant chrysoprase after that;
And next the noble jacinth, and then—
Magical charm for any plight,
Purple and indigo blending in one—
The amethyst. There the wall was set,
Jasper that shimmered like starlight and shone
In grandeur—all like the image of it
In the Apocalypse of the Apostle John.

86

As John devised, I too saw there
That the twelve steps were steep and wide;
And above, the city rose up square
And fair—as long as high, and as broad;
The golden streets glowed lustrous amber,
And the wall of jasper winked and gleamed
Like glass, and the mansions within were adorned
With every gem that men might find.
Each august line of that lofty domain
Was twelve thousand furlongs end to end,
In height, in breadth, and also in length—
As the measure was given the Apostle John.

And as John set it down still more I saw:
Each side of that city had three tall gates
Twelve all told on the outside wall,
And the crests were adorned with richly carved plates;
Each gate had one great Marjory pearl,
That perfect pearl that never fades;
And on each lintel a name was inscribed,
The princes of Israel properly ranked,
Each of the kings, by his birthright,
From highest to lowest the names were set down;
Such light shot over each prince's street
They needed there neither sun nor moon.

For the sun and moon they had little need,
For the Lord God Himself was their lamp and light,
And the Lamb was their lantern that never failed,
And all around Him the city blazed bright;
My sight pierced the buildings, however big-walled,
For no speckle appeared there to block my sight;
And there in the center of it all I beheld
The Throne where on golden pilasters it stood,
Even as John the Apostle said;
And the grand God of Heaven towered high on that
    throne
And a river ran over the world from His feet,
And brighter that river than sun or moon!

89

No sun or moon ever blazed so bright
As that fire-white flood that flamed from the floor;
It rolled with a rumble through every street
And showed not an atom of muck or mire.
In all that town no temple stood,
No chapel or church showed arch or spire;
For Almighty God was their minster instead,
And the Lamb their rich refreshment there.
Not one of the gates had a lock or bar,
But all stood open at every bright lane;
Yet none could rush for refuge there
Who bore any blemish below the moon.

90

Not even the moon would have will or might
In that city: Her form is too flawed, too grim.
And moreover, there where they know no night,
What use could it be for the moon to climb
Her compass and battle against the light
That chimes there brilliant beside the stream?
And plague-scarred planets have too low a state,
And the sun itself is too dingy and dim.
About that water stand trees that gleam
And bear the twelve fruits of life every season:
Twelve times a year they are weighted to the ground,
Renewing anew in every moon.

91

Below the moon so mighty a marvel
No mortal heart might long endure
As when my eyes caught sight of that castle
And saw its form and the whole of its wonder;
I stood as still as a dazed quail
For awe at the sight of that cynosure;
As a ghost I knew neither rest nor travail,
And yet I grew faint before that splendor;
And indeed, I truly dare to swear
Had an earthbound body seen the beauty I've seen,
Though all life's herbalists had him in cure,
His life would be lost below the moon.

92

Just as the wide white moon may rise
Before all the splendor of day sinks down,
So, bit by bit as I blinked my eyes,
I became aware of a grand procession.
That most renowned of noble cities
Suddenly filled—though I'd heard no summons:
Fair virgins, all in the same guise
As my comely queen in her streaming crown;
For they all came crowned in the same fashion,
In pearls and linen and costly array,
And on every virgin's breast was fastened
The priceless pearl of perfect joy.

93

With great joy they walked together
On golden streets that glowed like ice;
A hundred thousand at least there were,
Their identical livery like exquisite glass;
No man could have said who was happiest there.
And lo! as I looked, the Lamb walked past!—
All yellow gold His seven horns,
And like priceless pearls His garment flashed.
They turned toward where the throne arose,
And though they were many, none pressed for her way;
As mild as maidens seem at mass
Those queens walked on in their grand joy.

94

The grand joy that His coming stirred,
It would be too much for a tongue to tell;
The elders, when they beheld their Lord,
Kneeled to Him humbly, one and all;
And legions of angels called together
Waved rare incense sweet to smell;
Then glory and gladness anew poured forth
As they sang their praise of the priceless Jewel.
Those staves could strike through Earth to Hell
That the Virtues of Heaven lifted high,
Lauding the Lamb among all His people;
And my heart closed on a calm joy.

95

Unspeakable joy it seemed to gaze
On the Lamb: And marvel awoke in my mind;
Best was He, noblest, most worthy of praise
Of any on whom ever speech was spent.
He stood ascendant, His brow august,
Calm of countenance, in carriage a king.
And a knife wound wide and wet was exposed
Down under His heart, through the torn skin;
From His fair white side the bright blood streamed.
And I thought, dear God, who has done this to Thee?
In sorrow might any man's breast have burned
Before it could snatch such monstrous joy!

96

To men no joy like the Lamb's is known;
For though He was hurt—no mortal hurt more—
In His features I found no sign of His pain,
So glad His looks, so bright His glory!
And I looked among all His radiant thousand,
All in a transport of joy, and more
Than joy, and I saw there my little queen,
Great lady, and found she had left the shore.
Lord, how my heart leaped high when I saw her
Among all her peers, so white her hue!
And the sight so stirred me I swore I'd cross over
For my love's longing and the glory of joy.

97

Joy burst in through my eyes and ears,
And my mind, mortal, melted to madness.
My treasure was there and I burned to be with her
Beyond the water where I saw her in bliss.
Nothing under Heaven could hold me from there:
No blow, I thought, could block mere ghost.
I'd dive in the stream, and if nothing stirred,
I'd swim, and think blood and flesh well lost.
I was soon shaken from my senselessness.
When I tried to charge down to that water-way
In my mad pride, I was swiftly repulsed:
Such coin would not serve for my Prince's pay.

98

I was paid in a flash when I proudly burst in,
Attacking the stream with my addled plan,
For since my onrush was rash and wrong,
In a split second my siege was turned;
For just as I stirred to start from the bank,
The strain of it startled me down from my dream.
I awoke at once in the green garden,
My head lying on the little mound
Where my pearl had fallen from me to the ground.
I sat up, then sank once again in dismay,
And moaning to myself I said:
"Let all go now to the Prince's pay."

99

No pleasant pay was His hurling me forth
So suddenly from that sacred ground,
From sights more alive than all life on earth;
In searing anguish I leaned on the stone,
And helplessly I cried out to her,
"O pearl, pearl of rich renown,
All you have shown me was prized and dear
To me, mere flesh, in this holy vision.
And if it is true that you're taken to Heaven
And set in that garland I saw today,
Then I will serve on in this sorrow-dungeon
Believing that you are that Prince's pay."

100

To that Prince's pay I had always bent,
And I'd never before asked more than was given:
Had worked for my wages with true intent
As the pearl implored me, now so knowing,
When lifted, drawn into God's own presence,
To more of His mysteries I had been taken.
But always man longs for some luckier chance
Than any that ever descends upon him;
And so all my plot had been quickly broken,
My soul cast out from the Kingdom of Day;
Ah, mad is the mortal who strives against Heaven
And proffers Thee less than Thy just pay.

But to pay the Prince and be reconciled yet,
It is easy enough to become a good Christian;
For I have found Him day and night
A God, a Lord, and a firm friend.
On this little mound this luck I had,
Fallen there grieving the loss of my pearl;
Since then I've commended her ghost to God
In Christ's dear name—her ghost, and mine—
God who, in the form of bread and wine,
The priest reveals to us every day.
May He grant us our place as His serving men,
Pearls pleasing to the Prince's pay.

Amen. Amen.

PURITY

1

If a poet would fittingly sing of Dame Purity,
And describe all the qualities she requires as her due,
Many fair fables he'd find as he fashioned his song;
But to celebrate defilement would baffle his wits.
For wonderfully wroth is the One who wrought all things
With the vassal who follows Him and is found unclean.
Consider men of religion, who read and sing
And approach His holy presence and put on the cloth:
They take their way to His temple and draw there their hire;
Soberly, and with reverence, they rise to His altar
And handle His own body, and hold it their own.
What power His servants wield, if pure in spirit!
But if all their service is sham, mere show of courtesy,
Being all honesty outside—inside, false—
Then they themselves are sullied and stained in and out:
Loathing both God and His vessels, they vex Him to wrath.
So clean is He in His court, that King who rules all—
So honest toward all His household, so honorably served
By holy angels attired in all that is pure,
Perfect within and without, wearing mantles of light—
If He were not pleased by the pure, abhorring the foul,
How strange the contradiction! It could not be!
   Christ Himself once made this known among men
When He praised eight ways of life and promised rewards.
I remember one place among others, as Matthew records it,
Where He takes account of cleanness in the clearest of words:
Fair are the prospects of those who are perfect and pure,
For they shall behold our Lord with gladdened hearts;
And He also says that none shall see that sight
Who have any uncleanness upon them in spirit or flesh;
For He that has driven all foulness far from Himself
Will endure no soul gone dark with sin in His house.
Then never rise to His realm in rags and tatters

Nor yet in the hood of the wicked, with hands unwashed.
For what prince high in honor here on earth
Would be glad if a guest were to come in grotesque attire
When his host was seated on high in his solemnest robes,
Above all his dukes on the dais, the dinner served?
There the wretch in his rush comes running for the table
In stockings ripped at the knees and in patchwork rags,
His old shirt torn into shreds, and his shoes half gone!
For any or all of this, away they would haul him
With many a curse, and a cuff or two, perhaps;
They'd haul him away to the hall door and hurl the man out,
And tell him in plain terms to come back there no more
On pain of imprisonment or the pinch of the stocks.
Thus would the man be sent out for his savage dress
Though never in word or deed he did any more harm.

   But if such would be unwelcome to worldly princes,
The King of high Heaven is harsher toward him yet,
As Matthew says in the story concerning the lord
Who made for the marriage of his heir a marvelous banquet
And sent out his servant to summon his friends to assemble
And all attend the feast in their formal attire—
"For my fine bulls and my boars are fattened and slain
And my well-fed fowls are fat for the ax,
My poultry, fed in the pen, and my partridges too,
With sides of swine from the hunt, and swans and cranes,
All are prepared and roasted and ready for the table;
Come to my court and come quickly, before it's all cold."
   When they heard his call that they come to the court and dine,
The friends all sought excuses and stayed away;
One had bought a new house, he said, on his honor,
"And I'm just now leaving home to go look at the place."
   Another one also declined, and explained by saying,
"I've looked all over, lately, for yokes of oxen,
   And I've bought some now for my servants; and so I've no choice
   But to go where they're working, and watch how they pull in
        the plow."
"I just got married myself," said another man,

"Apologize for me at court; I really can't make it."
Thus did they all decline and draw away,
And no one would come to the castle, although they were urged.
   Then that mighty lord was much displeased,
And he listened in anger, and angrily he spoke.
"For their own affairs," he said, "they all forsake me.
Their insult is far more ugly than any Gentile's.
Then make your way, my men, to the main streets,
And at every wall of the city, seek about;
Approach every wayfarer there, on foot or horse,
Both women and men, both the better and the worse,
And ask them all politely to come to my feast,
And bring them all to my castle like barons of the best
Till all my palace walls are properly filled,
For those that I asked at first, I find, were unworthy."
   They went and invited all who walked that coast,
Brought bachelors in, whom they met by the banks of the sea,
Squires who sought out the castle on swift-running horses
And many a man on foot, both freeman and bondsman.
When they came to the court, they were given a noble welcome,
Met by the steward and soon ushered in to the hall;
Importuned there politely by the marshal
To sit as suited their stations and degrees.
The servants said to their sovereign after that,
"Lo, Lord, by your leave, loyal to your wish,
At your behest we have brought, as you bid us to do,
Strangers in from the streets; yet still there is room."
The lord replied, "Very well, look farther then;
Fare out into the fields and invite more guests,
Search in the gorse and the groves, get all that are there;
Whatever manner of man you meet, bring him in,
And be they fierce, be they feeble, fetch them all forth
Whether they're hale, or halt, or hobbling on a crutch,
Till every corner and crack of this castle is crammed.
For I swear that these same men that have sent their excuses
And turned their backs, untrue to me at this time,

Shall never sit in my castle or savor my food
Or sip any soup of mine though I see them starve."
  He spoke, and his servants went out in the world once more
And did as the lord had commanded and decreed;
They packed the palace with people of all degrees,
Not all with one woman's sons or with one man's line.
Whether worthy or unworthy, well were they lodged,
Ever the noblest first, those in fairest attire;
And those deemed best of all were taken to the dais,
And after them many a man to the meaner tables;
And all who sat there were seated to suit their dress.
Thus each won honor appropriate to his station.
Few men perfectly clean could be found at that feast,
Yet the simplest man in the hall was served to the full
With honor and with meat and with minstrels' songs
And with all the amusements a lord of the land should give;
And soon they began to be gay as they tasted good wine,
And each was soon at his ease with all the rest.

2

  Now, as the meal progressed, the prince resolved
To see in person the strangers assembled before him
To be sure they were all in good spirits, both rich and poor,
And to chat with them one by one, and warm their pleasure.
And so he went down from his room to the wide-floored hall
And went to the best on the bench and bid them be merry,
Warmed them with his welcome and walked to the next,
Stepped from table to table and talked with them gaily.
  But while he was crossing the floor he found with his eye
A man who had taken no thought what tatters he came in,
A serf in the thick of the throng, unfittingly clothed,
No festival frock but the filthy clothes he worked in,
A man not dressed for dealing with decent men.
The great lord was angry and gave the man what he asked for:
"Tell me, friend," said the duke, and dark was his look,

"How do you happen to come here in clothes so foul?
The suit you have on gives the holiday no honor;
These are no wedding weeds you wear on your back!
How do you happen to enter my house so boldly
In robes so ragged, and ripped all down both sides?
You're not a man of much worth in that matted gown;
You must think my hall and me some haven for beggars
To come so cavalierly into court.
You think me some ruffian who'll smile at the stink of your rags?"
The man was abashed at the other's angry words
And he hung down his grimy head and stared at the earth,
His wits thrown into confusion for fear of a blow,
And his brain could not summon a single word to speak.
Then wondrous loud the lord called out and shouted,
And he summoned his prison warders: "Seize him," he said;
"Bind up both his hands behind his back
And fasten fetters of iron firm round his feet.
Clamp him stiffly in stocks and shut him fast
Deep in my dungeon where sorrow dwells forever,
Grieving there and groaning and grinding his teeth
In bitterness, to teach him better manners."
  Thus has Christ compared the Kingdom of Heaven
To a sumptuous feast to which many shall find themselves called.
But take good care, if you come, that your clothes be clean,
And honor that holy day well, lest harm befall you
For daring to come near that noble peerage:
Hell itself He hates no more than the foul.
And what, in truth, are the robes in which they dress
Who show themselves adorned in the fairest attire?
In a word, they are the works a man has wrought,
His labors and all the love that lies in his heart;
If the labors of your life are clean and honest,
Fashioned in fair pattern, foot to hand,
And all your limbs draped beautifully and well,
Then may you see your Savior and sit in His hall.
  The faults are many by which man forfeits bliss
And fails to see his Savior: sloth is one;

And for pompousness and boasting and puffed-up pride,
Down the Devil's dark throat man rushes headlong;
For covetousness and cunning, for treachery,
For perjury, for murder, for drinking too much,
For felony and for fighting the failure may come;
For robbery, ribaldry, or trading in lies,
And for disinheriting or depriving widows,
For wrecking marriages or maintaining whores,
For treason and also betrayal—and tyranny as well—
And for false defamation and false and unfair laws.
A man may miss that joy so mightily praised
For such mistakes as these, and may suffer much pain
And never come in again to the King's court
And never, for sins like these, see God with his eyes.

3

But lo, I have listened and learned from learnèd men,
And also one sees the same on the strength of plain reason,
That that same splendid Prince whose sway is Paradise
Is displeased indeed by all that inclines toward evil;
But I never yet found written in any book
That He ever took wrathful vengeance on that which He made
Or avenged Himself for any vice or sin
Or so quickly came to the core of His holy wrath
Or ever so suddenly struck men down in anger
As for filth in flesh defiled by want of shame.
For I find the Almighty forgets His free manner then
And rises up outraged, with righteous wrath in His heart.

For consider that first of all falls, the fall of the fiend
While yet he was high in Heaven and hailed above others,
Of all God's splendid seraphim still the most fair:
Ungratefully, like a churl, he regarded that gift;
He had eyes for himself alone, and how handsome he was,
And so he forsook his Sovereign and said to himself,

"I'll set up a seat of my own, a throne in the polestar,
  And I'll stand as high as the Sovereign that set out the heavens."
As soon as he spoke, God's sentence fell upon him:
Jehovah by His judgment drove him into Hell;
Yet moderate was His anger, and measured with mercy:
He left still a tenth when He toppled the Devil's rich tower.
For though the fiend was overweening from fairness
And the glorious gleams that glittered there so white,
At once the judgment of God drove down upon him:
Thousands in a thick throng were thrown out of Heaven,
Fell headlong down from the firmament, fiends burned black,
Whirling down out of Heaven like hurtling snow,
Hurled down into their Hell-hole, swarming like a hive.
For forty days' time the fiends stood huddled together
Before that stinging storm would stint its might;
And as strained meal thickly smokes in a small sieve,
From Heaven to Hell that horrible shower hung
Round every end of the earth, everywhere alike.
Great was that destruction and dreadful God's vengeance,
And yet there was no rage, though the wretch remained proud
And, willful, would not acknowledge even now
His Lord, nor pray for pity, so proud his will.
However rank the offense, God's wrath was slight:
Though the Devil was cast into care, he kept to his ways.

  Or consider that later vengeance that landed on man
Through the fault of that first of men, who failed to keep truth,
Adam, who could not obey—ordained to bliss
In Paradise, where a place was prepared as his own
To live in love and joy for the length of all time
And then to inherit that hall that the angels had lost—
At last, at Eve's insistence, he ate of an apple
That poisoned the blood of all people produced from that root:
For God had forbidden the food that the poor fool touched,
And God's doom was the death that draws all men down.
But the punishment came in measure, and God was calm,
And He later amended all by a matchless maiden.

4

But all that might thrive was shattered in God's third thrust:
Mighty was His wrath, all mercy withdrawn
At sight of the filth of His people, by field and flood,
Who wandered about in the world and would know no lords.
And they were the fairest of form and of face as well,
The finest and merriest men that God ever made,
The sturdiest, most stalwart that ever stood upright,
And longer their lives lasted than all other men's;
For it was our first father that founded that line,
And the ancestor of them all was Adam himself
To whom God had given whatever was good upon earth
And all the blameless bliss that the body might have;
And those most like to that lord were the men who lived next,
For in truth, men so seemly would never be seen again;
And for them no law was laid down but the law of kind,
That they multiply and cleanly fulfill man's course.

And then men found out filth in fleshly deeds,
Contriving against their kind contrary works,
And spent their seed to no profit, each on another
And with others in turn in strange, ungodly ways.
Thus did they foul their flesh, and like fiends they looked
On the daughters of God's band and found them fair,
And they fell into fellowship with them like falcons or bulls
And by their grotesque perversions they got on them giants.
Merciless were those monsters, and mighty on earth,
And far and wide they were famous for furious deeds.
He who loved fighting most was famous as noble,
And whatever beast was most brutal was praised as the best.

And evil grew in earnest then on earth
And multiplied many fold among mankind,
And at last the monsters of the moors so marred all things
That the One who wrought all was troubled to wrath.
When He found every country on earth complete in corruption
And every man withdrawn from the ways of right,
A dark temptation to anger touched His heart.

Like a man with wrath within him, He said to Himself:
"I am much annoyed, now, that I ever made man.
And I shall undo and strike dead every dotard on earth
And shall kill in the field every creature clothed in flesh,
Both beasts and barons, birds and the fish in the streams:
All shall fall down and die and be driven from earth
That ever I planted a soul in, for sorely I rue
That ever I made them Myself; from this day forth
I shall watch and beware of the wickedness they keep."
  There lived in the world at that time one loyal man
Who ruled himself well and was righteous and ready to serve;
He followed the way of right and feared his Lord
And rejoiced in His goodness; and God was gracious to him.
His name was Noah, as men know well enough;
Three thriving sons he had, and they, three wives.
One son was Sem; the second was called Cam;
The third engendered was Japheth, joyful of heart.
  Now God in the time of His anger turned to Noah,
Flaming words of vengeance afire in His will:
"The mirth of all manner of creatures that move on the earth
Shall sink from My sight, for soon I shall hasten their end.
With their freakish, unholy labors they fill Me with loathing;
They vex Me with their filth, and with foulness annoy Me;
I shall scatter abroad My distress, destroy all together,
Both people and land and all that has any life.
But make for yourself a mansion, for this is My will,
A coffer closed in by trees and cleanly planed;
Make dwelling places within for both tame beasts and wild,
And calk all the seams with clay, and cover it well,
And outside daub every dent and plug all the holes;
And in length and breadth, lay out the ship as I tell you:
Hew the ship to the length of three hundred cubits,
And cut the crossbeams fifty cubits broad;
And build your ark up thirty cubits high,
And build a wide window in, wrought well at the top
In the compass of one cubit, and keep it square;
And make many mansions within and many a chamber,

Staterooms and stables and sturdily boarded pens.
For behold, I shall wake up a water to wash all the world,
And all the quick I shall kill with quakes and floods;
All that glides or crawls or has ghost of life
And dwells within the world I shall waste by My wrath.
But you I will deliver by this due warning,
For I find you righteous, and reason still reigns within you.
In time you shall enter this ark with all your sons
And your wife as well, and with you take
The mates of your merry sons; no more than your house
Will I save of all men's souls; I will smite all the rest.
Of every species alive bring in one pair;
Of each clean, comely kind bring seven mates,
But of each unclean kind keep a single pair
In order to salvage the seed of each separate species.
And match together the male and female beasts,
Pair by pair, each pleasing to the other.
Get all the feed to be found; fill up your coffer
For the sustenance of yourselves and also those others."
Quickly this good man goes to do God's behest,
Trembling in dread, for he dared not disobey.
When the ark was fashioned and framed and finally finished,
Jehovah came down once more and dealt him more words.

5

"Now, Noah," said the Lord, "is your labor done?
Have you closed the chest up tight, with clay all around?"
"Yes, my Lord, by your leave," the liege man replied,
"I've wrought it all as you wished it, as well as I could."
"Walk in, then," said God, "and your wedded wife with you,
And your three sons and their wives—and go there at once.
Bring in the beasts as I've bid you, and pen them up,
And when you are all well lodged, lock yourself in.
For when seven days are said, I will send to earth
Such a rushing, screaming wind and such shocks of rain

That all the world shall be washed of all its filth:
No flesh shall be left alive on any field
Save only the souls I have stowed away in this ark
And the seed which I shall save of the separate kinds."
Now Noah worked without stopping, starting that night,
And at last all were led to the ark as the Lord commanded.

    The seventh day came soon, and all were assembled
And housed in the hold, here wild beasts, here the tame.
And then the ocean swelled and the sea wall rose;
Overflows churned from wellheads in angry streams.
And no bank built was not soon burst asunder;
The mighty rolling deep rose up to the heavens,
And many a clustered cloud was cracked and cleft.
Every rain rift emptied and rushed to the earth
Nor ceased for forty days, and the flood still rose,
Overwhelming the widest plains and woods.
When all the water of the welkin washed the world,
All that death could draw down was drowned in those depths.
There was moaning enough among men when the mischief was
    known,
That nought but Death itself could endure the deep.
The water grew wilder yet and wrecked men's homes,
Hurled into every house, hid all within.
From the first, all that were able to flee took to flight;
Every mother and child were chased from their dwelling
And hurried to the high places—the highest they knew—
And hurtled in frantic haste to the highest hills;
But they fled to no avail, for the flood rolled on,
The terrible rain and tempest and turning waves,
And every lake filled level and lay on the banks,
And the dales, however deep, were drowned to the brinks.

    The mightiest of mountains were then no more,
And no more the folk who flocked there to flee God's wrath.
And all the wild beasts of the wood were floating on the water:
Some of them swam for dear life and thought to be saved,
Some scrambled up into treetops and stared up at Heaven,
And piteously they bleated and bellowed for fear;

Hares and harts together raced high on the summits;
Bucks, badgers, bulls, bolted up the banks;
And all cried out their care to the King of Heaven,
Cried to their Creator, called out for kindness
To Him who made earth confusion, His mercy surpassed,
And all His pity departed from the people He hated.
By now the flood flowed over their feet, and grew,
And every man saw well that soon he must drown.
Friends drew together and faced it, arm in arm,
To take what Destiny dealt them and die as one.
The lover looks to his lady and takes his leave,
To end life still as one, embrace for all time.
When the forty days were finished, no living flesh stirred;
The flood had devoured all with ferocious waves;
For it climbed above every cliff by fifteen cubits
And above the highest hill that hovered over earth.
Then darkening there in the mud lay man and beast
And all that ever lived; no struggle availed;
All save the one in the ark, and with him his band,
Noah who named in all troubles the name of our Lord.

    The eight in the ark were alive, as the Almighty chose,
For all who sailed in that ship were still God's men.
The ark was heaved on high by the whirling streams,
Cast over countries unknown and close to the clouds.
It weltered on wild water, went where it would,
Drove as on a dam break, dared all danger
Without a mast or a mainboom, much less a bowline,
Or cables or a capstan to clamp down her anchors
Or a hurrack or a hand-helm hasped to her rudder
Or any swaying sail to seek out Heaven,
But floated forth with the flight of the four winds
Wherever the water rushed or bounded back,
The ship rolled high as the gunnels and reared on end:
Had our Lord not held her helm she'd have had it hard.

    It was late in the life of Noah. To lay a true date,
He was six hundred years of age, and no odd years;
And it was the seventh day of the second month

THE GAWAIN-POET

That out of the wellheads of earth the water flowed;
And there followed three hundred fifty days of flood;
And every hill was hidden beneath gray waves
And all was wasted that dwelled within this world
That ever swam or flew or walked on foot.
And lucky was that remainder, riding the storm,
That all their species were saved and joined in the ship.
But then at length, when the Lord of the heavens liked,
He remembered in His mind the power of mercy
And awakened a new wind to blow on the waters,
And He lessened all that sea that was large before.
He blocked up all the pools and stopped up the wells
And bid the rains to cease; and the waters abated.
Then all the lakes took leave of one another,
When days of hardship had run to a hundred and fifty,
And the ship had been lifted up and lugged about
Wherever the winds and the water wished her to go.
She settled one summery day, sinking to the ground,
And came to rest at last on a high ridge of rock
On the Mount of Ararat, in Armenia's hills,
Which is called in the Hebrew tongue "The Hill of Thanes."
But though the great chest settled for good in the crags,
The flood was not finished yet or fallen to the bottom;
The highest of summits now showed themselves a little,
So the baron aboard his ship could see bare earth.

  He lifted up to his window and waved away
A messenger from that company, to seek land:
The proud raven it was, rebellious ever;
His color was blacker than coal and his heart untrue.
And he reaches out in flight and fans on the wind
And hales high on the heights to harken for tidings;
And, finding carrion, he croaks to himself in comfort:
Flesh cast up onto cliffs, where the clean land dries.
He catches the scent and the taste, and he settles there soon
And falls on the rotting flesh and fills his belly
And he soon forgets the command given yesterday,
The charge laid upon him by Noah, chief of the ship.

Now the raven turns in the wind and takes no thought
How other fowls may fare if they find no meat;
But the baron on board ship that abides his coming
Bitterly curses that bird, with all the beasts.
He seeks a nobler servant and settles on the dove.
He brought her up on the boards and blessed her, saying,
"Go, my worthy one; find dwelling places;
Drive above dark water and find dry land;
Bring back good news to the boat, bliss for us all;
Though that other bird be false, be faithful forever."
She sailed out into the sky on shining wings
And flew there all day long and dared not light,
Finding no fair place to set her foot,
But searching the stretching sea, saw only the ship,
And when evening came she settled again on the ark.
Noah let her come in and lodged her well.
Again on another day Noah remembered the dove
And bid her sail over the ocean and seek bare hills.
She skimmed the length of the sky and scouted the waves
Till nightfall came, and she flew once more to Noah.

6

One evening the dove flies hovering over the ark,
Then settles onto the prow and stands and waits.
And behold, she has brought in her beak a branch of olive
Handsomely embellished with leaves of green.
Such was the sign of salvation sent them by the Lord,
The settlement for themselves and the simple beasts.
What bliss there was then in that boat so long a-building!
What comfort in that chest sealed up with clay!
And merrily one fair morn in the first month,
First of all months of the year, and the first day,
They laughed, who lived in that boat, and they rose and looked
   out
And saw how the waters had waned, and the world was dry.

Then each one praised the Lord but remained there still
Till tidings came from the King who had closed them in.
And then God's word came down, and it gladdened them all:
He bid them to draw to the door, to be delivered.
Then swiftly they went to the entrance; the door swung wide;
And both the lord and his sons bent down and went out
And their wives walked after them, and the wild beasts next,
A clamorous crowd all clambering out in a crush.
But from each of the clean kinds Noah kept out one calf
And heaved it up on an altar and hallowed it well,
And of every true species he set up a sacrifice
That was clean and good, for God would have no other.
When all those beasts blazed bright and the breath of it rose,
The savor of sacrifice, and sought out Him
That saves or slays all things, He spoke to His man
To comfort him well with holy and courteous words:
"Never again from this day forth will I curse
All earth and all that is on it for any man's sins,
For I see that it is so that all man's wits
Are thrown into wickedness by the thought in his heart
And ever have been and shall be yet from childhood,
For always the mind of man is moved toward malice;
So never again will I strike with so swift a blow,
In all the days of this earth, as to end mankind.
But arise now, and move on, and make yourselves many;
Grow numerous as the grass, and grace be with you;
No end shall there be to your seasons of seed and harvest,
Of heat, hard frost, or heavy rain, or drought,
Neither the sweetness of summer or sad time of winter,
Nor night, nor day, nor the turning of the years;
But all shall run on, ever restless. Reign within them."
And with that He blessed each beast and turned him to the land.

And then all life spread wide when the wild were freed,
For every bird whom feathers served took flight
And fish that could master fins went forth to the flood
And beasts of forage went forth into bending grasses;
Snakes, in their way, slipped down to the secret earth;

The fox and the skunk went fleeing away to fair groves;
Harts to the high heath, hares to the gorse;
Lions and leopards went swiftly to lakeside caves;
Hawks and eagles rose up to the highest rocks;
Birds whose feet were webbed made way to the waters:
So each beast, like an arrow, sought his place,
And the four kinds in Creation claimed the Empire.

Such was the wrath and the woe for wicked deeds
That was sent from the Almighty Father on all His flock,
Those He had carefully cherished He chastised hard;
He voided the villainy that had vanquished His law.
Let man therefore beware, if he would worship
In the courteous court of the King that rules in bliss:
Let no man find himself so defiled by filth
That no water in the world might wash it away.
For no man under the sun has splendid works
If he's splattered over by sin and sits unclean;
One single sign of a spot may make him miss
The sight of that sovereign Lord who sits on high.
And so I shall seek to stand, in those shining mansions,
As bright as burnished beryl, as it behooves me,
Sound on every side and without a seam,
Without macule or mote, like a Marjory pearl.

7

After the King on His throne was greatly grieved
That ever He made man for earth and marked him to live,
Since man was fallen to filth, fierce was His vengeance:
He cut down all the creatures He first created;
He rued ever raising them up, and He ripped them from life
And undid all He had done, though He deemed it harsh;
For waves of sorrow sought the Sovereign's heart,
And He made then a covenant with all mankind,
In the vastness of His mind, in His merciful will,

That never again would He ever smite all things at once
Or kill again all that was quick, whatever the crime,
In all the length of time that the land shall last.
And He kept that covenant courteously ever after,
But He struck, nonetheless, with terrible vengeance at times.
Fiercely, for that same fault, He felled a rich kingdom
In righteous wrath that terrified many a man.
It was all for that same evil, ungodly error,
Venom and villainy and viciousness
That darkened the soul of man with his disloyal heart
Until he might not see with his eyes his Savior.
All sinfulness He hates like the stink of Hell,
But nothing troubles Him, neither by night or day,
Like the stain of harlotry, the scorn of self.
If the man defies instruction, die he must.

    But consider, sir, in your soul, though you live like a sot,
Though you build yourself a Babel, be sometimes reminded:
If the Lord who puts the light in living eyes
Moved about blind Himself it would be a great wonder,
And if He that fashioned the ears of all living men
Can listen to nothing Himself, lo, here is a marvel!
Take no heed of such talk devoid of truth;
There is no deed so dark He does not see it.
No son of earth is so sly in his work or so silent
That his deeds are not seen through before they're thought.
For He is the searching God, the seat of all action,
Of every rule the tester and root and heart.
Wherever He finds all is fair within a man,
His heart honest and whole, that man He honors,
And calls him courteously to His royal court;
But that other is punished and banished even from earth.
For in judging the knights of His band for acts of shame,
So repugnant to Him are their wrongs, He racks them with dread
And suffers them not for an instant but strikes them dead—
And that was revealed long ago by fiery destruction.

8

Sir Abraham was sitting one day on the ground
In front of the door of his house, in the shade of an oak;
Brightly the beams of the sun burned down out of Heaven
In the high heat of the homeland of Abraham.
He was huddled there in the shade, below shining leaves,
When his thought came aware of three tall men on the road;
They were noble lords and free and fair to behold,
As one guessed before they spoke or came again.
And the old knight lying there below the leaves
When he saw them coming went up to the three at once
And the good man greeted his guests as he might greet God,
And hailed them as one, and said to them, "Honored lords,
If ever your humble servant deserved any kindness,
Linger here with me a little, I humbly beg you;
Do not pass from your poor servant's place, I pray,
Until you have rested a little below these limbs.
And I shall be honored to bring for you basins of water,
And swiftly I'll see to the washing of your feet.
Rest yourselves here on this root, and I'll run in
And bring you a morsel of bread, a balm for your hearts."
"Do so," they said, "and serve us as you've promised;
We'll be waiting here by the bole of this same broad tree."
Then hurriedly Abraham shouted to Sarah, in the house,
And commanded her, "Be quick on your feet, this once!
Fix three plates of food, and find some cakes
And cover them up with hot ashes to get them warm;
While I go fetch some fat, you fan the fire,
And quick as we can we'll welcome our guests with pottage."
He hurried out to the cowbarn and caught up a calf
That was tender and not tough, told men to skin it,
Commanded his servants to cook the meat at once
And he would prepare it himself as he preferred.
The guests were standing bareheaded when he came back.
He caught up a clean cloth and cast it on the grass
And handsomely laid out upon it three unleavened cakes,

And he brought out butter next and put it by the bread.
He poured out suitable portions of milk between,
And he ladled out pottage and stew on a long, fine platter;
Like a steward, he served them sumptuously and well
With sour tastes and sweet and with such as he had.
In the guise of a mortal guest, God made good cheer
And was satisfied with His friend, and praised the feast;
Sir Abraham sat hoodless, his arms on his chest,
And administered meat to the three whose might wields all.
    Then the three there said, as they sat together,
When the meal was removed and they wished to make plain their
        thanks,
"Sir Abraham, I shall see to it soon," they said,
"That before the light of your life grows dark in the earth,
Sarah your wife shall conceive and bear a son,
And he shall be Abraham's heir and live after him
With honor and with wealth; and worthy lords
Shall hold as their heritage what I give to him."
The lady behind the door laughed aloud for scorn
And said to herself softly—Sarah the barren—
"Are you mad enough to believe what your mouth brings out,
And I so high in age, and my lord as well?"
For indeed, as Scripture says, they were sad with years,
Both lord and lady, and their labors had come to nought,
And Sarah was barren of womb since long before,
And even to this same time she was void of seed.
Then said our Lord where He sat, "So Sarah laughs,
Disbelieving the promise I've given here.
Does she think this mite too much for the might of My hand?
Nevertheless, I assure you I've spoken the truth.
I'll soon return, and I'll serve you as I have promised,
And I'll surely bring to Sarah a son and an heir."
Then out swung Sarah and swore by the heavens above
That for all their slander she'd never laughed at all.
"Now that's enough," said the Lord. "It isn't so,
For you laughed aloud, Sarah; but let it be."
With that they rose up quickly, for they must depart;

And like one man, they looked away toward Sodom.
For that city sat nearby, in a sunken vale,
Two miles and not much more away from Mamre.
And honest old Sir Abraham rose with the Lord
To attend Him with more talk and tell Him the way.
Then God went down the road, and the good man followed;
Sir Abraham stayed with his Lord to show him the path
That led to the city of Sodom, besotted then
In ugliness and filth. The Father rebuked them,
And spoke these words to the servant who pursued Him:
"How can I hide My heart from My faithful friend
And not speak out openly to him of all My intention,
Since he has been chosen as chief and father of My children,
From whom such a flock shall fall as will flood all the world,
And the blood of all his sons shall come to be blessed.
I had better be true with My servant and tell him My will,
And reveal all My purpose to Abraham at once.

9

"The roaring sounds of Sodom have sunk in My ears
And the grim guilt of Gomorrah has got up My wrath;
I shall move among that people and see for Myself
If they do as it seems from the din that drives aloft.
For the people have learned there an art that I little like,
And have found in their flesh perversions of ugly kinds;
Each man there takes as his mate a man like himself,
And they roll with them like fools, as though they were females.
I wrought them of separate kinds and warned them well,
And established their bond by the holiest of laws,
And linked them together by love, the sweetest of blessings;
The play of paramours I implanted Myself,
And made it, moreover, most splendid of all things:
When two who are true to each other are bound together,
Between a man and his mate such joy should come
That Paradise itself would prove little better,

THE GAWAIN-POET

As long as the sexes are honestly joined with each other
By a still and secret voice, unstirred by sight,
And the fire of love between them is lashed so hot
That all earth's floods of misfortune must fail to quench it.
But now they have altered My art, and they scorn all Nature;
They seize one another with scorn, in unclean ways;
But smartly will I smite them for smearing the world,
And My wrath will make of them symbols, world without end."
    Then Abraham was alarmed, and all his joy fell
At the thought of the heavy doom that the Lord had designed.
And, sorrowing, he said to Him, "Sire, by Your leave,
Shall sinful men and sinless suffer one pain?
For lo, is it like my Lord to let down judgments
By which both wicked and worthy shall fall by one wrath,
And weigh among the worse those who never wrought wrong?
That was never yet Your manner, who made us all.
If fifty good men could be found in yonder town,
In the city of Sodom and also in Gomorrah,
Fifty men still faithful to Your law,
And reasonable and righteous and ready to serve,
Shall they fall for the fault of the faithless all around them,
And shall they be joined in the judgment and get such justice?
That was never Your way before; let it not be now:
For You are a merciful God, and mild of heart."
"For fifty men," said the Father, "—and your fair words—
If fifty be found in that city, and clean of its filth,
I will gladly give grace and forgive all the rest their guilt,
And let them live on, untroubled, and leave them at peace."
"Ah, blessed is God," cried the man, "benign and noble,
Who holds in His hand all Heaven and all the Earth!
But though I have talked already, do not take it ill
If I talk just a trifle more—being dust and ashes.
What if I fail by five to find Your number
But the remnant all be righteous? What would You say?"
"Five short of fifty," said God, "and I'll still forgive all,
And hold back My hand from hurling them down to the earth."
"Suppose only forty are faithful, and all the rest false?

In that case must all of them fall and not one escape?"
"No, though just forty are sure, I'll stall for a time
And lay down all My wrath, little as I like it."
The good man bowed to God and gratefully thanked Him:
"Praised be the Savior, our Sovereign, so just in His wrath!
I am nothing but ugly earth and the blackest of ashes;
Who am I to match words with a Master of limitless might?
But since I've begun with my God, and He gives me His leave,
If I overstep like a fool, pray forgive me my error.
Suppose only thirty good men should be found there in Sodom;
Will You think it worthwhile to spare them for thirty men?"
Again the gentle Lord gave the old man his answer:
"For a group of thirty still good I'll give them peace
And drive My wrath at once from the depth of My heart,
And because of your courteous words give up all anger."
"What of twenty?" he said, "will You slay them then?"
"No, if you ask even that, I will give them grace.
For twenty true men I'll trouble them no more
But release all the region and write off all their debt."
"Now, worthy Lord," said Abraham, "one word more
And I swear I will struggle no further to save these men.
If no more than ten still trustworthy live in that town,
Will Your mind move to mercy and wait for their ways to mend?"
"It is granted," the great God said. "Gramercy, milord,"
Said Sir Abraham, and he ceased and sought no more.
    And then God went on His way by wide green paths
And Sir Abraham followed Him only with his eyes.
And as he was looking along where his gracious Lord passed,
He cried out after God with care in his voice:
"Milord, remember Your servant if You will!
Lot, my beloved brother, is living in the city.
He has his house in Sodom—Your poor humble servant—
Among those monstrous men who so mightily grieve You.
If the town must all be toppled, pray temper Your ire,
As far as Your mercy may move You, that Lot may be saved."
The old man goes his way then, weeping for grief,

Toward the Sea of Mamre, sunk in sorrow,
And there all night he lay in his house in longing;
And the Sovereign went to the city of Sodom and watched.

10

His warning was sent into Sodom at that time,
On that same evening, sent by means of two angels
Moving meekly together as merry young squires;
As Lot leaned at the door of his lodging, alone,
On a gracious porch that extended out even to the gates,
As royal and rich as the man of rank himself—
As he stared out into the street where big men played,
He saw there, advancing together, two comely men.
They were brave young barons both, with beardless chins
And splendid, rolling hair that shone like silk;
Their skin, where it showed, seemed the hue of the briar bloom,
And both were clean of countenance, clear of eye.
Their robes were of shining white and suited them well,
For their features were fine, and both young men were faultless.
Nothing about them seemed awkward—they walked like angels—
And so Lot saw as he stood there behind his gates.
He rose at once and ran out to them to meet them
And he bowed himself to them humbly, down to the ground,
And afterward, soberly: "Noble sirs, I beseech you,
Alight at my lodgings awhile and linger with us.
Come this once to the house of your humble servant.
I'll fetch you one of my vessels to wash your feet.
I ask no more than the honor of one night's visit;
When merry morning comes, you may go your way."
They said they had no strong desire to sleep in a house,
But quietly, there in the street where they were standing,
They would lie the length of the night, and lodge outdoors,
For the heavens on high were house enough for them.
But Lot implored them so long with pleasing words
That they granted his wish in the end and held back no longer.

Back to his mansion he brought them both,
A building splendidly furnished, for Lot was rich.
Lot's wife welcomed the visitors well, as she could,
And his two dear daughters greeted the guests demurely
And modestly, still maidens and yet unmarried,
Sweet and soft of speech and tastefully dressed.
    Then quickly noble Lot looked round about him
And commanded his men to prepare fine meat and drink:
"And whatever you make, make sure that it is unleavened,
For I shall not serve my guests either salt or yeast."
Now the wife was annoyed at that, I suppose, and in spite
Said softly to herself, "So they've no palate,
And care for no salt in their sauce. It seems nothing to them
That others might ask for some salt, though *they* be uncouth."
And so she served them mincemeat made with salt
And mocked the command of her lord, though he'd made himself
    plain;
And she salted their dishes in scorn, for *she* knew cooking.
Ah, why so mad, poor wretch? She too would be served!
They seated themselves at supper; soon dishes were brought;
The guests were gay and their speech was debonair.
(Their faces strangely shone when the two had washed
And the trestles were tilted up for the banquet tables.)
    When the two men had eaten and, afterward, talked for a while,
They spoke of sleeping—but the city was all awake:
All who might wield weapons, both weak men and strong,
Were gathered around Lot's gates, come for his guests.
A mighty crowd of people pressed to his doors,
And the guard was afraid, so ugly the growl they raised;
With burr-spiked clubs they battered the walls of the building,
And sharply, with riotous sound, they shouted words:
"If you love your life much, Lot, locked in your house,
You'll send out those young men we saw you take in
And they'll learn from us something of love, as our lust demands;
Such is the custom of Sodom to strangers who pass."
Lo, they spoke and spewed such dispiteous filth,
And yelped like dogs and yodeled and frothed like yeast

THE GAWAIN-POET

That the winds and weathers of the world have the stench in them
    yet
Of the vomit of vile words that defiled that night.
   At the sound, Sir Lot looked up, alarmed by the shouting,
And bitter shame shot through him; he shrank at heart.
For he knew well enough the custom those wretches kept,
And never was he so upset, his mind so shaken.
"Alas!" Lot whispered then, and quickly he rose
And excused himself with a bow and hurried to the gates.
He went without thought of his peril at wicked men's hands
But sailed out through the door to stand what he must.
Lot went forth at the wicket and swung the gate shut,
And the bolt on the gate shot home as it shut at his back.
Then mildly, with measured words, he spoke to the mob
For he thought that by courteous words he might chasten their
    hearts.
"Hear me, my worthy friends. Your ways are strange.
Calm down your dreadful din. Do not trouble my guests.
For listen! This self-defilement is villainous of you;
You are all of you worthy men, but your ways are wrong.
Yet I will provide you, I promise, with better pleasure.
I will give you the treasure of my house, my two fair daughters,
Both of them maidens unmarred by any man.
Though I say it myself, in all Sodom you'll find none fairer.
For my daughters are rich and ripe and ready for men;
To lie down with my loves will be pleasure indeed.
I will give you those two that are gracious and well made;
Behave with them as you will, but let my guests be."
At that word the arrogant rebels raised such a roar
That the words of the wretches' speech were pain in his ears:
"Has it slipped your mind that you stay here in Sodom as a stranger,
A country clod, a churl? We'll chop off your head.
Who asked your advice about how we entertain?
You who came here a boy—a rich man now!"
Thus the great mob mocked him and boomed in his ears,
And Lot was clamped to the gates by the press of the crowd.
But the bold young men leaped up and came bounding out,

And worked open the wicket and went to Lot
And seized him by the hands and hurried him in
And shut up the gates like stone with sturdy bars;
And they struck the mob with a spell so strong they staggered,
And the villains, blustering, blind as old Bayard himself,
Could make out not one mark or line of the mansion
But knocked at the gate all night, and all for nought.
Then each man went his way, his wishes fruitless,
And each one went to whatever rest he had coming.
But Lot's family would be wakened, though dwelling in Sodom,
To flee the most dreadful disaster that ever descended.

11

Redness struck the sky with the first streak of dawn
When the dark of night could endure in the town no more.
The angels rose up early and roused their friend
And admonished him to arise and flee God's wrath.
Quickly then Lot got up, alarm in his heart,
And the angels commanded him swiftly to snatch what he could—
"With your wife and your worthy vassals, and with your two
        daughters,
For surely, Sir Lot, you may save your lives even now.
Fly from this fell city, for fall it must;
With all your court make haste to the nearest hill;
Run your legs for dear life, looking straight ahead;
Let none be so bold as to slow for a backward glance;
See that your step not falter, but stretch on fast,
And until you have reached a rise, do not rest for an instant;
For we shall tear down this town to the last little stone,
And every last villainous man here shall vanish from earth,
And all the land that they live on we'll leave in flames,
And the city of Sodom shall suddenly sink in the ground,
And the ground of Gomorrah shall drop through the gorge of Hell,
And every last coast of this country shall clatter in a heap."
Then Lot lamented, crying, "Lord, what is best?

If I trust to my feet and foolishly think I can flee,
How can I hide me from Him whose wrath has been kindled,
And the fire of His breath that can fell and enflame all things?
I know not where I can creep to escape my Creator,
Or whether His fury will fall from before or behind."
But they said, "Do not fear, for the Father is friendly toward you;
Your fate is not sealed with Sodom's to brimstone and smoke.
Now choose for yourself a city of sanctuary
And for your sake He who sent us here will save it,
For you've strangely remained your own man in the midst of this
      filth,
And also Abraham asked, himself, that He save you."
"Lord, blessed is he among men!" said Lot.
"There is a city nearby that is known as Zoar.
 It stands on a rise surrounding a rounded hill;
 If it be His will, I would go there for my refuge."
"Go then," said the angel, "and that at once,
 With any of your house you wish to have with you.
 And keep to your way well, without looking back,
 For before the sun comes up the city will be struck."
    Then Lot awakened his wife and his two fair daughters,
 And went to the two young men the maidens were to marry,
 But they scoffed and thought him a crackpot and kept to their beds,
 And though Lot called them loudly, they lay there still.
 The angels hastened the others with awful threats
 And drove them out at the gates and down the street,
 And after Lot and his loves, his lovely daughters,
 They sought no others in all the city to save them.
 The angels led them in person as far as the wall,
 Preaching to them of their peril, and bidding them rush:
"Lest you too go down when the Lord destroys these devils,
 Bend your heads and run; be gone from here!"
 And run they did, and their robes flowed out behind,
 And before the first light out of Heaven, they came to a hill.
    And God began with His grim destruction above,
 And He wakened the wildest of weathers, and called out the
      winds,

And the winds rose up in wrath and wrestled together,
From all four sides of the world, wailing loud;
Clouds clustered together and cast up towers,
And thunderclaps came and made all Creation tremble;
The rain came rattling down, riddling the earth,
And balls of fire fell, and flakes of sulphur,
Smoldering and smoking, smashing the rocks,
Soughed around the city on all its sides,
Raced headlong into Gomorrah and moved the ground
And into Admah and Zeboim—all four cities—
All were inflamed by that rain, and roasted and burned;
And fiercely were they flayed who kept those fiefs.
For when Hell had heard the shriek of the Hound of Heaven,
He was all too glad, and he opened his gates in a flash,
Burst in an instant the bars above the abyss
So that all that region split wide in terrible rifts.
And the towering cliffs were torn into flying pieces
Like loose leaves of a book that is burst asunder;
And by now the breath of brimstone blended in
And the cities and their slopes all slid into Hell.
Redeless was that mob of men within
When they came aware of the wrath not one might escape.
Such shouts and shrieks of anguish shot to Heaven
That the clouds clattered with the noise, that Christ might relent.
    The sound reached Lot as he climbed the hill toward Zoar
And the women with him, following where he went;
Terror shook their flesh as they fled on together
Going at a dead run, not turning at all.
Lot and his lily-white daughters, loyal maidens,
Faithfully followed their faces, their eyes straight ahead;
But the grieving wife, who could never keep commands,
Turned once to snatch a glimpse of the grim destruction,
Quickly, over her left shoulder, looked back,
Glanced back once at the walls, and went no further
But stood there stiff as a stone, a steadfast image
As salt as any sea, and stands there yet.
Those who were with her went on and were unaware

Till they sank to their knees at Zoar, signing themselves,
And with love of the Lord looked up and praised Him gladly
Who saw His loyal servants and saved them from grief.
All was condemned and drowned and done by then;
The men of that little town had fled out in fear
And into a sea of confusion, on all sides, chaos,
And nought was saved but Zoar, set on a hill.
The three who were left went in, Lot and his daughters,
For Lot's wife was gone, still standing on the mountain
Turned to a statue of stone with the savor of salt,
For the poor foolish woman was ever found to be faithless:
First, at suppertime she served salt before God;
And after that she looked back, as the Lord had forbidden.
For the one she stands a stone, for the other, salt,
Delight of the lumbering beasts that live on land.
  Sir Abraham was up in the early hours
Who all that night took anguish to his heart,
And for love of Lot had lain in the dark awake
After he'd left our Lord who lives above.
And always the old man's eyes looked over to Sodom
That once was the sweetest city seen on earth
And like to that Paradise planted by God Himself;
Now it was plunged in a pit, filled over with pitch.
A terrible redness of smoke rose up from the blackness;
Such ashes flew up in the air, such fiery sparks,
As would rise from a furnace of slag boiling on a fire
When brightly burning brands are added below.
Such was the violent vengeance that voided those cities;
And thus that fair folk foundered and sank into earth.
Where the cities once were set, it is now all sea,
A sea that is dark and dim and supports only death.
Livid, bubbling, black, and bad to be near
As the ancient stinking tarn where sin is destroyed,
Where the smell and the taste are sharp enough to hurt;
And thus men speak of that waste as the Dead Sea.
For the works of death endure there even now
In that broad and bottomless lake as bitter as gall;

And nothing can lie in that lake and still keep life,
And every coast it touches it quickly destroys.
For lay there a lump of lead and it floats aloft,
But place a feather there and it plumbs the depth.
And wherever that water flows to wet the earth
There can never again be green, either grass or woodland;
And if murderers shove any man in the muck of that mere,
Though he lie there close to the bottom as long as a month,
He must ever live on in that lodging, and evermore lose,
And never be drawn down to death to the end of time.
And as it is cursed by Nature and all its coasts,
The clay that clings to that lake is all of corrosives,
Alum and bitumen, acrid both,
Sulphur grits and glass-gall and many more,
And washing over the water in waxy locks
One sees the foaming asphalt spicers sell,
And of such is all the soil along the sides
That cruelly corrodes both flesh and bone.
And by that tarn there are trees of a treacherous kind,
And they burgeon out and bear blossoms fair to see
And the fairest fruit a man can find on earth,
Oranges, pomegranates, and other things,
And all so red and ripe and richly hued
That one might well believe them sweet indeed;
But when that fruit is broken or bitten in two,
It reveals not the beauty of earth but blowing ashes.

12

These are signs and tokens still to be thought on,
Witnesses of the wicked works, and the wrath
Our Father sent forth on the filth that filled those lands;
By these all men may know He loves the pure.
And if He would have clean works, who is our Lord,
And if you have hopes of coming at last to His court
To stand before His throne and see His face,

What better can I say than this: Be pure.
Consider Jean de Meun's *Roman de la Rose*,
For he gives to men true rules for the winning of grace
From a lady to be loved: Look well and study
What bearing she respects, and what she loves best,
And in every house be that, in body and deed,
And follow in the footsteps of your fair one;
And if you will work in this way, then despite disdain
She will love you for your likeness to herself.
And likewise, if you would get love's grace of God
And loyally love your Lord and be His beloved,
Then pattern yourself on the Prince and make yourself pure;
Be evermore polished as bright as the Pearl Himself,
For listen, since first He lay in that loyal maiden
How splendid was that treasure chest that held Him,
Virginity unvanquished, no violence made Him;
But purer still her body when bearing God.
And then on the day He was born in Bethlehem,
What splendor those two had, although they were poor!
No bower was ever more bright than a barn was then,
No tapestried hall more fine than the sheepfold there,
No woman alive more glad than she who moaned,
For there man's worst disease was all made well,
And there, instead of rot, the scent of the Rose,
And there, where sorrow had wept, there was solace and song.
For angels with instruments came, fair trumpets and pipes,
Royally ringing viols and violins;
And all His courtly servants, to gladden her heart,
Leaned down around my Lady when she was delivered.
When that beautiful child was born, He was burnished so bright
That behold, both the ox and the ass bowed down at once;
They knew Him, by His cleanness, the King of all Nature,
For none before ever came forth so clean from his house.

   And if clean at His birth, how courtly He was later,
For all that leaned toward evil He loathed in His heart.
So noble He was by nature that He would not touch
Anything ungodly or inwardly stained.

Yet, loathing, He came to the low, to Lazaruses,
Some leper, someone lame, the stumbling blind,
The poisoned, the paralyzed, those pained by fever,
Men distraught or dropsical, even the dead.
They called on that courteous Lord and claimed His grace;
He healed them with His words and gave all they asked,
For whatsoever He touched turned clean again,
And cleaner than any man's craft could ever devise.
So pure the power of His hands that impurity fled
And so great the dexterity of the God and man
That the neatness of His fingers never failed Him,
And He neither cut nor carved with a knife or edge
But, instead, He broke His bread without any blade,
For in truth the cut came cleaner from His hands,
And the break proved more precise when it was parted,
Than all the carving tools of Toulouse could make it.

    Such is the purity of the Prince of that court;
How shall you come to His kingdom unless you be clean?
And yet we are all sorry sights and stained in and out;
Then how shall we hope to see that Sire on His throne?
But yes, that Master is merciful, marked though man is
And marred by mire as long as he lives on earth.
You that serve shame may shine again through shrift
And be purified by penance, become a pearl.
Where jewels are shown, the pearl is praised as priceless
Though it may be less dear than some other jewel in cost.
What can the cause be, then, but the cleanness of hue
That wins her honor above all other white stones?
For she shines so splendidly, so perfectly formed,
Without a fault or flaw—if she be fine—
And however old in use she may grow in this world,
As long as she lasts she can never lose her glow.
And if perchance she ceases awhile to be cherished
And declines to a dimmer hue in the hall where she lies,
She needs but to be washed with worship in wine
And her glow comes back more clear than it was before.
Just so, if the soul is dimmed by unworthy things,

If virtue grays but still man seeks to be saved,
By taking penance the soul may be polished again
Till it shines more bright than beryl or braided pearls.
　But beware, when once you're washed with the water of shrift,
And polished bright as the sheen of a newly scraped parchment,
Stain your soul in sin no more thereafter,
For then wrong deeds will displease the Lord indeed,
And tease the Sovereign to wrath more surely than ever
And to anger greater than if you had never washed.
For when a man's soul has been sealed and made sacred to God
He holds it wholly His and takes it to His heart.
If it falls away again, He feels it as much
As if it were snatched from His safe and stolen by thieves.
Beware of rack and ruin then, by His wrath;
For that which once was His should be white forever.
Though it be no more than a basin or bowl or cup,
A plate or dish, when once it has served the Prince,
He forbids that it ever be foully thrown to the ground.
Such is His hatred of wrong, who is righteous forever.
So it proved in Babylon once, in Belshazzar's time,
For sad misfortune befell him and struck all too soon
When he dared to defile the vessels ravished from the temple
And the service of the Sovereign some while before.
If you'll let me take the time I'll tell the tale,
How his doom was sealed when he would not serve them well,
The vessels his father had taken from the temple by force,
Robbing the old religion of all its relics.

13

　Daniel in his *Discourse* at one time set forth
(And the same is expressly proved in his *Prophecies*)
How the gentry of the Jews and of rich Jerusalem
Were driven by distress and drawn down to dust.
For in their faith that people was found false:

They had turned themselves to God to be His forever,
And He'd hallowed them as His own and had helped them in need
And saved them from so many sorrows it's strange to hear;
But they wandered away from their faith and followed false gods,
And that act awakened His wrath and raised it so high
That He fortified those faithful in the false law
To overthrow those false to the faith that was true.

    It was seen in the time when Zedekiah reigned
In Judea, the overlord to the lords of the Jews;
He sat on Solomon's throne, in solemn wise,
But slight was his loyalty to his noble Lord.
He turned to idolatry and abominations
And little cared for the laws of his allegiance;
And therefore the Father of Earth became his foe,
And Nebuchadnezzar knocked down his power with ease.
He pushed into Palestine with his many proud men,
And there he wasted with war the dwellings in the towns;
He herded up all Israel and led away the best
And gentlest blood in Judea, in the siege of Jerusalem.
He surrounded the massive walls with his mighty men
And at every gate left a duke, locking them in.
For the borough there was big, embattled aloft
And stocked within with sturdy knights to withstand them.

    And then on all sides they set off the siege of the city;
Skirmishes broke out, and bitter blows;
At every bridge a big wooden tower on wheels,
And seven times that day they assailed the gates.
Trueborn knights contended in those towers,
In big breastworks of board, built on the walls;
They fought and they fended off, and foes rolled together,
And two full years rolled round, and the town was not taken.
But the long siege went at last against the city,
For food was failing fast, and famine killed many.
Indeed, hot hunger within hurt the Jews far more
Than any attack of the army that lay outside.
Then redeless was that town, for all its towers,
For soon they became feeble, lacking food,

And the city was so pressed that they could not stray
A foot from the fortress to foray for new goods.
   Then the king of the country called for counsel
With the best of his barons, to plan his strategy.
In the stillness of night they'd steal out, and before a sound stirred,
They'd hurl through the enemy host before anyone knew.
But even before they were well past the watch at the wall,
A sudden shout sang out below the skies;
Then loud alarums rolled the length of the land;
Warriors, roused from their rest, ran for their arms.
They threw on heavy helmets, and leaped to their horses.
The cracking of clarions cried out clear, on high.
By now all the enemy host was hurling swiftly,
Following the foe, and quickly they found them,
Overtook them in no time and tilted them down
Till every prince had his peer pushed down to the ground.
And the king was caught with all Chaldea's princes,
And the gentry all overthrown on Jericho's plains,
And all were presented as prisoners to the prince,
Nebuchadnezzar, noble on his throne.
No man was ever more glad to meet his foes!
He spoke to them all with disdain, and spilt their blood;
He slew all the sons of the king in their father's sight,
And brutally he burned out both their eyes:
And he bid that that baron be brought into Babylon
And there be thrown in a dungeon to await his fate.
   Behold how the Lord has let His wrath have sway!
For neither Nebuchadnezzar nor all his nobles
Brought Zedekiah's pride to bitter pain,
But only his own churlish carriage before his Lord.
Had the Father been his friend, who kept him before,
And had he not turned against Him with unbelief,
Though all the people of India came to Chaldea,
And Turkey as well, they could never have taken the city.
   And Nebuchadnezzar would not yet leave that land
Till he'd overturned the town and torn it to the ground;
And he sent to Jerusalem a trusted duke

By the name of Nebuzaradan, to crush the Jews.
He was master of his men and mighty himself,
A leader to his horsemen in his onslaught.
He broke down the barriers quickly, and battlements next,
And he entered in eagerly, with ire in his heart.
The triumph was no great marvel, the men all away,
The best of them gone from the castle, who guarded the walls;
And those still there were so skinny and scant from hunger
That one wife would have done well for the healthiest four.
Nonetheless Nebuzaradan would not spare a soul
But put them all to the sword, with biting steel;
They struck down even the sweetest, most seemly maidens,
And they bathed babies in blood and spilled their brains:
Priests and prelates as well they put to death;
They split the wombs of wives and brazen wenches,
And the guts of women ran down into ditches;
And all that they could catch they carefully killed,
Or those who escaped, not swallowed by the sword,
Were stripped and caged, the cages strapped onto horses,
And fetters were put round their feet below full wombs;
They were brutally brought into Babylon to suffer,
To sit in sorrow as slaves, though once great ladies;
They were changed into churls and charged with heavy labor,
Carrying hay to the cart and milking cows,
Who once sat high in the hall as knights and dames.

14

But Nebuzaradan would not stint yet his ire
Until he had taken the temple itself with his troops.
He beats down the bars and he bursts open all the gates;
And all who served within were surprised and slaughtered.
He pulled down the priests by the hair and hacked off their heads,
Drove deacons to their death, bludgeoned down clerks,
Scythed down saintly virgins like so much grass.
Thus with the sweeping sword they swallowed them up.

THE GAWAIN-POET

Then like wretched robbers they ran to the relics
And stripped the church of all its sacred symbols,
The splendid brazen pillars painted with gold
And the central chandelier that lighted the place
And that bore aloft the lamp that should gleam forever
Before the Holy of Holies, where miracles happened.
They cast down the candlesticks and the costly crown
That stood on the altar, entirely wrought of gold;
The golden tray and the goblets garnished with silver,
The bases of golden posts, and beautiful basins,
Splendid platters and dishes of precious gold,
The incense vials and the vases wrought of fine jewels.
Now Nebuzaradan has seized those noble things,
Has gutted that precious place and packed his spoils;
The gold from the treasure box—a fortune in all—
And all the urns of the temple he packed together.
Swiftly and dispiteously he despoiled
What Solomon labored for many long years to build;
With all the wisdom he had he wrought there cleanly,
Devising the vessels of God and all the fair vestments;
By all the skill of his science, for love of his Sovereign,
He brought together the house and all its adornments;
But now, lo, Nebuzaradan has taken the treasures,
And afterward tears down the temple and burns it to ashes.
   Then with his legions of lords he rides through the land
And they harry each hidden corner of Israel:
With charging chariots he captures the chiefs,
And all their treasure he claims as chattel for the king.
To his king he presents the prisoners taken in booty,
Men who were worthy enough while their world lasted,
Many a high lord's son, and handsome maidens,
The proudest in all the province, and children of prophets:
Hananiah, Michael, Azariah,
And Daniel too, interpreter of dreams,
And many a wellborn mother's son—more than enough—
And mighty Nebuchadnezzar knows great joy.
Now he has conquered the king and captured the country

And struck down the dukes most daring and boldest in arms;
And the leaders of their law are laid to the ground,
And the prince of prophecy made prisoner.
But his joy was greater still when the jewels came,
For when he saw them gleaming, great was his wonder,
For vessels such as those heaped high in his hall
Nebuchadnezzar had never seen till then.
He seized them solemnly and exalted that Sovereign
More awesome than all others, Israel's Lord;
So mighty a god, such men, such marvelous vessels
Had never yet come from one country into Chaldea.
He put all the treasures away in a trusted place,
Royally and with reverence, as was right;
And afterward he reigned wisely, as you will hear.
Had he scorned those spoils he might well have suffered for it.

 The king reigned in royalty for the rest of his life,
The conqueror of all courts, and men called him Kaiser,
Emperor of Earth, and also Sultan,
And his name was graved as God of the Ground as well,
And all through the discourse of Daniel, who taught the king
That all goods come from God, and gave him proofs
Till the king was cleanly convinced that it was true,
And he humbled himself before God and all His works.
But all things draw down to darkness in the end;
Be a hero ever so high, he walks on earth;
And so at last, as he must be, Nebuchadnezzar,
For all his greatness and empire, is graved in the ground.
And it was his first-born son, bold Belshazzar
Who stood in his stead and stabilized the reign:
The bravest baron in Babylon, he thought,
Who neither in heaven nor on earth had any peer;
For he began with the glory the good king left him,
Nebuchadnezzar, who was his noble father.
Till then no greater king had come up in Chaldea,
And he would not honor the One who rules in Heaven.
False phantoms, fiends that were fashioned by hand
And cut from hard trees with tools, he tilted aloft,

And sticks and stones he mistook for the stoutest of gods
When they had been gilded and garnished with gold and silver.
And there he kneels and calls and cries for help,
And whenever they help him well, he rewards them at once,
And if they will grant him no grace, then grim at heart
He clutches an iron club and knocks them to bits.
Thus in pride and wrath he rules his realm,
In lust and lechery and loathsome works,
And though he had a wife, a worthy queen,
He had mistresses nevertheless, and called them ladies.
In the glow of concubines, in curious clothes,
In the study of rare new dishes and delicate tastes,
The mind of that man went all to misshapen things
Till the Sovereign on high decided He'd seen enough.

15

Now this bold Belshazzar bethought him at last
Of revealing his vanities for all to see;
It was not enough for the fool that his deeds were foul;
But all the wide world must be witness to his ways.
And so through all Babylon, Belshazzar broadcast the word,
And his cry went out through the country of Chaldea,
That every great lord on earth would be gotten together,
Assembled on a set day, for the sultan's feast.
To make that feast, the messenger was told,
The king of every country should come to the castle;
Every duke with his dearest lords and retainers
Should come to the court and acknowledge himself a liege man,
Reverence His Royal Highness and join in the revels
And look on his concubines and call them "milady."
    To praise his royalty many a rich lord came,
And many a baron bold, to noble Babylon.
So many the brave knights riding to the bastions,
Kings and mighty kaisers wending to the court,
Lords from so many lands, all leading their ladies,

To name the whole number of them would take no little time.
The worthy city was wide and long as well,
Placed on the fairest plain below the stars,
Proud on a sweeping prairie, fairest of them all,
Surrounded on all sides by seven great waters,
With a wondrously wrought wall, adorned to the top,
And craftily fashioned battlements cleanly cut,
Pinnacled towers between rising twenty full spear-lengths,
And, thickly crowded around them, crosswise palings.
The roof that rose above the grounds within
Was long and large and square on every side,
And every side stretched out for seven miles,
And the throne of the sultan was set in the very center.
It was truly a palace surpassing all others in splendor,
Both in construction and beauty, and walled all about;
The high-beamed chambers standing in the central hall
Were so broad between their pillars that horses could run there.
    At last, when the time appointed for the feast arrived
The mighty lords came together and met by the dais,
And Belshazzar was conducted to his seat,
Up the steep stone stairway to his throne.
Now all the floor of the hall was filled with knights,
And everywhere there were barons seated at the sideboards,
For none could come to the dais but the king himself
And his beautiful concubines in their blazing dress.
    When the faithful knights are seated, the feast begins;
Splendid trumpets strike up their song in the hall
And from every wall the echoes crack again;
From every trumpet golden banners hang.
Servants bear in the banquet on broad platters,
Silver brightly shined, to serve the guests,
Arbors over the platters, embellished above
With figures pared out of paper and painted with gold,
Angry baboons above and beasts below,
Birds in the foliage flickering between,
Richly enameled in azure and indigo;
And riding white horses they bore those platters in.

         THE GAWAIN-POET

And now there are kettledrum rolls and the notes of pipes,
And timbrels and tabors chattering, too, among them;
Cymbals and stringed instruments swell the sound,
And drumbeats bang out, battering thick and fast.
Thus they were served on every side of the hall,
Entertained with each course in sight of their lord
Where he and all his ladies lounged at the table.
So well he was served with wine that it warmed his heart,
And it burst up into his brain and blemished his mind,
And so greatly it weakened his wits he was well-nigh mad.
He rolls his eyes about and watches his wenches
And all the bold barons about him, there in that hall.

   And now the depth of dotage drove to his heart,
And by his own counsel he caught up a wild idea.
Mightily the master calls for his marshal
And commands him quickly to gather up all the coffers
And bring forth all the vessels his father seized,
Nebuchadnezzar, noble in his strength,
Who conquered with his knights and robbed the church
In Jerusalem, but kept his prize with courtesy.
"Bring those jugs to my board and fill them with beer;
Let all my ladies drink from them (ah, my loves!)—
Thus will I courteously prove, so that all may know,
There is no bounteous baron like Belshazzar."

   Soon the Treasurer was told all this,
And he with his keys unlocked the vault of the casks.
Many a brilliant burden was brought to the hall,
Many a sideboard covered with gleaming white cloth.
The jewels and blazing gems of Jerusalem
Were splendidly set out at the sides of the hall
And the noble altar of brass was lifted into place,
And the glorious crown of gold was raised aloft
That long before had been blessed with bishops' hands
And anointed carefully with the blood of beasts
In solemn sacrifice most sweet of savor
Before the Lord of the heavens to honor Him;
Now it is set for the service of black Satan

And before bold Belshazzar with boasts and pride,
And onto the altar that noble old vessel is raised
So curiously wrought by ingenious craft!
King Solomon worked for seven years and more
With all the wisdom the sovereign Lord had sent him
Devising ways for the vessels to be well wrought.
There were brilliant basins of fire-burnished gold
Enameled with azure, and pitchers of the same;
Clean-shining covered cups contrived as castles
Provided with, under the battlements, handsome outworks,
Filed-out figures and forms of various shapes;
The crowns of the covers that rested on the cups
Were artfully formed into slender, towering turrets,
And pinnacles were set there, projecting between,
And all embossed above with branches and leaves;
Magpies and parrots were pictured in the foliage
As though they were proudly pecking at pomegranates;
And the blossoms on the boughs were brilliant pearls
And all the fruit in those forms were flaming gems,
Sapphires and sardiners and seemly topaz,
Almandines and emeralds and amethystine stones,
Chalcedonies, chrysolite, clearest rubies,
Peridots and pynkardines and sprinkled pearls among them;
Thus decorated with trailing and crossing patterns
Was every beaker and bowl about the rim,
And the goblets of gold were graven all about,
And the vials were fretted with flowers and flies of gold.
 Up on that altar all was arrayed alike.
On a cart the candlestick was carried there soon,
The pillars so proudly embellished that many there praised it,
And praised the bases of brass that bore up the works
And the boughs beaming above, braided of gold
And burgeoning branches upon them, and birds on the branches
Of many and curious kinds and in curious colors;
And as if with wings in the wind, they waved their feathers.
Among the leaves on the limbs small lamps were set
And other artful lights that gleamed most fair;

And broad-cupped candlesticks were arranged all around it
With many a noble beast of brilliant gold.
It was never wrought for wasting wax in the hall
But intended to stand in the temple of the truth
Before the Sanctum Sanctorum, where steadfast God
Revealed Himself in spirit to special prophets.
You may well believe that the Lord who rules the welkin
Was much displeased by the play in the prince's palace
When His fairest jewels were fouled by filthy men,
Those gems that once were precious through His presence.
Solemnly in His sacrifice some were anointed
At the summons of God Himself who sits so high;
But now a braggart at his bench imbibes from those cups
Till drunk as the Devil himself, he dotes where he sits.

  And so the Maker of all the earth was outraged,
And so, at the height of their play, He sent them a sign;
But before He would do them harm, in the haste of His ire,
He sent to them a warning that all thought a wonder.
Now all this treasure of God is taken for gluttony,
Brought to a royal place and polished bright.
Belshazzar at once bids all of them drink.
"Weight yourselves with wine in this palace. Wassail!"
Swiftly all his swains sweep up to the altar
And catch up the cups in their hands to serve the kings;
Most willingly these others pour drink in the bowls,
And every master's man attends his lord.
There was a ringing, in truth, of royal bells
When the men in that mighty rock had caught up their cups,
The clattering of the cup lids cast to the floor,
And also splendid sounds of the psaltery sang.
Then the dolt on the dais drank all he could,
And afterward offered toasts to dukes and to princes,
Concubines and knights, because of his mirth;
And each, when his wine poured in, took a pull at the cup.
So long these lords delighted in sweet liquors
And gloried in false gods and called for their grace
Who were mere sticks and stones, and still forever—

Never a word slipping out, so wooden their tongues—
All the gaudy gods that the Gauls name yet,
Baalpeor, and Belial, and Beelzebub;
And they hailed them as highly as if all the heavens were theirs;
But Him that gives all good, that God they forgot.

16

And behold, a marvel came, which many men witnessed,
First the king himself and then all the court;
In the principal room of the palace upon a plain wall
Just opposite where the candlestick shone clearest,
There appeared a hand, with a stylus in the fingers,
A hand huge and dreadful, and it wrote grim signs:
No other form but a fist fixed to the wrist,
It carved into cold plaster, cutting out runes.
And when bold Belshazzar beheld that hand
Such fierce, dazing dread flooded his heart
That all there followed his face, and their color failed.
The terrible stroke of the blow strained all his joints;
His knees clench together, cold, and buckle,
And he claps his hands to his face, swelling his features.
He bellows like a bull when it bawls in terror,
His eye never going from the hand till all was graved
And rasped into the rough wall runish words.
When the hand had scraped its scripture in the wall
As a plowpoint carves its furrow into clay,
Both hand and stylus vanished from men's sight;
But the letters were left, writ large upon the wall.
    As soon as the king was calm enough to call out,
He commanded his book-learned counselors to go near
To see what the writing said and explain the signs,
"For terror shakes my flesh at the thought of those fingers."
Scholars went to their work, but do what they would,
There was not one there so wise he could read one word

Nor say what tribal lore it was, or language,
Or what the tidings told in those dark strokes.
Then bold Belshazzar became nearly mad;
He sent through all the city to seek out men
Skillful in witchcraft, and sent for wizards as well,
Men acquainted with magic and holy mysteries.
"Call all the clerks in Chaldea here to my court;
Make known to them this marvel we have seen
And cry aloud, 'That man who can tell the king
The meaning darkly muttered in these runes
That I may rightly know what the writing warns,
That man shall walk like a prince in robes of purple,
And a collar of clearest gold shall encircle his throat.
He shall be primate and prince of all my priests,
And the richest man in the realm to ride beside me
Save only two, and he shall be the third.' "
This cry was cast to the sky and many came,
The clerks were known as the keenest in all Chaldea,
Sage old lords who were subtle in sorcery,
And witches and walkyries went to that hall,
Diviners, demonologists, readers of dreams,
Exorcisers, sorcerers, and others,
And all who looked at the letters were no more enlightened
Than if they had looked at the leather of my left boot.
The king cried out in torment and tore his clothes,
And he cursed his learnèd clerks and called them churls
And got rid of them all at once by way of the gallows,
So witless was he now, and wild as a madman.
    The chief queen heard him raging in his chamber,
And after the cause of his anger was explained,
And she'd heard how fortune had changed in the chief hall,
To relieve her lord of his loss, the lady rose
And glided down the steps and approached the king;
She kneels on the cold of earth and courteously speaks
Words of worship and, afterward, wise advice.
"Most noble king," said the queen, "kaiser of earth,

Long may thy life last in length of days!
Why hast thou rent thy regal robes in dismay?
Though these cannot unlock the letters' secret,
Thou hast at hand a man, as I have heard,
Who possesses the spirit of the God who sees all things;
His soul is steeped with the wisdom of revelation
Which opens up things hidden, and strange marvels.
I mean that man who many times lifted thy father
From all the heat of his anger by holy speech.
When Nebuchadnezzar was troubled and annoyed,
He interpreted his dreams with perfect truth
And recovered him by his counsel from crushing fate;
All that the king could ask he completely explained
Through the lofty power of the living spirit within him
Of the God most glorious of all gods who govern.
For his learning in things divine and his trusty counsel,
Thy royal father, Belshazzar, ruled by his aid;
Men describe him as Daniel, deep of mind,
Caught and captured in the country of the Jews;
Nebuchadnezzar seized him, and now he is here,
A prophet of that province and prince of all clerks.
Send into the city and seek him today,
And win him by thy worship to grant thee thy wish;
And however murky the matter marked on the wall,
He will explain it as quickly as any clay tablet."

    The wise counsel of the queen was caught up at once,
And the man was brought before Belshazzar in a while.
When he'd come before the king and courteously hailed him,
Belshazzar accosted him, saying, "Good sir,
I am told by men that you have been, in truth,
Prophet of that province my father plundered,
And that you have within your heart a holy skill,
And your soul is filled with wisdom in dark sayings;
You are given the spirit of God who governs all.
And you can expound the secrets of Heaven's King.
A marvel baffles us here, and I would find out

The sentence of these strange words set in the wall,
For all Chaldea's clerks have miserably failed.
If you by your craft can conquer it, I'll requite you;
For if you can read it truly and turn it to reason,
Can first tell me the text of the interlocked letters
And afterward make known the matter and the meaning,
I will keep the promise I've solemnly sworn to you,
Array you in purple cloth, the most princely robes,
And a ring of blazing gold about your neck,
And you shall be third most noble of all my knights,
And a baron at my bench; you shall be no less."

17

Promptly the prophet Daniel spoke these words:
"Royal king of this realm, remember our Lord!
For it is most sure and certain the Sovereign of Heaven
Aided your father and cherished him on earth;
He made him the greatest of all earth's governors,
And allowed him to wield all the world in the way he liked.
That man whom God would have prosper, well will he thrive,
And he whose death He desires will drop like stone.
Whoever He would lift up is aloft in an instant
And whoever He would lay down lies down in a flash.
Thus came the great renown of Nebuchadnezzar;
The might of his reign was made by the might of God.
For that king believed in the Highest in his heart
And believed that his every power was borrowed from the Prince.
As long as that truth was clenched close to his heart,
There was no man on earth so mighty as himself.
But it happened, in due time, he was touched with pride,
For his suzerain was so large, his life so royal,
And he had such high regard for his own acts,
That he put from his thought the power of his Prince.
Then he began to blaspheme and blame the Lord,

And in words he made his might the equal of God's:
'I am sole god of the ground; I govern as I will,
Like Him that is high in Heaven and governs the angels;
If He established the earth and all that is on it,
I have built Babylon, most brilliant of cities
And established there every stone by the strength of my arms;
No might but mine might ever make such another.'
    "No sooner had these same words come out of his mouth
Than the Sovereign's answer sounded in his ears:
'Now this Nebuchadnezzar has said enough;
Now all your power is overthrown at once;
Removed from the sons of men, you shall live on the moors
And walk the wastes and dwell among wild beasts;
Like a beast, you shall bite bent grasses and bracken and herbs,
And run with the wolf and pasture with wild asses.'
For all his pride, he departed from his place,
His solemn and royal seat, and left his solace
And was outcast, full of care, to countries unknown,
Far into gloomy forests where men never came.
His wits no longer ruled, and for all he knew
He must be some humble beast, a bull or an ox.
He moved about on all fours, forage was his food,
And he ate, like any horse, of fallen herbs.
Thus the great king considers himself a cow.
And so he remained till seven summers were said.
    "By then, thick tufts of hair there were on his flesh,
And his body all adorned with the dew of Heaven;
His hair was tangled and matted, made shaggy and rough
Where it fell, grizzly, from his shoulders to his groin:
And intertwined twenty times, it reached to his toes,
With many a snarl where mire made it stick together.
His beard covered all his breast and reached bare earth,
And his eyebrows bristled like briars above his broad cheeks;
His eyes were hollow, hidden by hanging hair,
And all as gray as the kite, with great grim claws
That were crooked and keen as the talons of the kite;

THE GAWAIN-POET

His hue was like an eagle's and covered him over.
And then at last he learned who wields all might
And can make or unmake kingdoms as He wills.
Then he regained his wits, who had suffered woe,
And he came to knowledge and knew his littleness;
He learned to love his Lord and be loyal to Him,
For He and no other held all things in His hand.
Then soon he was sound again, his throne restored,
His barons gathered about him, glad he'd returned.
His head was suitably covered with its proper hue,
And just as quickly his kingdom was recovered.

"But you, bold Belshazzar, his bairn and heir,
See all these signs with your eyes and set them at nought;
For always you set your heart against high God,
Hurling boasts at Him in your blasphemous pride;
And now you've defiled His vessels in filth and vanity,
Those cups first consecrated for His house;
You've brought them out for your barons and filled them to the brim,
In a wicked hour, with wassail for your wenches.
Before your festival board you've brought in bowls
That bishops' hands once blessed with reverence,
And you've drunk from them to gods that never lived,
Made of mere sticks and stones, unable to stir.
And for that frothing filth, the Father in Heaven
Has sent down into this hall a terrible vision,
The fist with fearful fingers, that flays your heart—
Runes rasped on the wall with a rough pen.

"These, without more words, are the words here written
By each figure, as I find, in the Father's sentence.
Mene, Tekel, Upharsin, three signs in one;
And in three ways they warn you of coming doom.
And now gladly I'll give you the meaning of this.
Mene means no less than *Almighty God*
Has counted up your kingdom by careful numbers
And in good faith fulfilled it even to the end.
To tell you now of *Tekel*, the term means this:

Your royal reign has been set in the scales of balance
And is found much wanting in works of honor and faith.
And *Upharsin* shall follow for your faults, in certain truth;
For in *Upharsin*, in faith, I find these runes:
Down goes your principality; you shall be deprived;
The reign is taken from you and given to the Persians;
The Medes shall be masters here, and you shorn of might."

18

The king at once commanded that Daniel be clothed
In frocks of fine linen, as he before had promised.
Then Daniel soon was arrayed in costly purple,
And a collar of clear gold clasped to his neck.
And then a decree was drawn up by the duke himself:
Bold Belshazzar bids that all men bow,
And all the commons of Chaldea, liege men of the king,
To the prince third most precious of all his people
And higher than all the rest, save only two,
Retainer to Belshazzar in both castle and field.
At once all this was cried out and known in the court,
And the people who served that prince were all well pleased.
But however well Daniel was treated, the day passed over,
Night drew near with troubles enough for the duke;
For him there would dawn no day beyond that dark,
For the doom that Daniel read was bound to descend.
Solemnity and good cheer endured in the hall
And the fabulous feast went on till sunlight failed;
Then paler grew the blue of the broad sky;
Merry day grew dark, and the mist drove in
With the movement of the wind along low moors.
All the knights moved out and hurried home
To seek in their own halls supper and singing later.
And thus, late at night, the lord was left alone.
Then merrily servants escorted the king to his bed
To take what rest he pleased—and never rise.

THE GAWAIN-POET

For all around his castle his foes were gathered,
Who long had awaited their time to seize his lands.
Now on this same night they are suddenly assembled,
And not a man in the castle knew they were there.
And it was the mighty Darius, Duke of the Medes,
The proudest prince in all Persia, Porus, and India,
With many a mighty legion, bold men in arms
Who now have decided Chaldea's hour has come.
They throng there through the darkness in a crowd,
Cross over clear dark waters and scale the walls
And draw up long heavy ladders, lift them aloft;
They steal the town in silence; no shout goes up.
Within not more than an hour the knights are all in,
Arousing never a soul; they move in farther,
And silently they approach now the principal palace.
Then they run in in a rush, an enormous rout,
With the blasts of their blazing bugles bursting in shocks,
A clamor clattering to the sky, shaking men's hearts.
Sleeping men were slain before they could flee,
And every house was taken in no time at all.
Belshazzar was beaten to death in his bed,
His royal blood and his brains blending with the sheets.
The king was caught up in his curtain, by the heels,
And dragged away by the feet, and foully abused;
He who had been so doughty, drinking from the vessels—
Now the dog that lies in the ditch is more dear.

And the master of these Medes arose on the morn;
Royal Darius that day established his throne;
All the city is secure and makes its settlement
With the barons thereabout who follow him;
And thus was that land lost for the sin of its lord
And because of the fault of the foolish man who befouled
The ornaments of God's house, that once were holy.
He was cursed for his uncleanness, and caught by it,
Driven from dignity for his unworthy deeds,
Wrenched forever from the worship of the world

And no doubt kept by his former inclinations
From looking on our Almighty Lord above.
     And so I have thoroughly shown you in three ways,
Impurity is thrown down from the perfect heart
Of the blissful Lord who builds His home in Heaven;
It rouses Him to wrath and brings down His vengeance;
But purity is His pleasure, and true politeness;
And those that are seemly and sweet shall see His face.
May He send us grace that we may walk gay in our gear
And that we may serve in His sight, where joy never ends.

Amen.

PATIENCE

Prologue

Patience is a virtue, though few men find her sweet.
When heavy hearts have been hurt by scorn and the like,
Silent endurance assuages and soothes the burning,
For she kills every evil, and quenches malice.

For he who can suffer through sorrow may someday find joy,
But he who for pride will not bend finds pains all the more;
Then better to abide these buffets, be patient awhile—
Little though I like it—than always lash out.

I heard on a holy day, at a high mass,
How Matthew told that his Master taught His men:
Eight blessings He promised, each priceless gift
Appropriate to reward a particular virtue.

Blessed are all my people poor in heart,
For theirs is the Kingdom of Heaven to hold for all time;
Blessed also are all who abide in humility,
For they shall rule all this world and have their will.

And blessed also are those who in sorrow mourn,
For in every country their comfort shall come to them soon;
Blessed also is he that shall hunger for the right,
For he shall be freely fed and filled with all goodness.

Blessed are all men merciful of heart,
For all manner of mercy shall meet them in turn;
And blessed also are all who are pure in spirit,
For they shall see with their eyes the Savior's throne.

Blessed are they that endure and hold their peace,
For they shall be known as the noble Sons of God;
And blessed are they that by patience prove their hearts,
For theirs, as I have said, shall be the Kingdom.

These, all eight, are the honors that await us
If we will but love these ladies and live in their service—
Dame Poverty, Dame Pity, Dame Penance, the third,
Dame Meekness and Dame Mercy, and merry Dame Cleanness,

And also Dames Peace and Patience, in procession with the rest;
A man is blessed with but one, but still better with all.
And since to that fair lady Poverty I am forced,
I shall do what I can to win Patience, and dally with both.

For in my text these two are attached as a team,
Fettled in one form, the foremost and last,
And by rule and decree of their wisdom, they win the same prize,
And indeed, I affirm they are fashioned of one fair nature;

For where Poverty appears she will not be put out
But will live wheresoever she pleases, liked or disliked,
And where Poverty makes her way, however man moans,
For all his muttering, much must that man endure.

Perforce, then, Patience and Poverty are sisters,
And being besieged by both, I had better endure.
It is better, at last, to like them and look for their kindness
Than to wither away or be wroth and perhaps win worse.

If unto this destiny I am duly appointed,
What good can indignation do, or outrage?
For lo, if my liege lord likes, in this life, to command me
Either to ride or to run or to roam on his errand,

What good is my grumbling except to get greater griefs?
And if he commands me to talk, though my tongue be raw,
I must do what his power impels, despite displeasure,
And bow myself down to his bidding, be worthy my hire.

For did not Jonah resist in Judea once?
Searching after his safety he stumbled on terror.
Stay for a little time and take heed a while
And I'll tell you the whole tale as it's told in the book.

It came about once in the country of Judea
That the gentle prophet Jonah was charged with a mission;
The voice of the Lord came down to him, driving out gladness,
And God's stern words resounded in Jonah's ears.

"Arise," God said to Jonah, "and go forth at once,
And without any questions go quickly over into Nineveh
And all throughout that city say these words
Concerning that place, as I put them now in your heart;

"For I find all those within Nineveh's walls so wicked,
So mighty in malice towards Me, I'll stand no more
But soon will be wholly avenged for their venomous work.
Now set out at once and go swiftly, and speak as I've charged you."

And when that sound that had silenced the prophet had ceased,
He was outraged in his wits, and rebelliously thought:
"If I were to bow to His bidding and bear them this news,
And take me to Nineveh, my troubles would begin.

"He tells me Himself that those traitors are devils, and venomous;
If I came to them, then, with His tidings, they'd take me in a flash,
Pen me up in a prison, and put me in the stocks,
And break my bones on the warlock and burn out my eyes.

"This is a marvelous message for a mortal to preach
Among enemies by the hundreds and hell-bound fiends!
But if my Prince has plotted such pains for His prophet,
And because of some slip-up of mine has decided to slay me,

"Then whatever the cost," thought Jonah, "I will not go near
But will carry me some other way, where He keeps no watch;
I'll hie me over to Tarshish and hide there a while;
With luck, when I'm well lost, He'll leave me alone."

Then swiftly he started up, and he set out in haste,
This Jonah, to Port Joppa, chafing and fuming
That he would not put up with such pains at any price,
Nay, though the Father that formed him should therefore fall.

"Our Sovereign sits," thought he, "on so high His throne
In His luminous glory, He'd get but little grief
If I should be seized at Nineveh, stripped to the skin,
And stretched on a cruel cross in the company of thieves."

Thus Jonah speeds to that port and seeks his passage,
And finds there a ship fair rigged and ready for the waves;
He soon makes friends with the mariners, makes them payment
To sail him over to Tarshish as soon as they can.

Then he went onto the beams, and they heaved up the frame,
Caught up the broad cross-sail and bedded the cables;
The sailor waiting at the windlass weighed the anchor;
They lapped the second sail line snug to the bowsprit

And gathered in the guides; the great sail fell.
They lowered the larboard oars and leaned her to windward,
And the blithe wind at their backs found the bosom of the sail
And swung that sweet ship smoothly out to sea.

There was never a Jew more joyful than Jonah then,
When the heavy hand of his Lord he had boldly fled;
For he knew well enough that the One who wrought all the world
Could have no power to pursue His pawn on the sea.

Ah, poor witless wretch! In running from grief
He has put himself in position for perils far greater!
Monstrous indeed the mistake of his muddled mind;
Though he sought far-off Samaria, still God would see him!

Indeed, be assured He can see far and near as it suits Him;
For often enough He reveals how right was that king,
Noble David on the dais, who noted it once
And set it down in a psalm still seen in the Psalter:

"O, ye thick-skulled people, think a little while!
And though ye be steep in stupidity, strain to be wise:
Can you think Him deaf that has made all mortal ears?
He cannot be blind who first built all your eyes!"

But indeed, like a man in his dotage, he dreaded no evil,
This Jonah, far out to sea now and sailing for Tarshish:
But in truth he was overtaken all too soon
And so, alas, he shot far short of his aim.

For the King of all knowledge, He who foreknows all things,
Who ever remembers and wakes and who never lacks ways,
Called on that same craft that He carved with His hands
And quickly He caught it from sleep, for crossly He called:

"Eurus and Aeolus, in the east and north,
Blow, both, as I bid, on that gray-blue water."
Between the word and the act not an instant passed,
So willing were both those winds to work His will.

And now in the north and east there arose a roar
When the grim gales moved in on the gray-blue sea;
Rough thunderheads arose, and a redness below them,
And the sea moaned mightily, marvelous to hear.

The winds on the gray water so twisted together
That the waves went wild, and they rolled and weltered high
And crashed again to the abyss; and the terrified fishes
Fled, frenzied, to the floor of the ocean and hid.

When the roaring sky and the sea and the ship came together
There was little joy in the craft where Jonah sailed;
She pitched and reeled and rocked on the rolling waves,
And the gale hurled buffets that broke all her gear into bits.

Rudder and tiller were hurled in a heap to the seaways;
First the mast-stays fell, and the mast fell next;
The sail swayed to the sea, and the sweet ship walled
To drink in the ice-cold ocean; and then came their cry.

They cut the dangling cording and cast the cords over,
And many a bold boy leaped there to bale or to hurl;
They scrambled to scoop out the bilge and escape if they could,
For however heavy man's lot, he holds life sweet.

There was work enough for them, throwing the cargo over,
Their bags and their featherbeds and their bright fair clothes,
Their chests and all their coffers, their casks as well,
To lighten the hold on the chance that a leak might open.

And loud as ever the wind went howling over
And ever more angry the ocean, more ugly the currents;
And then the sailors, spent, could see no hope,
And each threw his wail to the god he trusted most.

Some there to Vernagu offered up their vows;
Some there turned to Diana and towering Neptune,
To Mahomed and to Magog, to the Moon and the Sun,
And each cried out to the god of his own belief.

And then the wisest came forward, one close to despair:
"My lords, we are plagued with a traitor, some lawless wretch
That has angered his god and now cowers here among us.
We'll all of us sink for his sins, and for his sake die.

"Then let every lad on this ship cast lots with the rest,
And the fellow that's lost all his luck, we'll lay him in the sea.
When the guilty one is gone for good from our midst,
The sovereign of the storm clouds will spare all the rest."

This was set and accepted; they assembled the others,
Dragged them from every dark corner to draw what they might;
The pilot leaped along lightly down under the hatches
To catch any cowards and bring them to cast their lots.

It befell that the pilot could find and bring forward no man
Save Jonah the Jew, asleep in a secret place;
In his fear of the violence of the storm he had fled
To the bottom of the boat; on a board he lay,

Huddled up by the hurrack; through Heaven's wrath
He lay in a sleep like a stupor, and slobbered as he snored.
The helmsman shoved him with a foot and shouted, "Stand!"—
And there the devil in his chains drew up from his dreams.

THE GAWAIN-POET

By the hair of his head the helmsman hauled him out
And carried him up by his chest and cast him on the deck;
And they all inquired in amazement what cause he had
To sleep so soundly in spite of the onslaught of sorrow.

Soon they decided the lots, and they dealt them all out,
And always the last of the lots would land on Jonah.
And then they cried out to him quickly and called in one voice,
"What the devil have you done, you doting wretch?

"What are you after on the ocean, out here among us?
Have you come with your blackhearted crimes to kill us too?
Have you got then, man, no god, no master to call on,
That you slide away into sleep, with slaughter in the wind?

"Where do you hail from? Why have you come off to sea?
Where in the world are you bound, and what is your errand?
For look, the lot is yours for your loathsome deeds;
Give glory therefore to your god before you go down."

"I was born a Hebrew," said Jonah, "and born of Israel;
And the god I worship is He who wrought all things,
The world and all the welkin, the winds, the stars,
And all that dwells within—with a word He made them.

"All this storm that we suffer was sent after me,
For alas, I've made God angry by guilt and deceit.
Carry me, then, to the guardrail and cast me to the sea,
For in truth, you haven't a hope under Heaven till it's done."

By sure signs that they well understood, he showed them
He'd fled forth from the face of the almighty God.
And such fear fell on them then, and flayed them within,
That they no longer dared to ill-treat him, but left him alone.

And men made their way in haste with mighty oars
To row at the sides, for the sail had sunk in the sea;
They strained and hauled on high there to steady the ship,
But all their work was in vain and availed them nothing.

In the foam of the cold flood they cracked their oars,
And then they had nought in their hands that could help them at all;
And then no comfort could they find, no counsel, no choice
Except that they judge this Jonah the Jew—and at once.

First they prayed to the Prince whom the prophets serve
That He grant them grace that they might not cause His anger
And never might bathe their hands in the blood of the innocent,
Though the man whom they heaved to the water here was His.

Quickly by the head and feet they lifted him then
And into that loathsome lake they let him fall.
As soon as he dropped from the deck, the tempest ceased,
And the sea became still once more as soon as she might.

And then, though their tackle was torn and twisted by the waves,
Currents stiff and smooth took the ship where she lay
And drove her clean on her course, keeping to the clear,
Till at last a lighter sea breeze laid her by the bank.

They lifted their love hymns aloft, with the land at their feet.
In the manner of Moses, to the mighty, most merciful God
They set up their sacrifice, made solemn vows,
And named Him their only God, and no god before Him.

But for all their joy and cheer, still Jonah trembles,
For he who would flee all grief finds fearful adventures:
What happened when Jonah went down in the dark of the water
No mortal could credit except in the true word of God.

2

Now was this Jonah the Jew condemned to be drowned;
From the side of that storm-beaten ship he'd soon been lowered;
And lo, as the Lord would have it, a great, rolling whale,
Beaten up from the abyss, bobbed near the boat.

When the whale was aware of the man who sought the water,
He suddenly turned on his tail, and his throat opened;
From the sailors that held Jonah's feet the sea beast took him:
Without ever touching a tooth, he tumbled in the throat.

Now the fish swings and sways by the ocean floor,
By many a great rough rock and by rattling shores
With the holy man in his maw half mad with dread,
And little the wonder of it if woe filled his heart;

For had not high Heaven's King, through His holy might,
Guarded this grieving man in the guts of Sheol,
What man could believe that by any law in all Nature
Life might be left for so long in a mortal thing?

But Jonah was spared by that Sire who sits on high,
Though he lay without hope of weal in the womb of the fish;
Driving on through the deep, and in darkness rolling,
Lord, cold was his comfort; his care was great!

And he knew all too well every care and discomfort that came—
How he slipped from the ship to the sea and was seized by the beast
And thrown in at the throat, and threatened no more
Than a mote at a minster door, so mighty those jaws.

He glides in past the gills through gluey filth,
Goes down a gullet a good rood wide, as he thought,
Falling down heel over head, and hurtling about
Till he hit at last in a chamber as huge as a hall;

And there he braces his feet and blinks in the dark,
And stands up in that stomach that stinks like the devil;
There in soft grease and sorrow and the stench of hell,
There stood his dwelling place who would suffer no sorrow.

He tries to discern in the dark what den would be best;
Explores every cavern corner and still cannot find
Either remedy or rest, only rankness and filth
Wherever he goes in those guts. Yet God is kind:

PATIENCE

And Jonah gave up his great pride, and he cried out to God:
"Now, Prince, I pray You, have pity on Your prophet!
Though I be a fool and fickle, and false in my heart,
Call back Your vengeance now, in the name of mercy!

"Though I be deceitful and loathsome and least of Your prophets,
You are God yet; all goods are in good truth Yours.
Have mercy now on Your man and his many misdeeds,
And willingly prove Yourself Lord both on land and on water."

He hauled himself up in a hollow and held himself there
Where no defilement of filth could fasten around him;
And there he sat unstained save only by darkness,
As he had in the hold of the boat, where he'd slept before.

So in the belly of the whale he waited, alive,
For three days and three nights, and thought on God,
His might, His mercy, His marvelous moderation;
And he knew Him now in care, who knew nothing in joy.

And onward rolls the whale in the wastes of the deep
Through many a rugged region, through pride of his will,
For that living mote in his maw had made him, no doubt—
Small as it was inside him—sick to the heart.

And Jonah, huddled there, hour on hour he heard
The flood on the great beast's back and beating on his sides.
And then at last, in a rush, he raised up his prayer
In this wise, as I read, and many were his words:

3

"Lord, I have called Your name when cares were strong:
Out of the hole, from the womb of Hell, You have heard me;
I called, and You have known my muted voice,
And have dipped me up from the deep to the depth of Your heart;

"The great wide flank of Your flood has folded around me
And all the pourings of the gulf and the bottomless pits,
And all Your coursing streams in uncountable channels
In one all-dashing dam have driven me under;

"And yet I said as I sat in the ocean bottom,
'Full of care, I am cast from Your clear eyes
And dissevered from Your sight; yet surely I hope
Hereafter to tread in Your temple, taken to You.'

"I am wrapped about in water, to my woe and dread;
The abyss binds this poor body I cower in;
The mighty rattling whirlpool plays on my head;
To the last boundary of the mountains, behold, I am fallen;

"The barriers of the steep banks bind me in;
To no landing place can I leap; my life is Yours.
And yet while Your justice sleeps, Lord, You will relieve me
By the might of Your mercy, mountain of my trust.

"For lo, when the onslaught of anguish had entered my soul,
Then I remembered at last my Lord Almighty,
Praying to Him that He pity His prophet and hear him,
That into His holy house my orisons might enter.

"I've spoken concerning Your mysteries many long days,
But now I know in truth that those witless men
That affirm their faith in the vain, and in vain things,
Believing it matters not, must lose all joy.

"But truly I swear to You now, I will take up the truth
And see to Your solemn service if You will save me;
And I'll offer up for my safety a sacred gift,
And I'll go wherever You guide me, I give You my word."

Then spoke our Father to the fish, and sternly He bid
That swiftly he vomit up Jonah upon dry land:
The whale went forth at His will to the waves' end
And there he coughed up the captive, as God had commanded.

Then Jonah sank to the shore in his filth-sopped clothes,
And well it might be that the robe he wore needed washing;
And the land that he looked to, the land that he lay beside
Was that same region that Jonah had shunned before.

And then the wind of the Word once more came down:
"Will you not now to Nineveh make your way?"
"Yes, my Lord," said the liege man; "lend me Your grace;
Only obeying Your bidding can bring me good."

"Rise and approach, then, and preach; behold the place!
My words are within you. Make your way thither and speak!"
In silence, swiftly, the prophet stood up on his feet,
And that same night he came near to the city of Nineveh.

The city was spread out wide and was strangely broad,
And to walk the length of that city took three full days:
But Jonah went straight to the place, and he stopped not once.
And with no man he saw did he stop to speak one word.

And then he cried out so clearly that all there could hear,
And the true tenor of his theme he told as commanded:
"Forty days shall come and shall come to an end,
And then shall your towers be taken and turned into nought.

"Truly this same town shall be tumbled to the ground
And upside-down shall be dumped in the deep abyss
And be swallowed swiftly down by the swarthy earth,
And all that live in this place lose limb and life."

His words sprang up in the city and were spread all about
To young and to old and to all who had homes in that place;
Such terror overtook them, such trembling and dread
That all there changed their cheer and were chilled at the heart;

And still the prophet spoke on, saying ever the same:
"Verily, God's vengeance shall void all this town!"
And then without a sound the city wept,
And for fear of the Lord, they lamented in their hearts.

They caught up haircloth coats that cruelly cut
And they bound them tight to their backs and their bare sides,
Dropped thick dust on their heads and dolefully begged
That their penance please the Lord who would punish their wrongs.

And they cried in all the streets till the king heard them,
And quickly the king rose up and came down from his throne;
He stripped off the noble robe from his naked back
And stood in the center of the crowd that cried for mercy;

Hoarsely he called for a haircloth, and hasped it around him,
And sewed poor sackcloth around it, and sighed from his heart;
As if dazed, he lay in the dust, with dripping tears,
Wondrously weeping for all his wicked deeds.

Then said the king to his servants, "Assemble swiftly
And drive through the land the decree I shall utter now:
That every quick creature within this city's walls—
Both animals and men, both women and children,

"Each prince, each priest, and every prelate among us—
All shall faithfully fast for their false works;
Seize women's children from suck, wail though they will;
No beast shall feed in the broom nor yet on bent grasses

"Or pass to his pasture or pick any leaf at all;
No ox shall go to his hay or horse to water;
But all shall ask Him for mercy with all their strength;
Our roar shall rise up to Heaven, that He may repent.

"For will He blame and judge if we please Him at last,
Who sits in splendor on high, in His sweet nobility?
Such is the power of that Prince that, displeased as He is,
He may yet in His mountainous mind find mercy for us.

"If we leave off all delight in our loathsome sins
And walk in the straight ways of which He has told us,
He will abandon His anger and all His wrath
And forgive us this guilt, if we know Him God, and believe."

Then all believed in His law and left their sins;
They performed the whole of the penance the king decreed;
And God through His goodness forgave them, as he predicted;
Despite the warning He'd sent, He withdrew His wrath.

4

Great was the sorrow that settled on Jonah then.
He waxed as wroth as the wind toward our Lord;
So hot was the anger in Jonah's heart that he shouted
A prayer to the high Prince, and in pain he lamented:

"I beseech you, Sire, now sit and judge Yourself.
Was this not my very word that has now come to pass,
The same that I spoke in my country when You sought me first
And said I must traipse to this place and teach Your will?

"I knew all along Your courtesy and patience,
Your liberality, Your loving grace,
Your long endurance of loss, Your slowness to anger;
However huge the offense, You have always shown mercy.

"I knew all the time that as soon as I'd said what I could
To menace those proudhearted men making merry there,
They could win You to peace with a prayer and a little pain;
And therefore I wanted to fly away far into Tarshish.

"Now, Lord, flick out my life. It lasts too long.
Bid me to drop to my death rattle. Drive me to the end.
For sweeter it were, I swear, to be struck down dead
Than to preach any longer Your lore that must leave me a liar."

The voice of our Sovereign then sounded in Jonah's ears,
Upbraiding the prophet and answering him crossly:
"Hear Me, wretch. Is it right to so rise up in anger
For any deed I have done or deemed for you yet?"

Joyless and muttering, Jonah raised himself up
And stalked to the eastern side of that high place
And prepared himself to abide on a great broad field
To wait for that Dwelling Place that would one day come.

He wrought himself a hut there, as well as he could,
Of polypod ferns and hay and various leaves,
For the place was bare and there were no bending groves
That would shield him from sun or soothe him with cool shade.

He bent down and crawled in his burrow, his back to the sun,
And there, sadly, he slumbered all that night;
While he slept, God in His grace grew out of the soil
The fairest climbers above him that ever man saw.

And when at last God sent down dawn and day,
Jonah awoke in his dwelling place under the woodbine,
And he looked above at the leaves that trembled green.
So splendid a love-cell had never been seen until then.

For the room was broad at the bottom and vaulted above,
Enclosed on either side, like a stately house,
An entrance on the north and nowhere else,
But all shut tight in foliage, shaded and cool.

Gladly he looked at those green and glorious leaves
That waved in the gentle wind and were so cool;
The sun shone bright around it, yet no shaft found
So much as a slit to slip through to strike the man.

The prophet was pleased indeed with his pleasant house;
He lies there, lolling inside, and looks toward town
So comfortable he was now, with the woodbine around him,
That he thought, all the length of that day, Oh, the devil with food.

And he laughed as he looked about at the lodgings he'd found
And he heartily wished that the hut were in his own land,
High upon Ephraim or Hermon's Hills—
"A comelier cottage, in truth, I could never keep!"

And when night drew near and he knew it was time for sleep,
He slipped into slumber down under the silent leaves.
And God caused a worm to gnaw at the woodbine's roots,
That the woodbine might all be withered when Jonah awoke.

He commanded the Western Wind to awaken softly,
And He spoke to tell Zephyrus, "Blow now soft and warm
That no cloud may quicken before the cruel sun,"
And He brought the sun up, broad and burning like a torch.

And when the man awoke from his wondrous dreams
And looked at his woodbine, the limbs were limp and scarred,
And withered and wasted were all those worthy leaves,
And searing sun had scorched them while Jonah slept.

The beams of the sun grew brighter and brutally burned;
The warm wind of the west had his way with the leaves.
Then the man crouched without cover and could not hide,
The woodbine taken away; and he wept for sorrow.

With anger harsh and hot, he howled in outrage:
"Ah, you Maker of Man, how mighty Your works,
To pick on Your poor prophet before all others!
Will You never have pity, but play every prank You can think of?

"I made me a comfort, but lo, You have caught it away,
My beautiful woodbine that proudly protected my head;
I see You are set upon stealing away all solace.
Why will You not give me death? I endure too long!"

And again to the stubborn Jonah our Sovereign spoke:
"Is this your righteousness, rebel, this riot of pride,
To grow all at once so wroth on account of a woodbine?
Why are you grown so peevish, poor thing, for so little?"

"It is *not* little," cried Jonah, "—but in Justice's name,
I would I were out of this world and wrapped in the clods!"
"Think, then, man! If your work to you seems dear,
Then little wonder if My work seems worthy of saving.

"You are riled and worked up to wrath for your woodbine's sake,
 Yet it took neither trouble nor one hour's time to tend it—
 It was made at a single stroke, unmade at another—
 And yet so great is your anger you ask Me for death!

"Blame Me not, then, for thinking My work worth preserving,
 Or for showing My mercy to sinners who seek forgiveness.
 First I made them Myself in My own image,
 And then I looked after them long, and I led their way:

"And if I should lose all My labor of all this time
 And topple that town to the earth when it turned from My face,
 Well might sorrow for the city sink to My heart,
 And well might I mourn at the malice of so many men!

"And some, moreover, as madmen, must count as mere innocents,
 Like babes at the breast that have been thus far without taint;
 And some, foolish women without enough wit to choose
 The left hand from the right, though it win them the world;

"And then there are poor dumb beasts that abide in that city,
 They know no sins, nor know how to sink into sorrow.
 Why should I smite them, then, if soon they will turn
 And care and acknowledge Me king and accept My law?

"If Heaven were hasty, like you, what harms we might see!
 Could I not endure but as you do, not many would thrive!
 But I cannot be so malicious, dismissing all mildness,
 For the might to kill must be kept by the rein of kindness.

"Be not such a Grendel, good man, but go your way;
 Whether in pain or in pleasure, be brave and be patient,
 For the man too quick to cut up his outworn clothes
 Will gather together old tatters and weave in the wind."

Oppressed by my poverty, then, and with pains enough,
 It behooves me to suffer in silence and still hold my peace;
 For the penance and the pain may prove at last
 That Patience is a virtue, though few find her sweet.

SIR GAWAIN
AND THE GREEN KNIGHT

Part One

1

After the siege and assault was ended at Troy,
The battlements breached and burnt to brands and ashes,
Antenor, he who the trammels of treason there wrought,
Was well known for his wrongs—the worst yet on earth.
Aeneas the noble it was and his kingly kinsmen
That afterward conquered kingdoms and came to be lords
Of well-nigh all the wealth of the Western Isles;
For royal Romulus to Rome rushed swiftly
And with great splendor established that first of all cities
And named it his own name, as we now know it;
And Ticius to Tuskan went and built there his towers;
And Langaberde in Lombardy lifted up houses;
And far over the French flood Felix Brutus
On the slopes of many broad hills established Britain
                              with joy,
            Where war and wrack and wonder
            Have sometimes since held sway,
            And now bliss, now blunder,
            Turned like dark and day.

And after Britain was built by that brave baron,
Bold lords were bred there, men who loved battle,
And time after time they would turn to the tools of destruction;
More monsters have been met on the moors of that land
Than anywhere else I know of since earliest times.
But of all who built castles there, of Britain's kings,
Arthur was highest in honor, as all men know;
And so I intend to recount a tradition of the region,
A strange and surprising thing, as some men hold,
And awesome even among the adventures of Arthur.
If you will listen to my lay but a little while
I will tell it all, and at once, as I heard it told
                                    in town,
            Rightly, as it is written,
            A story swift and strong
            With letters locked and linking,
            As scōps have always sung.

3

King Arthur lay at Camelot over Christmas
With many a gentle lord, his gallant-hearted men,
The noble knights of the Round Table, names of renown,
With great revels and good, and gladness of heart.
Tournament trumpets rang there time and again,
And knights jarred knights, with jubilant hearts, in the joust,
And later they came into court to dance caroles;
For the feast was in full swing for fifteen days
With all the dinners and diversions devised by man,
Such explosions of joy, it was beautiful to hear—
Joyful din all day long, and dancing all night;
Happiness reigned on high there in halls and in chambers
Where lords and ladies delighted themselves as they liked.
With all the goodwill in the world they dwelled there together,
The most renowned of knights—next to Christ himself—
And the loveliest ladies that ever yet lived in the land,
And their king the comeliest king that had ever held court;
For all those excellent people were still in their youth
                                        on that dais;
             Most highborn under Heaven,
             Their king of all kings best—
             Where but there has there been
             A company so blessed?

4

While the New Year was still young—it was newly fallen—
The nobles sat two to a serving on the dais,
For the king and all his knights had come down to the hall
When the chanting of mass in the chapel had come to an end;
Joyful cries were cast up by the clergy and others,
Praising Noel anew and naming it often;
And now the great lords rushed about giving out handsels,
Cried out the gifts on high and gave them in person;
They debated busily, briskly, about those gifts,
And the ladies laughed, delighted, even though they lost
(And she who won was not sorry, you may be sure);
Thus they all made merry till dinner was made.
Then, when they all had washed, they went to their seats,
Arranged by standards of rank, as seemed to them right,
Queen Guinevere, resplendent, seated in the center,
Placed on the blazing dais, adorned all about
With the finest of silks on all sides, and streaming above her
A tapestry-tent out of world-famous Tars and Toulouse
Embroidered and splendidly spangled with sparkling gems
That might well prove priceless if anyone wanted to buy them
                              some day;
             But the fairest of all to see
             Was the gem with eyes of gray;
             Fairest of all was she,
             As all our poets say.

5

Now Arthur the King would not eat until all were served,
So brimming he was with youth and boyish high spirits;
He loved all the luster of life, and he little liked
Either to lie in bed late or too long to sit,
So busy his youthful blood, his brain so lively;
And also for other reasons he waited there, restless:
He had sworn by his sovereignty he would start no meal
On the festival of the New Year before he was given
Some strange tale about some most mysterious thing,
Some Monstrous Marvel that merited belief,
Of the Old Ones, or of Arms, or of other adventures,
Or until some stout lancer had sought of him some sure knight
To join with him in the joust and in jeopardy lay
Mortal life against life, each leaving to the other
His fling at the fairer lot, as Fortune might fashion.
Such was the King's custom when the court came together
At each of the fine feasts he held with his freemen
                                        in the hall;
              Therefore, bold in his manner,
              He stands at his place, tall,
              Waiting, young on the New Year,
              Laughing and talking with them all.

6

There at his station the King stood, straight and proud,
Taking politely of trifles to all the high table;
The good Sir Gawain was stationed by gray-eyed Guinevere,
And Agravain of the Gauntlet on Gawain's left,
Sure knights both and sons of the King's own sister.
Above, at the head of the table, sat Bishop Baldwin,
And Ywain, son of Urien, ate with the Bishop.
All these were seated on the dais and served with distinction,
And down below many another knight ate at the sideboards.
Then quickly the first course comes in, with a clarion of trumpets
Hung brightly with many a blazing banderole,
And now the kettledrums barked, and the brilliant pipes
Warbled wildly and richly, awakening echoes
That lifted high every heart by their heavenly sound.
Then in flooded wonderful cates, the finest of foods,
Mountains of splendid meats, such a marvel of dishes
It was hard to find places to place there, in front of the people,
The vessels of silver that held all the various stews
                              on hand.
                    Soon each to suit his wishes
                    Turned gladly, gay of mind,
                    For every two, twelve dishes,
                    Cold beer and brilliant wine.

But now I will speak no more of their sumptuous banquet,
For as every man must know, there was nothing missing.
Another strain of music now sang through the hall ·
Encouraging each of the nobles to eat all he might;
And strangely, almost as soon as that sound died out
And the first course had been courteously served to the court,
There haled through the door of that hall an ungodly creature,
A man as enormous as any known on earth:
From his wide neck to his rib cage so square and so thick,
His loins and his legs so long and so loaded with power,
I must hold that man half giant under Heaven—
And yet for all that, a man he must still have been,
And the handsomest creature that ever yet rode horseback;
For his chest and his shoulders were huge as any boulder
And yet his waist and his belly were worthily small,
And indeed all his features were princely and perfectly formed
                and clean:
        But astounded, every man there
        Stared at the stranger's skin,
        For though he seemed fine and fair,
        His whole great body was green!

8

He came there all in green, both the clothes and the man,
A coat, tight-fitting and long, fastened to his sides;
On his shoulders a beautiful cloak that was covered inside
With pelts perfectly pured, resplendent cloth
Bright with a trimming of blaunner, and a hood to match,
Loosened now from his locks and lying on his shoulders;
Close-fitting, tightly stretched hose of that same vivid green
Clung to his calves; at his ankles hung gleaming spurs
Of gold on embroidered bangles richly barred;
The guard-leather under his legs, where the large man rode,
And everything on him, in fact, was entirely green—
Both the bars of his belt and the beautiful stones
Artfully arranged over all his array
Upon settings of silk on himself and the cantle of his saddle;
It would be too much to tell half the trimmings and trifles
Embroidered in brocatelle, with birds and flies,
Gay weld-glints of green gleaming gold at the center,
The beautiful bridle with its metal all brightly enameled,
The stirrups the stranger stood on stained the same way,
And the saddlebow also, and the mighty steed's fine skirts
Where they glistered and gleamed and glinted, all of green stones.
For the charger on which he came was completely the color
                              of the man—
        A great horse huge and heavy
        And hard to keep in hand,
        Who bridled and bristled roughly
        But knew the knight's command.

Splendid that knight errant stood in a splay of green,
And green, too, was the mane of his mighty destrier;
Fair fanning tresses enveloped the fighting man's shoulders,
And over his breast hung a beard as big as a bush;
The beard and the huge mane burgeoning forth from his head
Were clipped off clean in a straight line over his elbows,
And the upper half of each arm was hidden underneath
As if covered by a king's chaperon, closed round the neck.
The mane of the marvelous horse was much the same,
Well crisped and combed and carefully pranked with knots,
Threads of gold interwoven with the glorious green,
Now a thread of hair, now another thread of gold;
The tail of the horse and the forelock were tricked the same way,
And both were bound up with a band of brilliant green
Adorned with glittering jewels the length of the dock,
Then caught up tight with a thong in a criss-cross knot
Where many a bell tinkled brightly, all burnished gold.
So monstrous a mount, so mighty a man in the saddle
Was never once encountered on all this earth
　　　　　　　　　　till then;
　　　　His eyes, like lightning, flashed,
　　　　And it seemed to many a man,
　　　　That any man who clashed
　　　　With him would not long stand.

But the huge man came unarmed, without helmet or hauberk,
No breastplate or gorget or iron cleats on his arms;
He brought neither shield nor spearshaft to shove or to smite,
But instead he held in one hand a bough of the holly
That grows most green when all the groves are bare
And held in the other an ax, immense and unwieldy,
A pitiless battleblade terrible to tell of.
The head alone was a full ell-yard in length,
The branching pike-steel of blinking green and gold,
The bit brilliantly burnished, with a broad edge
So carefully ground it could cut like the blade of a razor;
The stout shaft which the stern-faced hero gripped
Was wound around with iron to the end of the wood
And was all engraved in green with graceful figures;
And a leather cord lapped around it to lock on the head
And, below, lapped round the handle to hold it in tight;
And what seemed hundreds of tassels were tacked to the cord
On buttons of bright green, brochéed and embroidered.
Thus came the dreadful knight to King Arthur's hall
And drove full tilt to the dais, afraid of no man.
He never hailed anyone there but, haughtily staring,
He spoke, and the first words he said were these: "Where is
The ruler of this rout? For readily would I
Set eyes on that sovereign and say a few words with him, man
                                 to man."
             He glanced at the company
             And looked them up and down;
             He stood and seemed to study
             Which knight had most renown.

11

All the lords sat silent and looked at the stranger
And each duke marveled long what the devil it meant
That a hero and horse should have taken such a hue,
As growing-green as the grass—and yet greener, it seemed;
More brightly glowing than green enamel on gold.
And every man there stood musing and came more near
Wondering what in the world this creature was up to,
For many a marvel they'd met with, but nothing like this.
They thought it must be magic or illusion,
And for that reason many a lord was too frightened to answer;
Astounded at the sound of his voice, they sat stone still,
And a deathly silence spread throughout the hall
As if they had slipped off to sleep; their sounds sank away
                        and died;
          But some (I'm sure) kept still
          From courtesy, not fright;
          Since this was Arthur's hall,
          Let him address the knight.

12

King Arthur stared down at the stranger before the high dais
And greeted him nobly, for nothing on earth frightened him.
And he said to him, "Sir, you are welcome in this place;
I am the head of this court. They call me Arthur.
Get down from your horse, I beg you, and join us for dinner,
And then whatever you seek we will gladly see to."
But the stranger said, "No, so help me God on high,
My errand is hardly to sit at my ease in your castle!
But friend, since your praises are sung so far and wide,
Your castle the best ever built, people say, and your barons
The stoutest men in steel armor that ever rode steeds,
Most mighty and most worthy of all mortal men
And tough devils to toy with in tournament games,
And since courtesy is in flower in this court, they say,
All these tales, in truth, have drawn me to you at this time.
You may be assured by this holly branch I bear
That I come to you in peace, not spoiling for battle.
If I'd wanted to come in finery, fixed up for fighting,
I have back at home both a helmet and a hauberk,
A shield and a sharp spear that shines like fire,
And other weapons that I know pretty well how to use.
But since I don't come here for battle, my clothes are mere cloth.
Now if you are truly as bold as the people all say,
You will grant me gladly the little game that I ask
     as my right."
   Arthur gave him answer
   And said, "Sir noble knight,
   If it's a duel you're after,
   We'll furnish you your fight."

13

"Good heavens, I want no such thing! I assure you, Sire,
  You've nothing but beardless babes about this bench!
  If I were hasped in my armor and high on my horse,
  You haven't a man that could match me, your might is so feeble.
  And so all I ask of this court is a Christmas game,
  For the Yule is here, and New Year's, and here sit young men;
  If any man holds himself, here in this house, so hardy,
  So bold in his blood—and so brainless in his head—
  That he dares to stoutly exchange one stroke for another,
  I shall let him have as my present this lovely gisarme,
  This ax, as heavy as he'll need, to handle as he likes,
  And I will abide the first blow, bare-necked as I sit.
  If anyone here has the daring to try what I've offered,
  Leap to me lightly, lad; lift up this weapon;
  I give you the thing forever—you may think it your own;
  And I will stand still for your stroke, steady on the floor,
  Provided you honor my right, when my inning comes,
                                to repay.
                    But let the respite be
                    A twelvemonth and a day;
                    Come now, my boys, let's see
                    What any here can say."

14

If they were like stone before, they were stiller now,
Every last lord in the hall, both the high and the low;
The stranger on his destrier stirred in the saddle
And ferociously his red eyes rolled around;
He lowered his grisly eyebrows, glistening green,
And waved his beard and waited for someone to rise;
When no one answered, he coughed, as if embarrassed,
And drew himself up straight and spoke again:
"What! Can this be King Arthur's court?" said the stranger,
"Whose renown runs through many a realm, flung far and wide?
What has become of your chivalry and your conquest,
Your greatness-of-heart and your grimness and grand words?
Behold the radiance and renown of the mighty Round Table
Overwhelmed by a word out of one man's mouth!
You shiver and blanch before a blow's been shown!"
And with that he laughed so loud that the lord was distressed;
In chagrin, his blood shot up in his face and limbs
     so fair;
    More angry he was than the wind,
    And likewise each man there;
    And Arthur, bravest of men,
    Decided now to draw near.

15

And he said, "By heaven, sir, your request is strange;
But since you have come here for folly, you may as well find it.
I know no one here who's aghast of your great words.
Give me your gisarme, then, for the love of God,
And gladly I'll grant you the gift you have asked to be given."
Lightly the King leaped down and clutched it in his hand;
Then quickly that other lord alighted on his feet.
Arthur lay hold of the ax, he gripped it by the handle,
And he swung it up over him sternly, as if to strike.
The stranger stood before him, in stature higher
By a head or more than any man here in the house;
Sober and thoughtful he stood there and stroked his beard,
And with patience like a priest's he pulled down his collar,
No more unmanned or dismayed by Arthur's might
Than he'd be if some baron on the bench had brought him a glass
of wine.
        Then Gawain, at Guinevere's side,
        Made to the king a sign:
        "I beseech you, Sire," he said,
        "Let this game be mine.

"Now if you, my worthy lord," said Gawain to the King,
"Would command me to step from the dais and stand with you there,
That I might without bad manners move down from my place
(Though I couldn't, of course, if my liege lady disliked it)
I'd be deeply honored to advise you before all the court;
For I think it unseemly, if I understand the matter,
That challenges such as this churl has chosen to offer
Be met by Your Majesty—much as it may amuse you—
When so many bold-hearted barons sit about the bench:
No men under Heaven, I am sure, are more hardy in will
Or better in body on the fields where battles are fought;
I myself am the weakest, of course, and in wit the most feeble;
My life would be least missed, if we let out the truth.
Only as you are my uncle have I any honor,
For excepting your blood, I bear in my body slight virtue.
And since this affair that's befallen us here is so foolish,
And since I have asked for it first, let it fall to me.
If I've reasoned incorrectly, let all the court say,
                             without blame."
          The nobles gather round
          And all advise the same:
        "Let the King step down
        And give Sir Gawain the game!"

Then King Arthur commanded the knight to rise,
And promptly Gawain leaped up and, approaching his lord,
Kneeled on one knee by the King and caught up the weapon;
And gently the King released it and lifted up his hand
And gave God's blessing to him, and bid Sir Gawain
To be hearty both in his heart and in his hand.
"Take care, cousin," said the King, "as you set to your carving;
For in truth, I think, if you tackle the matter rightly
You'll take without much trouble the tap he returns."
Then Gawain turned to the knight, the gisarme in his hand.
The Green Knight waited boldly, abashed not a bit.
And then up spoke the knight in green to Sir Gawain:
"My friend, let's go over our terms here before we go further.
And first, let me ask you, my boy: What is it men call you?
Now let me hear the truth. Let me know I can trust you."
"On my faith," said the noble knight, "Sir Gawain is the name
Of the baron who gives you this blow, befall what may;
And twelve months from now I will take from you another,
And with any blade you may wish—but from nobody else
                    alive."
          The Green Knight answered then,
          "I am proud, by Heaven above,
          To get from the famous Sir Gawain
          Whatever he may have.

18

"By crimus," the Green Knight said, "Sir Gawain, I'm glad
To be getting from your own hand the handsel I've asked.
You've recited without a mistake my whole agreement—
Quite glibly, in fact, all the terms of my trade with the King—
Except that you still have to promise me, sir, by your honor
To seek me yourself, alone, wherever you think
You will find me in all the wide world, and win there such wages
As you pay out today before all these princes on the dais."
"Where shall I seek you?" said Gawain, "Where is your castle?
By our Lord, sir, I haven't the least idea where you live;
I know neither your court, Knight, nor your name;
But tell me your name, and tell me truly the way there,
And I swear I will work all my wits to wend my way to you,
And that I can swear to you by my certain troth."
"That is enough for the New Year; I need no more,"
Said the warrior all in green to the worthy Gawain;
"If I tell you truly, after I've taken your tap—
If you lay on too lightly—if quickly I tell you all
Concerning my castle and country and what I am called,
Then you may ask me my path and hold to your pact.
And if I can bring out no sound, all the better for you!
You may linger here in your land and look no further
                              and relax;
            Take up your tool, Sir Gawain,
            And let's see how it smacks."
        "Just as you wish, my friend,"
            Said he—and stroked his ax.

19

On the ground, the Green Knight got himself into position,
His head bent forward a little, the bare flesh showing,
His long and lovely locks laid over his crown
So that any man there might note the naked neck.
Sir Gawain laid hold of the ax and he hefted it high,
His pivot foot thrown forward before him on the floor,
And then, swiftly, he slashed at the naked neck;
The sharp of the battleblade shattered asunder the bones
And sank through the shining fat and slit it in two,
And the bit of the bright steel buried itself in the ground.
The fair head fell from the neck to the floor of the hall
And the people all kicked it away as it came near their feet.
The blood splashed up from the body and glistened on the green,
But he never faltered or fell for all of that,
But swiftly he started forth upon stout shanks
And rushed to reach out, where the King's retainers stood,
Caught hold of the lovely head, and lifted it up,
And leaped to his steed and snatched up the reins of the bridle,
Stepped into stirrups of steel and, striding aloft,
He held his head by the hair, high, in his hand;
And the stranger sat there as steadily in his saddle
As a man entirely unharmed, although he was headless
                              on his steed.
            He turned his trunk about,
            That baleful body that bled,
            And many were faint with fright
            When all his say was said.

20

He held his head in his hand up high before him,
Addressing the face to the dearest of all on the dais;
And the eyelids lifted wide, and the eyes looked out,
And the mouth said just this much, as you may now hear:
"Look that you go, Sir Gawain, as good as your word,
And seek till you find me, as loyally, my friend,
As you've sworn in this hall to do, in the hearing of the knights.
Come to the Green Chapel, I charge you, and take
A stroke the same as you've given, for well you deserve
To be readily requited on New Year's morn.
Many men know me, the Knight of the Green Chapel;
Therefore if you seek to find me, you shall not fail.
Come or be counted a coward, as is fitting."
Then with a rough jerk he turned the reins
And haled away through the hall-door, his head in his hand,
And fire of the flint flew out from the hooves of the foal.
To what kingdom he was carried no man there knew,
No more than they knew what country it was he came from.
What then?
The King and Gawain there
Laugh at the thing and grin;
And yet, it was an affair
Most marvelous to men.

Though Arthur the highborn King was amazed in his heart,
He let no sign of it show but said as if gaily
To the beautiful Guinevere, with courteous speech:
"Beloved lady, today be dismayed by nothing;
Such things are suitable at the Christmas season—
The playing of interludes, and laughter and song,
Along with the courtly caroles of knights and their ladies;
Nevertheless, I may now begin my meal,
For I've seen my marvel, that much I must admit."
The King glanced then at Sir Gawain, and gently he said,
"Now, sir, hang up your ax. You've hewn enough."
On the drapes of the throne, above the dais, they hung it,
Where every man might see for himself the marvel
And tell of the wonder truly by that token.
Then the two of them turned to the table together,
The King and the good Sir Gawain, and quickly men served them
With double helpings of delicacies, as was right,
All manner of meats, and minstrelsy as well;
In joy they passed that day until darkness came
                              in the land.
            And now think well, Sir Gawain,
            Lest you from terror stand
            Betrayer of the bargain
            That you have now in hand!

Part Two

1

Such was the earnest-pay King Arthur got early,
When the year was young, for his yearning to hear men boast;
Though words of daring were few when they went to their seats,
Now they have hard work enough, and their hands are full.
Sir Gawain was glad to begin those games in the hall,
But if the end should be heavy, it ought not surprise you.
For though men grow merry of mind when there's much to drink,
A year turns all too soon, and all things change:
The opening and the closing are seldom the same.
And so this Yuletide passed, and so the year passed,
And each season, in order, succeeded the other:
For after Christmas, in came crabbed Lenten
That tries the flesh with fish and foods more plain;
And then the weather of the world contends with winter:
Cold clutches the earth, the clouds lift up;
And then the rain falls, shining, in warm showers,
Falls on the fair plains, and flowers come,
And green are the robes of the ground and all the groves,
And birds begin to build and sing on the boughs
For joy as summer's softness settles down
                                    on the banks;
              The blossoms swell to flowers
              By hedgerows rich as kings;
              And deep in the fair forest,
              Royal music rings.

2

Now comes the season of summer; soft are the winds;
The spirit of Zephyrus whispers to seeds and green shoots.
Joyful enough is that herb rising up out of earth,
When the dampening dew has dropped from all her leaves,
To bask in the blissful gaze of the bright sun.
But harvest time draws near and soon grows harsh
And warns it to ripen quickly, for winter is coming;
With draft, he drives the dust along before him,
Flying up from the face of the earth to the sky.
Wild winds of the welkin wrestle with the sun,
And leaves tear loose from their limbs and alight on the ground,
And gray is all the grass that was green before;
Then all that rose up proud grows ripe and rots,
And so the year descends into yesterdays,
And winter returns again as the world requires,
                              we know.
              Comes the Michaelmas moon
              And winter's wages flow;
              And now Sir Gawain soon
              Remembers he must go.

But yet while the holiday lasts he lingers with Arthur,
And the King makes a festival of it, for Gawain's sake,
With rich and splendid revels of all the Round Table—
Courteous knights and the comeliest of ladies—
But all had leaden hearts for love of the hero.
Nevertheless, they hid every hint of sorrow;
Though joyless, they made jokes for the gentle knight's sake.
Then sadly, when dinner was over, he spoke to his uncle
And talked of the trip he must take, and told him simply,
"Now, liege lord of my life, I must ask to leave you.
You know of the terms I have taken. I ask no better.
To worry you with my troubles would waste your time;
I must leave to take my blow tomorrow at the latest,
And seek the knight in the green as God may guide me."
The noblest barons in the palace gathered together,
Ywain, and Eric, and many another man—
Sir Dodinal le Sauvage, the Duke of Clarence,
Sir Lancelot, Sir Lionel, Sir Lucan the good,
Sir Bors and also Sir Bedevere, big men both,
And many another noble, with Mador de la Port.
This company of the court came nearer to the King
To give the knight their counsel, with care in their hearts;
Deep was the secret grief of that great hall
That so worthy a knight as Sir Gawain should go on that quest,
To suffer one sad stroke and strike no more
                           that day.
        Sir Gawain feigned good cheer
        And said, "Why should one fly
        From fortune dark and drear?
        What can man do but try?"

4

He stayed there all that day and dressed the next morning.
He asked them, early, for his arms, and all were brought:
First a carpet of scarlet was spread on the floor
And covered with gilt gear that gleamed aloft;
The strong knight stepped up onto it, handled the steel,
Dressed in a costly doublet wrought at Tars,
On his head a hood made craftily, closed at the top,
Lined and bound within with a brilliant blaunner;
Steel sabots they set on that sure knight's feet,
And they lapped his legs in lovely greaves of steel
With kneeplates pinned at the joints and polished clean
And cinched around his knees with knots of gold;
Cuisses, next, that cunningly enclosed
His thick and brawny thighs, they attached with thongs;
And then a woven byrnie with bright steel rings,
Set upon costly cloth, encircled the knight,
And beautifully burnished braces about both arms,
And tough, gay elbow cups, and gloves of plate,
And all the goodly gear that might give aid
                              on that ride:
          Coat-armor of the best,
          His gold spurs pinned with pride,
          A sword the knight might trust
          On a ceinture of silk at his side.

And when the knight was hasped in his splendid harness,
Every last latchet and loop all gleaming gold,
Worthily dressed as he was he went to hear mass,
Made offering, honored his Lord at the high altar.
Then Gawain came to the King and all the court,
And gently he took his leave of lords and ladies;
They walked with him, kissed him, commended him to Christ.
Now Gringolet was ready, girt with a saddle,
Glorious, gleaming with many a golden fringe,
The riveting newly wrought for the coming ride,
The bridle bound about and barred with gold,
The proud skirts and the breast-harness splendidly tricked,
The crupper and caparison matching the saddlebows;
And all was clamped on red cloth by golden nails
That glittered and glanced like the gleaming beams of the sun.
Then he caught up the helmet and hastily kissed it,
A helmet heavily stapled and padded within;
It towered high on his head and was hasped in back,
With a lightly hanging veil laid over the visor
Embroidered and bound fast with the best of gems
On a broad silk border, and birds on all the seams—
Brightly painted parrots preening in among
Love knots and turtledoves—so thickly embroidered
The women must have worked on it seven winters
                              in the town;
          But greater yet the price
          Of the circlet round his crown:
          A rich and rare device
          Of diamonds dripping down.

6

Then they showed him his shield, of shining gules,
With the pentangle upon it, painted in gold;
He bore it up by the baldric and hung it on his neck,
And that shield was fair to see, and suited him.
And why the sign of the pentangle suited that prince
I intend to stop and say, though it slows my tale:
That star is the same that Solomon once set
As an emblem of truth by its own just claim and title;
For that fair figure is framed upon five points,
And every line overlaps and locks with another,
And everywhere it is endless—thus Englishmen call it,
In every dialect, "the endless knot."
And therefore it suited this knight and his splendid arms,
Five ways ever faithful on five different sides.
Like purified gold, Sir Gawain was known for his goodness,
All dross refined away, adorned with virtues
                                        in the castle.
            And thus on coat and shield
            He bore the New Pentangle;
            A man still undefiled,
            And of all knights most gentle.

First, in his five senses they found him faultless;
And next, he was found unfailing in his five fingers;
And all his faith was fixed on the five wounds
That Christ received on the cross, as the creed tells;
And whenever this man was hard-pressed, in murderous battle,
His steady thought, throughout, was this alone:
That he drew all the force he found from the five joys
That the holy Queen of Heaven had through her child;
And for this reason the hero had handsomely painted
On the inside of his shield an image of the Virgin,
So that when he glanced there his courage could not flag.
And these, I find, were the fifth five of the hero:
Franchise and *Fellowship* before all things,
And *Cleanness* and *Courtesy* that none could corrupt,
And *Charity*, chief of all virtues. These five things
Were fixed more firmly in him than in all other men.
Now all these fives, in truth, were firm in him
And each was locked with the other that none might fail,
And fashioned firmly on five unfailing points,
No two on the same side, yet inseparable
Throughout and at every angle, a knot without end,
Wherever the man who traced it started or stopped.
And so on this shining shield they shaped the knot
Most regally, in gold on a crimson field:
The pentangle of perfection it was to men
of lore.

And now Sir Gawain gay
Caught up his lance of war;
He gave them all good-day
And thought: *For evermore!*

8

He struck the steed with his spurs and sprang on his way
So swiftly that Gringolet's shoes struck fire on the stone;
And all who saw that sweet knight sighed in their hearts,
And each man there said the same to every other,
Grieving for that knight: "By Christ, it's sad
That you, lad, must be lost, so noble in life!
It would not be easy to find this man's equal on earth.
It would have been wiser to work more warily;
We might one day have made him a mighty duke,
A glowing lord of the people in his land;
Far better that than broken like this into nothing,
Beheaded by an elf for undue pride.
Who ever heard of a king who'd hear the counsel
Of addle-pated knights during Christmas games?"
Many were the warm tears that watered their eyes
When that handsome hero rode from the high hall
                              that day.
                    He paused at no abode
                    But swiftly went his way
                    Down many a devious road,
                    As all the old books say.

9

Now through the realm of Logres rides the lord,
Sir Gawain, servant of God. No pleasant game.
Often he sleeps alone at night, and friendless,
Where he finds at lunchtime little enough that he likes.
He had no friend but his horse in the hills and forests
And no one but God to talk with on the way.
Soon the knight drew near to northern Wales,
And he fared over the fords and past the forelands
Over at Holy Head till he came to the hillsides
In the wilderness of Wyral; few lived there
Who loved with a good heart either God or man.
And always he asked of all he met as he passed
Whether they'd ever heard word of a knight of green,
Or knew, in some nearby kingdom, a Green Chapel.
But all of them shook their heads, saying never yet
Had they heard of any hero with the hue
                    of green.
            He left the roads for the woods
            And rough-grown higher ground,
            And many would be his moods
            Before that place was found.

A hundred cliffs he climbed in foreign countries,
Far removed from friends, riding as a stranger;
At every hill or river where the hero passed
He found—strange to say!—some foe before him,
And a foe so foul and so fell he was forced to fight.
He met so many marvels in those mountains,
A tenth would be too tedious to tell.
Sometimes he takes on dragons, sometimes wolves,
Sometimes wood-satyrs dwelling in the rugged rocks;
At times he battles bulls and bears and boars
And giants puffing and snorting down from the hilltops;
Had he not been sturdy and doughty, or served his God,
He'd doubtless have died or been murdered there many times over;
For if warring worried him little, the winter was worse,
When the cold, clear water showered from the clouds
And froze before it could fall to the faded earth;
Nearly slain by sleet, he slept in his irons
Many more nights than he needed in the naked rocks
Where the cold stream fell down crashing from the mountain's crest
And hung, high over his head, in hard icicles.
Thus in peril and pain and terrible plights
The knight roams all through the region till Christmas Eve—
                         alone.

        Earnestly that night
        He lifted up a moan
        To the Virgin, that she guide
        His way, reveal some home.

11

By a mountain that morning merrily he rides,
And into an old, deep forest, weird and wild,
High hills on either hand, and below them a holt
Of huge and hoary oaks, a hundred together;
Hazel and hawthorn were twisted there all into one,
And rough, ragged moss grew rampant all about,
And many small sorrowing birds upon bare twigs
Piteously piped there for pain of the cold.
Sir Gawain on Gringolet glided along below them
Through many a quagmire and bog, a man all alone
Brooding on his sins, lest he never be brought
To see the service of that Sire who the selfsame night
Was born of a lady to allay all human griefs;
And therefore, sighing, he said: "I beseech Thee, Lord,
And Mary, mildest mother and most dear,
Grant some haven where I may with honor hear mass
And also Thy matins tomorrow—meekly I ask it—
And thereto promptly I pray my Pater and Ave
                              and Creed."
                    He rode on in prayer
                    And wept for each misdeed,
                    On four sides signed the air
                    And said: "Christ's cross give speed."

12

Nor had the hero signed himself but thrice
Before he beheld in that wood a moated dwelling
Above a lawn, on a mound, locked under boughs
Of many a boar-proud bole that grew by the ditches:
The comeliest castle that ever a knight had kept,
Ascending like a prayer, and a park all about,
With a sharp-piked palisade, all thickly pinned,
Surrounding many a tree for more than two miles.
The hero stared at that stronghold where it stood
Shimmering and shining through starlit oaks,
Then humbly he took off his helmet and nobly gave thanks
To Jesus and St. Julian, gentle lords both,
Who had guided him courteously and had heard his cry.
"I pray, let them grant me lodgings," said the lord,
Then with his gilt heels goaded Gringolet,
Who chose, entirely by chance, the chief of the gates
And brought the hero in a bound to the end of the bridge
>   in haste:
>   The bridge was sharply raised,
>   The gate bars bolted fast;
>   The walls were well arrayed:
>   They feared no winter's blast.

On his great white horse the warrior waited on the bank
Of the steep double ditch that drove against the wall.
The rock went down in the water wonderfully deep,
And above, it hove aloft to a huge height:
Of hard-hewn stone it rose to the high tables
Built up under the battlements, by the best law,
And above stood splendid watch stations, evenly spaced,
With loopholes craftily fashioned and cleanly locked.
A better barbican he had never beheld.
And then he beheld, beyond, the noble hall:
Towers built on top branched thickly with spires,
Finials floating upward, fearfully tall,
With carved-out capitals, ingeniously wrought;
Chalk-white chimneys his eye caught there in plenty
Blinking on the high rooftops, all of white.
So many were the painted pinnacles springing up
Among the castle crenels, and they climbed so thick,
The castle seemed surely to be cut out of clean white paper.
The freehearted knight on his horse thought it fair indeed
If he might come safely at last to the cloister within
To hold up there in that house while the holy days lasted,
                            in delight;
            Then there came to his call
            A porter, courtly, polite;
            Taking his place on the wall,
            He hailed the errant knight.

14

"Good sir," called Gawain, "would you kindly go my errand
To ask the great lord of this castle to take me in?"
"Gladly, by Peter," said the porter; "I'm sure, in pure truth,
You'll be welcome, sir, to stay here as long as you like."
The serving man came back again to him swiftly
And brought a great company with him to greet the knight.
They let down the drawbridge, and joyfully they rushed out
And kneeled down on their knees on the cold earth
To welcome him in the way that seemed to them worthy;
They yielded the mighty gate to him, swinging it wide,
And he hurried to raise them up, and rode over the bridge.
Several men steadied his saddle while he lighted,
Then stabled the dancing steed—men sturdy enough!
Knights and squires came down to Sir Gawain then
To lead the bold knight blissfully to the hall.
When he hefted off his helmet, men hurried to his side
To snatch it from his hand, all too eager to serve him,
And they took his sword of steel and his glinting shield.
Then nobly the good knight hailed every one of those nobles,
And many proud lords pressed closer to honor the knight;
And still hasped in his armor they led him to the hall
Where a fair fire burned fiercely on the hearthrock;
And the lord of the castle himself came down from his chamber
To meet with due ceremony the man on the floor.
He said: "You are welcome to rest here as long as you wish;
All I have is yours to use as you will

> and please."
> "I thank you, sir," said Gawain;
> "May Christ with words so free
> Greet you." The two good men
> Embraced in courtesy.

15

Sir Gawain gazed at the lord who so graciously met him
And thought it no common knight that kept that castle;
An immense man, indeed, mature in years;
A beard broad and bright, and beaver-hued;
His stance was proud and staunch, on stalwart shanks;
His face flashed like fire; his speech was free:
Surely a man well suited, Sir Gawain saw,
To lead as lord in a land of gallant men.
The lord led him to a chamber and quickly commanded
Lads delivered to the knight as loyal servants,
And soon there stood at his bidding servants a-plenty
Who brought him to a bright room with the finest of beds;
Curtains of clearest silk and clear gold hems,
Curious covertures with comely panels,
Bright blaunner above, embroidered at the sides,
The draperies running on ropes by red-gold rings,
Tapestries tacked to the walls from Tars and Toulouse,
And under his feet on the floor, fair rugwork to match.
There he was unlocked, with laughing speeches,
From his interlinked coat of mail and his colorful robes;
And swiftly the servants sought for him splendid robes
To put on or put aside, picking the best.
As soon as Sir Gawain had chosen, and was dressed
In one that perfectly fit him, with flowing skirts,
He looked like Spring itself, as indeed it seemed
To all who gazed at him: a glory of color
Shining and lovely, and not a bare limb showing.
Christ never had made a more handsome knight than he,
                                        they thought.
                    Wherever on earth he were,
                    It seemed that Gawain might
                    Be prince and without peer
                    In fields where bold men fight.

THE GAWAIN-POET

16

A chair before the hearth where charcoal burned
Was readied for Sir Gawain, and suitable covering—
Cushions upon counterpanes, both quaintly wrought—
And then a costly mantle was cast on the man,
Of a bright, fine fabric beautifully embroidered
And fairly furred within with the finest of pelts,
All of English ermine, and a hood of the same;
And Gawain sat in that settle, handsome and shining,
And soon he had warmed himself, and his spirit quickened.
They built up a table then on gilded trestles
And covered it with a cloth of clean, clear white,
A napkin and a salver and silver spoons;
When he wished, Sir Gawain washed and went to his place.
Serving men served him suitably enough
With stews of many sorts, all artfully seasoned—
Double helpings, as was right—all kinds of fish,
Some kinds baked in bread, some broiled on the coals,
Some boiled, still others in stews that were sweet with spice,
And all of the sauces there skillfully made to delight him.
Again and again the good man called it a banquet,
Most courteously, and the courtiers urged him on
                              and said:
          "Now take this penance, lad,
            And thou shalt be comforted!"
          And ah, what joy he had
          As the wine got into his head!

Then they sought and inquired, in a delicate way,
By putting to him personal, casual questions,
That he tell them in courtesy what court he came from;
The knight confessed that he'd come from the court of King Arthur,
The rich and royal king of the Round Table,
And that he who sat in their castle was Gawain himself,
Come there that Christmastime, as chance had fallen.
When the lord of the castle learned what lad he had there
He laughed aloud, so pleased was he with his luck,
And all the men around him were overjoyed
And gathered together around Sir Gawain that instant,
For all mortal virtue, both prowess and perfect taste,
Were summed up in that name universally praised;
He was honored above all other men on earth.
Softly then each courtier said to his comrade,
"Soon we shall see some ingenious examples of tact,
And faultless, mellifluent figures of fine conversation;
What speech can achieve we'll soon find out without asking,
For before us sits the embodiment of good breeding!
God has indeed been gracious unto us
To grant us the gift of so grand a guest as Sir Gawain
At this time when all men take joy at His birth, and feast
      and sing.
  The whole art of manners
  No man's more fit to bring;
  It may be, too, his hearers
  Will learn of love-talking."

18

By the time the dinner was done and the knight stood up
It was late enough; dark night was driving in;
The chaplains made their way toward the chapel
And rang the resounding mass bells, as was right,
For the solemn evensong of Christmastide.
The lord listened and went in, and also the lady,
And reverently she walked to her closed pew;
Sir Gawain in gay robes went gliding after.
The lord took him by the sleeve and led him to a seat
And looked after him kindly and called him by his name,
And called him the welcomest man in all the world;
And earnestly Gawain thanked him, and they embraced
And sat there together soberly through the service.
It pleased the lady then to look at the knight,
And with all her ladies in waiting she left her place;
Fairest of all was she of body and face,
Of shape and color and all other qualities—
More lovely than Guinevere, Sir Gawain thought;
He crossed the chancel to cherish her chivalrously.
Another lady led her by the left hand,
A woman much older than she—an ancient, in fact—
And highly honored by the nobles gathered around her.
Hardly similar were those ladies in looks,
The younger ripe with vigor, the other one yellowed,
The one shining radiant, rich red everywhere,
On the other, rough, wrinkled cheeks that hung down in rolls,
One in sheer kerchiefs and clusters of clear pearls,
Her breast and the flesh of her bright throat showing bare,
Purer than snow on the slopes of December hills,
The other one with a gorger covering her neck,
Her black chin hidden in the depths of chalk-white veils,
Her forehead folded in silk and everywhere enveloped,

Ornamented and trellised about with trifles
Until nothing was left in view but that lady's black brows,
Her nearsighted eyes, her nose, and her naked lips
(Lips that were sour to see and strangely bleared);
A wonderful lady in this world men might well call her
                    —to God.
              Her body was short and thick,
              Her buttocks splayed and wide;
              But lovelier was the look
              Of the lady at her side!

19

When Gawain's glance met the glance of that gracious lady
He left the lord with a bow and lightly stepped to them;
He bid good-day to the elder, bowing low,
And he took the more lovely politely in his arms.
He kissed her cheek and most courteously gave her greetings;
They ask to be better acquainted; he pleads in turn
That they make him their own true servant, if it please them.
They take him between them and, talking and laughing, lead him
To the chamber, to the hearth, where they call at once
For spices, which the servants speedily bring them
Together with heart-warming wine whenever they ask it.
Again and again the lord of the castle leapt up
To make sure that all were merry on every side;
He took off his hood with a flourish and hung it on a spear
And challenged them all to capture it; for whoever
Should best please the company, that Christmas, should have it;
"—And I shall strive, on my soul, to struggle with the best,
With my good friends' help, before I give up my clothes."
Thus with laughing words the lord made merry
In order to please Sir Gawain with games that night
        by the fire.
          Such, as the hours ran,
          Was the reign of that good sire;
          Then at last Sir Gawain
          Rose and prepared to retire.

20

On the morning when every man looks back to that time
When Christ was born to die to redeem mankind,
Joy wakes for His sake in all the world;
And so it did there that day in due celebration;
Strong men furnished the dais with elegant foods
All day long and again for the great, formal dinner;
The ancient woman was given the highest seat,
And the lord of the castle, I trust, took his place beside her;
Gawain and the lady gay were seated together
At the middle of the feastboard, where the foods came first;
And the rest were seated about all the hall as seemed best,
Each man suitably served in his degree.
There was such meat, such mirth, such marvelous joy
That to tell of it all would soon prove tedious
Even if I were to choose only striking details;
Suffice it to say that the knight and that splendid lady
Found one another's company so amusing,
Through their courtly dalliance and their confidences,
Their proper and courteous chat—all perfectly chaste—
That to play like theirs no other fencing sport
                                    compares.
              Kettledrums and brasses
              Rattled and sang on the stairs;
              Each man minded his business,
              And they two minded theirs.

Pleasure filled the palace that day and the next,
And the third day passed, as pleasing as the others;
Their joy on the day of St. John was cheering to hear,
But then fell the close of the feast-time, as all of them knew;
The guests would go off again on the gray of the morning,
So all that night they stayed wide awake, drank wine,
And danced their courtly caroles continuously.
At last, when it was late, they took their leave,
Each one to wend his way down his wandering road.
Gawain too said good-day, but the lord drew him back
And led him to his own chamber, and to the chimney,
And there he held him awhile and heartily thanked him
For the pleasure and the great prestige he'd brought by his presence
In honoring the house at that holy season
And ornamenting the castle with his courtliness.
"As long as I live, in truth, I'll be the better
For Gawain's being my guest at God's own feast!"
"I thank you, sir," said Gawain; "but let me assure you,
The honor is all your own. May God defend it.
And I am your servant, my lord, to command as you will
In large things and in small, for my debt to you
                              is great."
               The lord of the castle said,
               "Then stay another night!"
               But Gawain shook his head;
               It lay outside his might.

Then most kindly the lord of the castle inquired
What dire and dreadful business drew him out
From the court of the king, and at Christmas, to ride alone
Before the holiday holly was hauled out of town.
"Indeed, sir," said the knight, "it's just as you've guessed;
A high and hasty errand hales me from the hall,
For I am summoned in person to seek out a place
That I haven't the faintest idea where to turn to find;
For all the length and breadth of Logres, Lord help me,
I must somehow make it there by the morning of New Year's.
And for that reason, my lord, let me ask you this:
That you tell me truly if ever you've heard any tale
Of a Green Chapel, and where on God's earth it stands,
Or the knight who keeps that chapel, a man all of green.
For there was established between us a solemn agreement
That I look for that man in that place, if my life should last;
New Year's morning is now no great while off,
And by God's son, I'd be gladder to greet that man
Than any other alive, if God will allow it.
And so, by your leave, I'd better be looking for him,
For I've barely three days left to be done with this business,
And by heaven I'd rather fall dead than fail in this."
Then the lord laughed. "I insist that you linger, now;
For I'll tell you the way to the place when your time is up.
Worry no more about where you will find the Green Chapel:
For you shall bask in bed, my boy, at your ease,
While your days pass, and put out on the first of the year
And come to your mark by mid-morning to do as you like
out there.
    Stay till New Year's day,
    Rest and build up your cheer;
    My man will show you the way;
    It's not two miles from here."

THE GAWAIN-POET

Sir Gawain grew jubilant then. He laughed for joy.
"I thank you now for this above everything else,
  For luck is with me at last; I shall be at your will,
  To stay or to do whatever may please you most."
The lord threw his arm around him and sat down beside him,
And he asked that the ladies be called, to bring still more joy;
There was happiness then on all sides as they sat there together,
And the lord of the castle let out such explosions of laughter
He seemed half out of his wits, hardly sure who he was.
Before long he called to the knight, and cried out loudly,
"You've sworn you'll be my servant and do as I say:
  Will you hold to your hasty promise here and now?"
"Certainly, my lord," said the good Sir Gawain,
"As long as I'm here in your castle, I'm yours to command."
"You've had a hard trip," said the lord, "and you've come a long
      way,
  And I've kept you cavorting all night; you haven't caught up
On either your food or your sleep, I know for a fact.
You shall therefore lounge in your bedroom and lie at your ease
Tomorrow till time for high mass, and then take your dinner
When you wish, along with my wife, who'll sit beside you
And keep you company till I come back to court.
                    You stay here;
            And as for me, I'll rise
            At dawn and play the hunter."
            Gawain grants all this
            And bows, as does the other.

24

"—And one thing more," said the lord; "we'll make a pact:
Whatever I win in the woods, I will make it yours,
And anything you may win you'll exchange with me;
Such is the swap, my sweet. Swear on your word,
Whether the bargain should bring you to better or worse."
"By God," said the gallant knight, "I gladly accept;
And I'm glad to discover milord has a gambling heart!"
"Who'll bring us the beverages to bind this bargain?"
The lord of the place called out. The people all laughed.
They drank and dallied together and dealt in small talk,
Those splendid lords and ladies, as long as they liked,
And then, in the French manner, with many pretty words,
They stood and said *bonsoir* and spoke in whispers,
Kissed with great courtliness and took their leave.
Attended by fleet-footed servants and flaming torches,
Each of the company came at the last to his bed
                for rest;
        But often before they go
        The lord brings up the jest;
        No man knew better how
        To entertain a guest.

Part Three

1

Early, before it was daylight, the hunters arose,
The guests who wanted to go, and called to their grooms,
Who bustled about and saddled the big white horses.
They trimmed their tackle and tied up the saddlebags
And fixed themselves up in their finest attire for the hunt,
Then leaped to their horses lightly, lifted their reins,
And turned, each man to the hunting trail he liked best.
The lord of the land was by no means the last of those
Arrayed for riding, his retinue around him;
When he'd heard hunters' mass and had snatched a hasty breakfast,
He flew with his hunter's bugle to fields of bent grasses;
By the time the day's first rays had dawned on the hills,
He and his men were all mounted and ready to ride.
Kennelmen keen in their craft now coupled the hounds,
Caught up the kennel doors, called out loudly to the dogs,
Blew mightily on their bugles three bare motes,
And the hounds bugled back—bright music in the morning!—
And those that dashed off too soon were driven to place.
A hundred hunters were there, I've heard; all hunters
of the best.

> The keepers took their posts
> And signaled the hounds' release;
> And hard on their bugle blasts,
> A roar rose up in the trees.

At the first cry of the quest all the wild creatures quaked;
Deer drove down through the dales, half crazy with dread,
Raced for the ridges, reversed again in a rout,
Driven back by the bellowing shouts of the beaters.
They let the harts with their high-arching antlers escape
And also the brave old bucks with their broad-palmed horns,
For in close season, the lord of the castle commanded,
No man should make so much as a mark on the males;
But the hinds were all held in with a "Heigh!" and a " 'Ware!"
And the does all driven with a din to the depths of the vales.
You could see on all sides the slanting of arrows,
For at every turn in the forest a feather flashed,
A broad steel head bit deep into hurtling brown,
And Christ, how they brayed and bled and buckled on the bank!—
And always the kennelhounds howling on their heels,
And hunters with horns lifted high not a rod behind,
Their clear bugles cracking as if all the cliffs had exploded;
And any deer that escaped the arrow
Was dragged down into its death at the dog stations,
Driven there from the high ground, harried to the water—
So skillful were the men at the lower stations,
So great the greyhounds who got to the deer in a flash
And savagely shook out their life, more swift, I swear,
                              than sight!
              The lord now leaped like a boy,
              Now riding, now running in delight;
              And thus he drove, in his joy,
              Bright day into dark night.

Thus plays the lord of the hunt at the edge of the limewoods,
And good young Gawain lies in his gay bed:
While daylight slides down the walls, he lies concealed
Under a quaintly made coverture, curtains drawn.
As he lay there half asleep, there slid through his thought
A delicate sound at his door. It was softly drawn open;
He squirmed his head up stealthily from the bedclothes
And caught up a corner of the curtain just a little
And peeked out warily to see what it was.
In slipped the lady of the hall, so lovely to behold,
And silently, secretly, drew the door closed behind her
And bore toward the bed. Sir Gawain blushed.
He lay back craftily, letting on that he slept.
She soundlessly stepped to him, stole up close to his bed
And lifted the curtain and stealthily crept in
And softly seated herself on the bedside, near him,
And stayed there, watching to see the first sign of his waking.
Sir Gawain lay still for a good long while
Studying in his conscience what this situation
Might lead to or mean. Something most strange, he was certain.
And yet he mused to himself, "It might be more seemly
To ask and find out in plain words what it is that she wishes."
And so he awakened and stretched and turned toward her
And unlocked his eyelids and let on that he was surprised,
Exclaimed and signed himself to be safer, through words,
                                        with his hand.
                    Red and white together
                    Her pretty cheeks and chin;
                    Lightly she leaned nearer,
                    With laughing lips, to begin.

"Good morning, my good Sir Gawain," the gay lady said;
"You're an unwary sleeper to let one slip in like this;
 I've taken you just like that! You'd better call 'Truce'
 Or I'll make your bed your prison, believe you me!"
 Thus the lady laughingly let fly.
"And good morning to you, gay lady," said Gawain with a grin,
"I give myself up to your will, and glad to be caught!
 I surrender my arms at once and sue for kind treatment—
 That being, if I'm not mistaken, my only course."
 Thus Gawain replied to the lady and laughed as he spoke;
"But lovely lady, if you would grant leniency
 And unlock your prisoner and allow him to rise,
 I'd be glad to be free of this bed and be dressed somewhat better,
 And I might enjoy even more exchanging terms."
"No sir! Not on your life!" that sweet one said,
"You'll not budge an inch from your bed. I've a better idea:
 I'll lock you up even tighter—inside my two arms.
 Then I can chat all I please with the knight I've caught.
 For I see that, sure enough, you're the sweet Sir Gawain
 Whom all this wide world worships, wherever you ride;
 Your honor and handsome bearing are highly praised
 By lords and ladies alike, and by all that lives;
 And now here you are, I find, and we're all alone:
 My lord and most of his men are miles away,
 The others still in their beds, and my ladies too,
 And the door is closed and locked with a good strong bolt.
 Since here in my house lies the knight whom all the world loves,
 I'll make good use of my time, while my time may last,
                         with chatter.
                You're welcome to my body:
                Do anything whatever.
                Of absolute necessity,
                I'm yours, and yours forever!"

THE GAWAIN-POET

"Upon my soul!" cried Sir Gawain. "I'm certainly honored!—
 Though alas, I'm by no means the marvelous man you speak of;
 I'm wholly unworthy to soar to such splendid things
 As you've just suggested; I know it myself, I assure you.
 But God knows I'd be glad, if you thought it good,
 To contribute to the pleasure of your virtue
 By speech or some other low service. I'd think it sheer joy!"
"Upon *my* soul, Sir Gawain," said the lady,
"If I did not prize the princely glory and prowess
 That please all others, I'd be guilty of puffed-up pride!
 There are lovely ladies enough, my lord, who would liever
 Have you, dear heart, in their clutches, as I have here—
 To dally with, draw out thy pretty nothings,
 Take comfort from, find ease for all their sorrows—
 Than keep all the gold or great estate they own.
 As sure as I love that Lord who rules your life,
 I have at hand what every woman hopes for
                                through grace."

> No one could be pleasanter
> Than she so fair of face;
> But always Gawain answered her
> In turn, with perfect taste.

6

"Madam," said merry Sir Gawain, "may Mary defend you,
 For truly, I find you freehearted, the noblest of women;
 No doubt there are men who deserve their renown for their deeds,
 But as for myself, the praise exceeds my merit;
  You're so good yourself that you see in me only the good."
"By Mary," said the beauty, "I beg to differ.
 Were I as worthy as all other women alive
 And were all the wealth in the world within my grasp
 And were I to have my choice of the husband I'd cherish,
 In the light of the lordly virtues that lie here in you—
 Handsome, courteous, debonair as you are
 (Virtues I'd only heard of before, but believed in)—
 Then I swear I would care for no sovereign on earth but sweet
     Gawain."
"Alas," said the knight, "you have chosen my better already.
 But I'm proud of the noble price you put upon me,
 And I swear myself your servant and you my sovereign,
 And may I become your true knight, and Christ give you joy."
Thus they chatted of this and that till mid-morning,
 And always the lady let on that she loved him most dearly,
 But Sir Gawain remained, in his graceful way, *en garde*.
 Though I were the loveliest lady in the land, she thought,
 Even so, his mind would be drawn to the dark that he need not
                 long await,
             The stroke that must destroy him,
             Swift and sure as fate.
             When the lady asked to leave him,
             He did not hesitate.

The lady gave him good-day, then laughed and looked sly,
And as she stood she surprised him with stern words:
"May He who speeds our speech pay you well for my pleasure;
But as for your being the brilliant Sir Gawain—I wonder."
"Why?" asked the knight at once, in some distress,
Afraid that perhaps he had failed at some point in his manners.
But the lady blessed him and brought out no charge but this:
"So good a man as Sir Gawain is granted to be
Could not easily have lingered so long with a lady
Without ever asking a kiss—in courtesy's name—
By means of some delicate hint between dainty speeches."
Sir Gawain answered, "Indeed, it shall be as you wish:
I shall kiss at your command, since knights must obey,
And also for fear of displeasing you. Plead it no more."
With that she came more near him and caught him in her arms,
Lovingly leaned toward him and kissed him on the lips;
Then courteously they commended each other to Christ,
And without a word more, the lady went out through the door.
Then good Sir Gawain prepared in all haste to get up,
Called to his chamberlain, picked out his clothes for the day,
And as soon as he had himself dressed, hurried down to hear mass
And then to the splendid breakfast the servants had set him;
All that day till the moon rose, Gawain made merry
                              with pleasure.
              There never was a knight more bold
              Between two ladies more clever,
              The young one and the old,
              And great was their joy together.

And still the lord of the land looked after his sport,
The hunt of the barren hinds in the holts and heaths.
By the time the sun went down he'd slain such a number
Of does and other deer you'd have doubted your eyes.
At the end of the hunt, the game was gathered up quickly
And all the slaughtered deer stacked up in a pile;
The hunters of highest rank stepped up with their servants
And selected for themselves the fattest of the slain
And broke them open cleanly, as the code required;
They checked a sample of those that were set aside
And found on even the leanest two fingers of fat;
They slit the cut still deeper, seized the first stomach
And cut it with a sharp knife and scraped the white flesh;
Then they struck off the legs and stripped the hide,
Broke the belly open and pulled out the bowels
Deftly, lest they loosen the ligature
Of the knot; they gripped the gullet and disengaged
The wezand from the windhole and spilled out the guts;
Then with their sharp knives they carved out the shoulders
And held them by small holes to preserve the sides
Intact, then cut the breast and broke it in two.
For the next stage they started again with the gullet,
Opened it neatly, as far as the bright fork,
Flicked out the shoulder fillets and after that
Clipped away the meat that rimmed the ribs;
They cleaned the ridge of the spine, still working by rule,
From the center down to the haunch which hung below;
And they hefted the haunch up whole and carved it away
Reducing it to "numbles"—a word all too apt,
> I find.
>> By the fork of all the thighs
>> They cut the folds behind;
>> At last they split the sides
>> Making the back unbind.

THE GAWAIN-POET

9

They cut off, after that, the head and the neck,
And then they swiftly severed the sides from the chine,
And they flung the corbies' fee far up in the trees;
Then finally they thurled each thick side through
By the ribs and hung them on high by the hocks of the legs,
And each man there got the meat he had coming to him.
From one of the finest of the deer they fed their dogs
With the lights, the liver, and the leather of the paunches
Mingled in with bread that was soaked in blood.
They blew the call of the kill; the kenneldogs bayed;
Then the men took their meat and turned toward home,
Their bugles striking out many a brilliant note.
By the time all daylight was gone, the hunters were back
Within the walls of the castle, where Gawain awaited
                                        their call.
                    Joy and the hearthfire leap;
                    The lord comes home to the hall;
                    When he and Sir Gawain meet
                    Their cheer lends cheer to all.

10

The lord then commanded the people all called to the hall
And summoned the ladies downstairs, and their ladies in waiting,
To stand before those now assembled, and he sent his men
To haul in the venison and to hold it high;
Then gaily, in his game, he called to Sir Gawain
And told him the tally of those tremendous beasts
And showed him the fine meat they'd cut from the ribs.
"What do you think of our sport? Have I earned your praise?
Have I duly proved myself your dutiful servant?"
"You have indeed," said he; "so fine a hunt
I haven't seen in the winter for seven years."
"I give it all to you, Gawain," the man said then,
"For according to our contract, it's yours to claim."
"So it is," said the knight, "and I say the same to you:
  What I have honorably won within your walls
  I'll be equally quick to acknowledge wholly yours."
With that he closes his arms round the lord's neck
And gives him the sweetest kiss he can summon up.
"There you have my achievement today. That's it.
  I swear if there were more I'd make it yours."
"Hmmm. Very nice," said the lord, "I thank you kindly;
  But it might seem better yet if you'd breathe in my ear
  Whom you won this treasure from by your wits."
"That was not in our contract," said he, "ask no more.
  You've gotten what is yours; more than that you must
                              not bid."
              They laughed in their merry manner
              And their talk was clever and good;
              When they turned then to their dinner
              They found no lack of food.

11

Later they gathered in the chamber, by the fireplace,
Where servants waited on them, bringing in wine;
And after a while, in high spirits, they settled again
On the same contract for tomorrow as they'd made today,
That as chance might fall, each would exchange with the other
Whatever he won that day, when they met at night.
Before all the court they agreed upon the covenant,
And, laughing, saluting once more with wine, they sealed it.
At last, late, the lord and the knight took their leave,
And every man there made his way in haste to his bed.
By the time the cock had crowed and cackled but thrice
The lord had leaped from his bed, as had all his men;
The hunter's mass and breakfast were both behind them
And the company dressed for the woods before any light showed,
                            for the chase;
            With hunters and with horns
            They cross the meadow brush;
            Unleashed, among the thorns,
            The hounds are running in a rush.

12

Soon by the side of a quagmire the hounds hit a scent;
The hunting-lord cheered on the hounds that had hit it first,
Shouted out wild words with a wonderful noise;
And when those hounds heard him shout they hurried forward
And fell on the trail in a flash, some forty at once,
And then such a howl and yowl of singing hounds
Rose up that the rocks all around rang out like bells;
Hunters cheered them on with their horns and their voices;
Then, all in a group, they surged together
Between a pool in those woods and a rugged crag,
The dogs in a scrambling heap—at the foot of the cliff
By the quagmire's side where rocks had tumbled roughly—
Rushed to make the find, and the men rushed behind them.
They surrounded the knobby rocks and the bog as well—
The men—for they knew well enough he was hiding there
        someplace,
The beast whose trail the bellowing bloodhounds had caught;
They beat the bushes and shouted "Get up! Up!"
And angrily out he came to attack the men—
One of the most amazing swine ever seen,
An ancient loner who'd long ago left the herd,
For he was an old one, and brawny, the biggest of them all,
A grim old devil when he grunted, and he grieved them plenty,
For the first thrust he made threw three to the earth
And gave their souls God-speed as quick as that.
The hunters hollered "Hi-y" on high, and cried out "Hey! Hey!"
And lifted their horns to their mouths to recall the hounds;
Many were the bugle notes of the men and the dogs
Who bounded after that boar with boasts and noise
                        for the kill;
            Again and again, at bay,
            He rushes the hounds pell-mell
            And hurls them high, and they,
            They yowp and yowl and yell.

280   THE GAWAIN-POET

13

Up stepped sturdy men to shoot at him,
And their arrows hurtled at him and hit him like rain,
But hitting his plated hide, the arrowheads failed
And their barbs would not bite in through the bristles of his brow
Though the force of the blow made the smooth shafts shatter to bits;
Then, insane with anger, he turns on the archers,
Goring them horribly as he hurls himself forward,
And not a few were afraid and fled before him.
But the lord on his light horse lunged in after the boar,
Boldly blowing his bugle like a knight in battle;
He rallied the hounds and rode through heavy thickets
Pursuing the savage swine till the sun went down.
Thus they drove away the day with their hunting;
And meanwhile our handsome hero lies in his bed,
Lies at his ease at home, in all his finery
                                        so bright.
                    The lady by no means forgot him
                    Or to bring him what cheer she might;
                    Early that day she was at him
                    To make his heart more light.

14

The lady came up to the curtain and looked at the knight;
Sir Gawain welcomed her worthily at once,
And quickly the lady returned his greeting with pleasure
And with a loving look she delivered these words:
"Sir, if you're really Sir Gawain, it's surely most strange—
A man whose every act is the apex of virtue
And yet who has no idea how to act in company;
And if someone teaches you manners they slip your mind;
All I taught yesterday you've forgotten already,
Or so it seems to me, by some very sure signs."
"What's that?" said the knight. "I swear, I'm still in the dark.
If things really stand as you say, I'm sadly at fault."
"I taught you, sir, of kissing," said the lady gay;
"Where favor is conferred, you should quickly claim it,
For such is the practice prescribed by the code of Courtesy."
"Away with you, my sweet," said the sturdy knight,
"I didn't dare ask a kiss for fear you'd deny it.
If I asked and you refused I'd be most embarrassed."
"Well mercy!" said the merry wife, "how *could* I refuse you?
You're a great strong knight; you could take what you wished, if you
      wanted—
If a woman were so churlish as to refuse you."
"True, by God," said Gawain, "your reasoning's good;
But where I come from force is not much favored,
Or any gift not given with free good will.
I stand at your commandment, to kiss when you wish;
Come, start whenever you like, and stop whenever
             you please."
      She bent to him with a smile
      And gently kissed his face;
      And now they talked a while
      Of love, its grief and grace.

                                     THE GAWAIN-POET

15

"I should like to know, milord," the lady said then,
"—If my asking were not to annoy you—what is the reason
That one so young and so valiant as you are now,
So courteous and so knightly as you're known to be,
[Has said not one single word of his struggles for Love,]*
When in all the romance of Chivalry, what is most praised
Is the game of love, the ground of all deeds of arms?
For to tell of the desperate gambles of trusty knights
Is both the title and text of every tale—
How lords have ventured their lives for their ladies' love,
Endured for them long and dreary, doleful hours,
And later avenged them valiantly, casting out grief,
And brought by their own joy, joy to all the hall.
It's said, sir, that you're the most splendid knight of your time;
You're raved about and honored on every side;
Yet I've sat beside you here on two occasions
And I haven't heard from your mouth so much as a mumble,
Neither less, nor more, on Courtly Love.
You who are so keen in advice, and so courteous,
Ought to be eager to give a poor young thing some guidance
And teach her some trifling details of true love's craft.
Why? Are you ignorant, really, for all your renown?
Or is it perhaps that you think me too stupid to learn?
                    For shame!
            I come here alone and sit
            To learn. In heaven's name,
            Come, teach me by your wit
            While my lord's away on his game."

---

* Based on the proposed emendation of Sir Israel Gollancz.

16

"In good faith, Madam," said Gawain, "may God preserve you!
It's a very great pleasure to me, and game enough,
That one so worthy as you would come to me
And take such pains for so poor a man as to play
With your knight with looks of any sort. I'm charmed!
But to take such travail on myself as to tell *you* of love—
To touch on the themes of that text, or tell of love's battles,
You who, we both know well, know more of the tricks
Of that art by half than a hundred such men as I
Know now or ever will know in all my life—
That would be manifold folly, my fair one, I swear.
Whatever you ask I will do, to the height of my power,
As I'm duty bound, and for ever more I'll be
Your ladyship's humble servant, as God may save me."
Thus did she tempt the knight and repeatedly test him
To win him to wrong (and whatever things worse she plotted).
But so fine was his defense that no fault was revealed,
Nor was there evil on either side or ought
                    but bliss.
      They laughed and chatted long;
      At last she gave him a kiss
      And said she must be gone
      And went her way with this.

Then Gawain got himself dressed to go to his mass,
And soon after that their dinner was splendidly set,
And so the knight spent all that day with the ladies;
But the lord again and again lunged over the land
Pursuing his wretched boar that rushed by the cliffs
And broke the backs of the best of the hounds in two
Where he stood at bay, until bowmen broke the deadlock
And forced him, like it or not, to fight in the open;
So fast their arrows flew when the archers assembled—
Yet sometimes the stoutest there turned tail before him—
That at last the boar was so tired he couldn't run
But dragged himself with what haste he could to a hole
In a mound beside a rock where water ran;
He gets the bank at his back and he scrapes the ground
And froth foams at the corners of his ugly mouth
And he whets his huge white tusks. The hunters around him
Were tired, by this time, of teasing from a distance,
But brave as they were they didn't dare draw nearer
      that swine;
    He'd hurt so many before
    That none was much inclined
    To be torn by the tusks of a boar
    So mighty and out of his mind,

18

Till up came the lord of the hunt himself, on his horse,
And saw him standing at bay, the hunters near by;
He steps from his saddle lightly, leaves his mount,
Draws out his sun-bright sword and boldly strides close,
Wades through the water toward where the beast lies in wait.
But the creature saw him coming, sword in hand,
And his back went up, and so brutal were his snorts
That many there feared for their lord, lest the worst befall him,
And then the boar came rushing right straight at him
So that baron and boar were both of them hurled in a heap
In the wildest of the water; but the boar got the worst;
For the man had marked him well, and the minute he hit,
Coolly set his sword in the slot of his breastbone
And rammed it in to the hilt, so it split the heart.
Squealing, the boar gave way and struggled from the water
in a fit.

> A hundred hounds leaped in
> And murderously bit;
> Men drove him up on the land
> And the dogs there finished it.

19

From many a blazing horn came the blast of the kill,
And every man there hallooed on high in triumph,
And all the bloodhounds bayed as their masters bid,
Those who were chief huntsmen in that chase.
Then the lord, who was wise in woodcraft,
Began the butchering of the mighty boar.
First he hacked off the head and set it on high,
Then roughly opened him up, the length of the backbone,
Scooped out the bowels and cooked them on hot coals,
And mixed them in with bread to reward his hounds;
Next he carved out the flesh in fine broad cuts
And drew out the edible inner parts, as is proper,
And he fastened the sides together, still in one piece,
And afterward hung them to swing from a sturdy pole.
Now with this same swine they started for home,
And before the lord himself they bore the boar's head,
The lord who had won him himself in the stream by force
                                        alone.
        The great lord could not rest
        Until his prize was shown;
        He called, and at once his guest
        Came to claim his own.

20

The lord was loud with mirth and merrily laughed
When he saw Sir Gawain, and cheerfully he spoke;
The noble ladies were called and the court brought together,
And he showed off the slices of meat and told the tale
Of the might and length of the boar, and also the meanness,
And the fight that beast had fought in the woods where he'd fled.
Sir Gawain commended his hunt most generously
And praised it as a proof of remarkable prowess,
For so much meat on a beast, the good man said,
He'd never seen, nor the sides of a swine so enormous.
When they held up the huge head, our hero praised it
And, for the lord's sake, said it half scared him to death!
"Now Gawain," said the lord, "this game is yours,
By the covenant we made, as you recall."
"So it is," said Gawain, "and just as surely
All I've gained I'll give to you, and at once."
Embracing the lord of the castle, he kisses him sweetly,
And after a moment he gives him a second kiss.
"And now we're even," said Gawain, "for this evening.
Since first I came, up to now, I'm in no respect
in your debt."
    "Good St. Giles," said the lord,
    "You're the best I ever met!
    Keep on like this, on my word,
    And you'll be a rich man yet!"

They raised the tables to the trestles then
And covered them with linen cloths. Clear light
Leaped up the length of the walls, where the waxen torches
Were set by the servants sweeping through the hall.
There was soon much merriment and amusement there
In the comfort of the fire, and a good many times
At supper and later they launched some noble song,
Old and new caroles and Christmas carols
And every kind of enjoyment a man could name;
And always our handsome knight was beside the sweet lady,
And so remarkably warm were her ways with him,
With her sly and secret glances designed to please,
Our Gawain was downright alarmed, and annoyed with himself,
And yet in all courtesy he could hardly be cool to her;
He dallied, delighted, and nervously hoped he'd escape
                              disgrace.
                    They amused themselves in the hall
                    And, when it suited their taste,
                    Went with the lord, at his call,
                    To sit by his fireplace.

The two men talked there, sipping their wine, and spoke
Of playing the same game again on New Year's Eve;
But the knight asked the lord's permission to leave in the morning,
For the twelvemonth-and-a-day was drawing to a close;
The lord would not hear of it; he implored him to stay
And said, "Now I swear to you on my word as a knight,
You'll find your way to the Chapel to finish your business,
My lad, on New Year's Day, a good deal before prime;
So come now, relax in your bed, catch up on your rest,
And I'll go and hunt in the holts and hold to my bargain
And later exchange with you all I chase down and bring in.
For I've tested you twice, my friend, and found you faithful,
But it's always the third strike that counts; so think of tomorrow;
Eat, drink, and be merry, boy! *Carpe diem!*
The man who goes hunting for grief, he'll get it in no time."
It was true enough, Gawain saw, and he said he would stay.
Bright wine was brought to them, and then to bed
                              by torches' light.
                    Sir Gawain lies and sleeps
                    Soft and still all night;
                    Before it's dawn, up leaps
                    That crafty older knight.

After mass the lord and his men made breakfast—
A beautiful morning it was!—and he called for his mount;
And every hunter who'd ride to the hounds behind him
Was dressed and horsed and waiting at the door of the hall.
The fields were fine to see, all shining with frost,
The sun rising brilliant red on a scaffold of clouds,
Warm and clear, dissolving the clouds from the welkin.
The hunters uncoupled the hounds by the side of a holt
And the rocks in the undergrowth rang at the sound of their horns.
Some few of the dogs fell at once on the scent of the fox,
A trail that is often a traitoress, tricky and sly:
A hound cries out his find, the hunters all call to him,
The other hounds rush to the young hound busily sniffing,
And they all race off in a rabble, right at last,
That first hound leading the pack. They found the fox quickly
And when they spied him plain, they sped in pursuit,
Fiercely and angrily shouting with voices of outrage.
He twists and turns through many a tangled thicket
And he doubles back or he hides in the hedges to watch them;
At last by a little ditch he leaped a thorn-hedge
And stole out stealthily down the long slope of a valley
And laughed, believing his wiles had eluded the hounds;
But before he knew it he'd come to a hunting post
Where suddenly there whirled at him three hounds at once,
all gray!

> He quickly bounded back,
> And his heart leaped high in dismay;
> But taking another tack,
> To the woods he raced away.

Lord, how sweet it was then to hear those hounds,
When the whole of the pack had met him, all mingled together!
Such scorn those hounds sang down on that fox's head
It seemed as if all the high cliffs had come smashing to the ground;
Here he was hallooed when the huntsmen met him,
Yonder saluted with savage snarls,
And over there he was threatened and called a thief—
And always the hounds on his tail to keep him a-running.
Again and again when he raced for the open they rushed him
And he ran for the woods once more, old Reddy the sly;
He led them every which way, the lord and his men,
Over hill and dale, that devil, until it was midday—
While at home the handsome knight lay asleep in his bed,
In the morning's cold, inside his handsome curtains.
But for love's sake the lady could not let herself sleep long
Or forget the purpose so firmly fixed in her heart;
She rose up quickly and hurried to where he lay,
And she wore a splendid gown that went clear to the floor
And luxurious furs of pelts all perfectly pured,
No colors on her head but costly gems
All tressed about her hairnet in clusters of twenty;
Her beautiful face and her throat were revealed uncovered,
And her breasts stood all but bare, and her back as well.
She glides through the doorway and closes the door behind her,
Throws the wide window open and calls to the knight
And warms his heart at once with her glorious voice
                              and cheer:
              "Lord, man, how can you sleep
                When the morning shines so clear?"
                Though sunk in gloomy sleep,
                He could not help but hear.

25

From the depths of his mournful sleep Sir Gawain muttered,
A man who was suffering throngs of sorrowful thoughts
Of how Destiny would that day deal him his doom
At the Green Chapel, where he dreamed he was facing the giant
Whose blow he must abide without further debate.
But soon our rosy knight had recovered his wits;
He struggled up out of his sleep and responded in haste.
The lovely lady came laughing sweetly,
Fell over his fair face and fondly kissed him;
Sir Gawain welcomed her worthily and with pleasure;
He found her so glorious, so attractively dressed,
So faultless in every feature, her colors so fine
Welling joy rushed up in his heart at once.
Their sweet and subtle smiles swept them upward like wings
And all that passed between them was music and bliss
                              and delight.
                How sweet was now their state!
                Their talk, how loving and light!
                But the danger might have been great
                Had Mary not watched her knight!

For that priceless princess pressed our poor hero so hard
And drove him so close to the line that she left him no choice
But to take the full pleasure she offered or flatly refuse her;
He feared for his name, lest men call him a common churl,
But he feared even more what evil might follow his fall
If he dared to betray his just duty as guest to his host.
God help me, thought the knight, *I can't let it happen!*
With a loving little laugh he parried her lunges,
Those words of undying love she let fall from her lips.
Said the lady then, "It's surely a shameful thing
If you'll lie with a lady like this yet not love her at all—
The woman most brokenhearted in all the wide world!
Is there someone else?—some lady you love still more
To whom you've sworn your faith and so firmly fixed
Your heart that you can't break free? I can't believe it!
But tell me if it's so. I beg you—truly—
By all the loves in life, let me know, and hide nothing
                    with guile."
            The knight said, "By St. John,"
            And smooth was Gawain's smile,
        "I've pledged myself to none,
            Nor will I for awhile."

"Of all the words you might have said," said she,
"That's surely cruellest. But alas, I'm answered.
 Kiss me kindly, then, and I'll go from you.
 I'll mourn through life as one who loved too much."
 She bent above him, sighing, and softly kissed him;
 Then, drawing back once more, she said as she stood,
"But my love, since we must part, be kind to me:
 Leave me some little remembrance—if only a glove—
 To bring back fond memories sometimes and soften my sorrow."
"Truly," said he, "with all my heart I wish
 I had here with me the handsomest treasure I own,
 For surely you have deserved on so many occasions
 A gift more fine than any gift I could give you;
 But as to my giving some token of trifling value,
 It would hardly suit your great honor to have from your knight
 A glove as a treasured keepsake and gift from Gawain;
 And I've come here on my errand to countries unknown
 Without any attendants with treasures in their trunks;
 It sadly grieves me, for love's sake, that it's so,
 But every man must do what he must and not murmur
                              or pine."
                 "Ah no, my prince of all honors,"
                  Said she so fair and fine,
                 "Though I get nothing of yours,
                   You shall have something of mine."

She held toward him a ring of the yellowest gold
And, standing aloft on the band, a stone like a star
From which flew splendid beams like the light of the sun;
And mark you well, it was worth a rich king's ransom.
But right away he refused it, replying in haste,
"My lady gay, I can hardly take gifts at the moment;
Having nothing to give, I'd be wrong to take gifts in turn."
She implored him again, still more earnestly, but again
He refused it and swore on his knighthood that he could take
    nothing.
Grieved that he still would not take it, she told him then:
"If taking my ring would be wrong on account of its worth,
And being so much in my debt would be bothersome to you,
I'll give you merely this sash that's of slighter value."
She swiftly unfastened the sash that encircled her waist,
Tied around her fair tunic, inside her bright mantle;
It was made of green silk and was marked of gleaming gold
Embroidered along the edges, ingeniously stitched.
This too she held out to the knight, and she earnestly begged him
To take it, trifling as it was, to remember her by.
But again he said no, there was nothing at all he could take,
Neither treasure nor token, until such time as the Lord
Had granted him some end to his adventure.
"And therefore, I pray you, do not be displeased,
But give up, for I cannot grant it, however fair
                or right.
      I know your worth and price,
      And my debt's by no means slight;
      I swear through fire and ice
      To be your humble knight."

"Do you lay aside this silk," said the lady then,
"Because it seems unworthy—as well it may?
  Listen. Little as it is, it seems less in value,
  But he who knew what charms are woven within it
  Might place a better price on it, perchance.
  For the man who goes to battle in this green lace,
  As long as he keeps it looped around him,
  No man under Heaven can hurt him, whoever may try,
  For nothing on earth, however uncanny, can kill him."
  The knight cast about in distress, and it came to his heart
  This might be a treasure indeed when the time came to take
  The blow he had bargained to suffer beside the Green Chapel.
  If the gift meant remaining alive, it might well be worth it;
  So he listened in silence and suffered the lady to speak,
  And she pressed the sash upon him and begged him to take it,
  And Gawain did, and she gave him the gift with great pleasure
  And begged him, for her sake, to say not a word,
  And to keep it hidden from her lord. And he said he would,
  That except for themselves, this business would never be known
                        to a man.
              He thanked her earnestly,
              And boldly his heart now ran;
              And now a third time she
              Leaned down and kissed her man.

And now she takes her leave and leaves him there,
For she knew there was nothing more she could get from the man.
And when she was gone from him, Gawain got up and got dressed,
Rose and arrayed himself in his richest robes,
And he laid away the love lace the lady had given
And hid it well, where later he'd find it still waiting;
Then, at once, he went on his way to the chapel
And approached a priest in private and asked him there
To purify his life and make plainer for him
What a man had to do to be saved and see Heaven.
He confessed his sins in full, spoke of all his misdeeds,
Both major sins and minor, and asked God's mercy,
And he asked the priest for perfect absolution.
The priest assoiled him and made him as spotless of guilt
As he would if the Day of Doom were to fall the next morning.
And after that Sir Gawain made more merry,
Dancing caroles and joining the hall's entertainments,
Than ever before in his life, until dark, when the owl
                         sang low.
               And all who saw him there
               Were pleased, and said: "I vow,
               He was never so debonair
               Since first he came, as now."

31

Now let us leave him there, and may love be with him!
For the lord of the hunt is still riding, and all his men.
And behold, he has slain that fox whom he hunted so long!
As he leaped a bramble to get a good look at the villain,
Where he heard the hounds all hurrying Reddy along,
Who should appear but Renard himself from a thicket,
And all the rabble in a rush, and right on his heels.
The hunter was quick to spot him, and oh, he was sly!
He waited, half hidden, then whirled out his sword and struck.
The fox darted back—he intended to turn for the trees—
But a hound right behind him shot forward before he could stir,
And there, just ahead of the horses' hooves, they hit him,
And they howled, and oh, how they worried that wily one!
The lord came down like lightning and caught up his legs
And snatched him up in a flash from the teeth of the dogs,
And he held him up over his head and hallooed like a fiend
And all the hounds there howled at once.
The hunters came galloping up with their horns all blaring,
Sounding the recall on high till they came to the hero;
When the whole of the kingly company had come close
And every last baron that had him a bugle was blowing
And all of the others who didn't have horns were hallooing,
Right there was the merriest music a man ever heard,
The hymn that went up for the soul of Renard from horn
and throat.
They grant the hounds their reward
And fondle their heads and dote;
And then they take Renard
And part him from his coat.

And then they headed for home, for night was near,
And splendidly they sang with their shining horns;
The lord alights at last at his well-loved home,
Finds a fire awaiting him there, and his friend,
The good Sir Gawain, so gay tonight in the hall,
Brimming with mirth and love with the merry ladies;
He wore a blue robe with skirts that swept the flagstones,
His surcoat was softly furred and suited him well,
And his hood, of the same material, hung on his shoulders,
And both were bordered all about with white fur.
In the middle of the floor he met the lord
And greeted him gladly, and graciously said to him:
"I shall for once be first to fulfill the pact
We swore to one another and sealed with wine."
Then Gawain embraced the lord and kissed him thrice,
The sweetest and solemnest kisses a man could bestow.
"By Christ," said the elder knight, "you're quite a man
In business, if all your bargains are good as they seem."
"Yes. Well, no worry there," said Gawain at once,
"Since I've paid in full and promptly all I owe."
"Mary," the other answered him, "mine's not worth much,
For I hunted all day long, and all I got
Was this foul-smelling fox—the devil take him!—
It's hardly decent pay for such precious things
As you've kindly pressed upon me, these kisses so sweet
                                    and good."
            "Enough now," said Sir Gawain,
            "I thank you, by the rood."
            Then how the fox was slain
            He told them as they stood.

With mirth and minstrelsy, and meat at their pleasure,
The two made as merry as any man living might—
With the laughter of the ladies and lighthearted joking,
Both the knight and the hall's noble lord, in their happiness—
Only a drunk or a madman could make more merry.
They laughed, and all the hall laughed with them and joked
Until the time came round at last for parting,
When finally they were forced to turn to their beds.
And now my sweet knight says adieu first to the lord,
Bowing humbly and graciously giving his thanks:
"For the splendid welcome you've given me here at your home,
At Christmastime, may the King of Heaven reward you.
I'll make myself your servant, if you so desire;
But tomorrow, milord, as you know, I must move on;
But give me someone to show me the path, as you promised,
The road to the Green Chapel, where as God sees fit
I must meet on New Year's Day my appointed fate."
"In good faith," said the lord, "I'll do so gladly,
All I may ever have promised, I'll pay *in full*."
He assigns a servant to Gawain to show him the way
And guide him in through the hills, that he make no mistake,
And show him the easiest path through the woods to the green
       one's cell.
    The lord thanks Gawain gravely
    For more than he can tell;
    Then to each highborn lady
    Sir Gawain says farewell.

34

With sorrowing heart and with kisses he spoke to them both
And urged the two to accept his undying thanks,
And they returned the same again to Gawain,
And with heavy sighs of care they commend him to Christ.
Then Gawain said goodbye to all the hall;
To every man he'd met he gave his thanks
For his service and companionship and the kindness
With which they'd all attended his every wish;
And the servants there were as sorry to see him go
As they'd been if he'd lived with them all their lives as their lord.
Then the torchbearers took him upstairs to his room
And led him to his bed to lie down and rest.
And did he sleep soundly then? I dare not say!
There was much concerning the morning our knight might turn
in his thought.
Then let him lie there still:
He is near to what he's sought;
If you'll listen for a while,
I'll tell what morning brought.

Part Four

1

Now New Year's Day draws near; the night slides past:
Dawn drives out the dark, as the Lord commands;
But the wintry winds of the world awaken outside
And clouds cast down their chilly load on the earth;
There's enough of the North Wind's needle to trouble the naked;
Snow and sleet hurl down to make wild creatures cower,
And howling winds come hurtling down from the heights
And drive huge drifts to the depth of every dale.
The young man listened well, where he lay in his bed,
And although his eyelids were locked, he got little sleep;
By every cock that crowed he could tell the hour.
He was up and dressed before any faint sign of dawn,
For there in his chamber there flickered the light of a lamp.
He called to his chamberlain, who cheerfully answered,
And he bid him to bring in his byrnie and the saddle of his horse;
The other was up at once and arranging his clothes,
And he dressed our knight at once in his noble attire.
First he put on soft cloth to ward off the cold,
And then all his other equipment, carefully kept:
His chest- and belly-plates, all polished to a glow,
The rings of his rich byrnie rubbed free of all rust;
And all was as fresh as at first, so that well might he thank
                            his men.
            He put on every piece,
            All burnished till they shone,
            Most gay from here to Greece;
            And he called for his horse again.

2

When Gawain garbed himself in his handsome clothes—
His cloak with its crest of gleaming needlework,
The velvet cloth set off by splendid stones,
Brightly embellished and bound by brilliant seams,
Beautifully furred within with the finest of pelts—
He by no means left behind that lady's gift,
The last thing on earth it was likely he'd forget!
When he'd lightly belted his sword to his lean hips
He circled the sash around him twice,
Winding the girdle around himself with relish,
That green device that seemed only gay decoration
On the proud and royal red of Gawain's robe;
But it wasn't because of its worth he wore that sash,
Or pride of its pendants, polished though they were,
But in hopes of saving his head when he had to endure
Without argument, when the time came for that ax
                        to fall.
            Now Gawain, tan and proud,
            Works his way through the hall,
            Nodding and bending to the crowd
            And once more thanking them all.

And now the great, tall Gringolet was ready,
The war horse carefully stabled while Gawain was here,
And how that proud steed pranced in his rage to run!
Sir Gawain stepped up beside him, inspecting his coat,
And said, "Here's a castle that knows how to keep its guests;
Good fortune to the man who maintains such groomsmen,
And the lady of this place, may love be with her!
May they who see to their guests so splendidly
And welcome them so well be richly rewarded—
And all of you here—when you come to the Kingdom of Heaven!
And if I may stay alive awhile on earth,
May I see some way to repay you at last for such kindness!"
He steps in the stirrup and strides aloft;
They show him his shield, and he swings it onto his shoulder,
Then touches Gringolet once with his gilded heels,
And the charger lunges, lingering no longer
                              to dance.
              High on his horse he rides,
                Armed with his spear and lance;
              "This castle be kept by Christ!"
              He cried, "May He give it *bonne chance!*"

They dropped the drawbridge down, and the men at the gates
Unbarred the blocks, and both halves opened wide;
He blessed the company quickly and crossed on the planks,
And he praised the porter who knelt by the prince of the hall,
Praying to God that He grant all good fortune to Gawain,
And thus he rode off before dawn with his single servant,
The man sent to show him the path to the place appointed
Where Sir Gawain was doomed to suffer that sorrowful stroke.
They rode by hills where every bough hung bare
And climbed in the bloom of cliffs where coldspots hung—
The dark sky overcast, the low clouds ugly;
Mists moved, wet, on the moor, and the mountain walls
Were damp, every mountain a huge man hatted and mantled;
Brooks boiled up muttering, bursting from banks all about them,
And shattered, shining, on the stones as they showered down.
The way through the wood wound, baffling, out and in
Till the hour of sunrise came and the sun rose cold
                              and bright.
            They rode on a high hill's crown,
            The snow all around them white;
            The servant beside him then
            Reined up and stopped the knight.

5

"Sir," the servant said, "I've brought you this far.
You're pretty near right up on top of that famous place
You've asked about and looked for all this while;
But let me say this, my lord—because I know you,
And because you're a man I love like not many alive—
If you'll take my advice in this, you'll be better off.
The place you're pushing to is a perilous place,
And the man who holes up in those rocks is the worst in the world,
For he's mighty, and he's cruel, and he kills for pure joy;
No man between Heaven and Hell is a match for that monster,
And his body's bigger than the best four
In Arthur's hall, or Hector, or anyone else.
It's there he plays his game, at the Green Chapel,
Where no man passes, however proud in battle,
But he cuts him down for sport by the strength of his arm;
He's a man without moderation, a stranger to mercy,
For chaplain or plowman, whoever goes past that chapel—
Monk, mass-priest, mortal of any kind—
That green man loves his death as he loves his own life.
So I say to you, sir, as sure as you sit in your saddle,
Go there and you go to your grave, as the green man likes;
Trust me, for if you had twenty more lives, he'd take
                                   them too.
                    How long he's lived, God knows!
                    —Or who he's cut in two;
                    But sir, against his blows
                    There's nothing a man can do.

6

"And so, milord, I plead with you, leave him alone!
Go home some other route, by Christ's own side—
Ride through some far-off country, and Christ be with you!
And I'll go back home, I promise you on my honor,
And swear me by God and by all the beloved apostles,
By the wounds and by all that's holy—and all other oaths—
I'll keep me your secret, sir, and say never a word
Of your fleeing from any man living that ever I heard of."
"I thank you," said Gawain, and grudgingly he added:
"Good fortune to you, my friend, for wishing me well;
As for your keeping the secret, I'm sure I believe you;
But however well you held it in, if I left here
Flying in fright from the place, as you feel I should,
I'd prove myself a cowardly knight and past pardon.
I'll make my way to the Chapel to meet what I must
And have what words I will with the one you tell of.
Whether for better or worse, I'll try my hand
                      on this hill.
            Cruel as he may be,
            However quick to kill,
            God can find the way
            To save me, if He will."

"Mary," the other man said, "since you've as much
 As said you've set your heart on suicide,
 And losing your life would please you, who can prevent it?
 Here's your helmet, then, and here's your spear.
 Ride on down this road past the side of that rock
 Till it sets you down in the stones on the valley floor;
 Look down the flats to the left a little way
 And there, not far away, you'll find the Chapel
 And the burly knight that keeps it not far off.
 And now goodbye, by God's side, noble Gawain.
 I wouldn't ride further for all the gold on earth—
 Or walk even one step more in these weird woods."
 With that the serving man jerked at his horse's reins
 And stabbed his horse with his heels with all his might
 And galloped along the land and left our knight
                              alone.
               "By Christ," said Gawain now,
               "I'll neither whine nor moan;
                 To the will of God I bow
                 And make myself His own."

He put his spurs to Gringolet, plunged down the path,
Shoved through the heavy thicket grown up by the woods
And rode down the steep slope to the floor of the valley;
He looked around him then—a strange, wild place,
And not a sign of a chapel on any side
But only steep, high banks surrounding him,
And great, rough knots of rock and rugged crags
That scraped the passing clouds, as it seemed to him.
He heaved at the heavy reins to hold back his horse
And squinted in every direction in search of the Chapel,
And still he saw nothing except—and this was strange—
A small green hill all alone, a sort of barrow,
A low, smooth bulge on the bank of the brimming creek
That flowed from the foot of a waterfall,
And the water in the pool was bubbling as if it were boiling.
Sir Gawain urged Gringolet on till he came to the mound
And lightly dismounted and made the reins secure
On the great, thick limb of a gnarled and ancient tree;
Then he went up to the barrow and walked all around it,
Wondering in his wits what on earth it might be.
It had at each end and on either side an entrance,
And patches of grass were growing all over the thing,
And all the inside was hollow—an old, old cave
Or the cleft of some ancient crag, he couldn't tell which
                                    it was.
              "Whoo, Lord!" thought the knight,
              "Is *this* the fellow's place?
                Here the Devil might
                Recite his midnight mass.

"Dear God," thought Gawain, "the place is deserted enough!
And it's ugly enough, all overgrown with weeds!
Well might it amuse that marvel of green
To do his devotions here, in his devilish way!
In my five senses I fear it's the Fiend himself
Who's brought me to meet him here to murder me.
May fire and fury befall this fiendish Chapel,
As cursed a kirk as I ever yet came across!"
With his helmet on his head and his lance in hand
He leaped up onto the roof of the rock-walled room
And, high on that hill, he heard, from an echoing rock
Beyond the pool, on the hillside, a horrible noise.
Brrrack! It clattered in the cliffs as if to cleave them,
A sound like a grindstone grinding on a scythe!
Brrrack! It whirred and rattled like water on a mill wheel!
Brrrrrack! It rushed and rang till your blood ran cold.
And then: "Oh God," thought Gawain, "it grinds, I think,
For me—a blade prepared for the blow I must take

                  as my right!
        God's will be done! But here!
        He may well get his knight,
        But still, no use in fear;
        I won't fall dead of fright!"

And then Sir Gawain roared in a ringing voice,
"Where is the hero who swore he'd be here to meet me?
 Sir Gawain the Good is come to the Green Chapel!
 If any man would meet me, make it now,
 For it's now or never, I've no wish to dawdle here long."
"Stay there!" called someone high above his head,
"I'll pay you promptly all that I promised before."
 But still he went on with that whetting noise a while,
 Turning again to his grinding before he'd come down.
 At last, from a hole by a rock he came out into sight,
 Came plunging out of his den with a terrible weapon,
 A huge new Danish ax to deliver his blow with,
 With a vicious swine of a bit bent back to the handle,
 Filed to a razor's edge and four foot long,
 Not one inch less by the length of that gleaming lace.
 The great Green Knight was garbed as before,
 Face, legs, hair, beard, all as before but for this:
 That now he walked the world on his own two legs,
 The ax handle striking the stone like a walking-stave.
 When the knight came down to the water he would not wade
 But vaulted across on his ax, then with awful strides
 Came fiercely over the field filled all around
                                    with snow.
              Sir Gawain met him there
              And bowed—but none too low!
              Said the other, "I see, sweet sir,
              You go where you say you'll go!

"Gawain," the Green Knight said, "may God be your guard!
You're very welcome indeed, sir, here at my place;
You've timed your travel, my friend, as a true man should.
You recall the terms of the contract drawn up between us:
At this time a year ago you took your chances,
And I'm pledged now, this New Year, to make you my payment.
And here we are in this valley, all alone,
And no man here to part us, proceed as we may;
Heave off your helmet then, and have here your pay;
And debate no more with me than I did then
When you severed my head from my neck with a single swipe."
"Never fear," said Gawain, "by God who gave
Me life, I'll raise no complaint at the grimness of it;
But take your single stroke, and I'll stand still
And allow you to work as you like and not oppose
                              you here."
               He bowed toward the ground
               And let his skin show clear;
               However his heart might pound,
               He would not show his fear.

12

Quickly then the man in the green made ready,
Grabbed up his keen-ground ax to strike Sir Gawain;
With all the might in his body he bore it aloft
And sharply brought it down as if to slay him;
Had he made it fall with the force he first intended
He would have stretched out the strongest man on earth.
But Sir Gawain cast a side glance at the ax
As it glided down to give him his Kingdom Come,
And his shoulders jerked away from the iron a little,
And the Green Knight caught the handle, holding it back,
And mocked the prince with many a proud reproof:
"*You* can't be Gawain," he said, "who's thought so good,
A man who's never been daunted on hill or dale!
For look how you flinch for fear before anything's felt!
I never heard tell that Sir Gawain was ever a coward!
I never moved a muscle when *you* came down;
In Arthur's hall I never so much as winced.
My head fell off at my feet, yet I never flickered;
But you! You tremble at heart before you're touched!
I'm bound to be called a better man than you, then,
                        my lord."
           Said Gawain, "I shied once:
           No more. You have my word.
           But if my head falls to the stones
           It cannot be restored.

13

"But be brisk, man, by your faith, and come to the point!
Deal out my doom if you can, and do it at once,
For I'll stand for one good stroke, and I'll start no more
Until your ax has hit—and that I swear."
"Here goes, then," said the other, and heaves it aloft
And stands there waiting, scowling like a madman;
He swings down sharp, then suddenly stops again,
Holds back the ax with his hand before it can hurt,
And Gawain stands there stirring not even a nerve;
He stood there still as a stone or the stock of a tree
That's wedged in rocky ground by a hundred roots.
O, merrily then he spoke, the man in green:
"Good! You've got your heart back! Now I can hit you.
May all that glory the good King Arthur gave you
Prove efficacious now—if it ever can—
And save your neck." In rage Sir Gawain shouted,
"*Hit* me, hero! I'm right up to here with your threats!
Is it *you* that's the cringing coward after all?"
"Whoo!" said the man in green, "he's wrathful, too!
No pauses, then; I'll pay up my pledge at once,
                                        I vow!"
                    He takes his stride to strike
                    And lifts his lip and brow;
                    It's not a thing Gawain can like,
                    For nothing can save him now!

He raises that ax up lightly and flashes it down,
And that blinding bit bites in at the knight's bare neck—
But hard as he hammered it down, it hurt him no more
Than to nick the nape of his neck, so it split the skin;
The sharp blade slit to the flesh through the shiny hide,
And red blood shot to his shoulders and spattered the ground.
And when Gawain saw his blood where it blinked in the snow
He sprang from the man with a leap to the length of a spear;
He snatched up his helmet swiftly and slapped it on,
Shifted his shield into place with a jerk of his shoulders,
And snapped his sword out faster than sight; said boldly—
And, mortal born of his mother that he was,
There was never on earth a man so happy by half—
"No more strokes, my friend; you've had your swing!
I've stood one swipe of your ax without resistance;
If you offer me any more, I'll repay you at once
With all the force and fire I've got—as you
                              will see.
              I take one stroke, that's all,
              For that was the compact we
              Arranged in Arthur's hall;
              But now, no more for me!"

15

The Green Knight remained where he stood, relaxing on his ax—
Settled the shaft on the rocks and leaned on the sharp end—
And studied the young man standing there, shoulders hunched,
And considered that staunch and doughty stance he took,
Undaunted yet, and in his heart he liked it;
And then he said merrily, with a mighty voice—
With a roar like rushing wind he reproved the knight—
"Here, don't be such an ogre on your ground!
Nobody here has behaved with bad manners toward you
Or done a thing except as the contract said.
I owed you a stroke, and I've struck; consider yourself
Well paid. And now I release you from all further duties.
If I'd cared to hustle, it may be, perchance, that I might
Have hit somewhat harder, and then you might well be cross!
The first time I lifted my ax it was lighthearted sport,
I merely feinted and made no mark, as was right,
For you kept our pact of the first night with honor
And abided by your word and held yourself true to me,
Giving me all you owed as a good man should.
I feinted a second time, friend, for the morning
You kissed my pretty wife twice and returned me the kisses;
And so for the first two days, mere feints, nothing more
                              severe.

              A man who's true to his word,
                There's nothing he needs to fear;
              You failed me, though, on the third
                Exchange, so I've tapped you here.

16

"That sash you wear by your scabbard belongs to me;
  My own wife gave it to you, as I ought to know.
  I know, too, of your kisses and all your words
  And my wife's advances, for I myself arranged them.
  It was I who sent her to test you. I'm convinced
  You're the finest man that ever walked this earth.
  As a pearl is of greater price than dry white peas,
  So Gawain indeed stands out above all other knights.
  But you lacked a little, sir; you were less than loyal;
  But since it was not for the sash itself or for lust
  But because you loved your life, I blame you less."
  Sir Gawain stood in a study a long, long while,
  So miserable with disgrace that he wept within,
  And all the blood of his chest went up to his face
  And he shrank away in shame from the man's gentle words.
  The first words Gawain could find to say were these:
"Cursed be cowardice and covetousness both,
  Villainy and vice that destroy all virtue!"
  He caught at the knots of the girdle and loosened them
  And fiercely flung the sash at the Green Knight.
"There, there's my fault! The foul fiend vex it!
  Foolish cowardice taught me, from fear of your stroke,
  To bargain, covetous, and abandon my kind,
  The selflessness and loyalty suitable in knights;
  Here I stand, faulty and false, much as I've feared them,
  Both of them, untruth and treachery; may they see sorrow
                                    and care!
              I can't deny my guilt;
              My works shine none too fair!
              Give me your good will
              And henceforth I'll beware."

At that, the Green Knight laughed, saying graciously,
"Whatever harm I've had, I hold it amended
Since now you're confessed so clean, acknowledging sins
And bearing the plain penance of my point;
I consider you polished as white and as perfectly clean
As if you had never fallen since first you were born.
And I give you, sir, this gold-embroidered girdle,
For the cloth is as green as my gown. Sir Gawain, think
On this when you go forth among great princes;
Remember our struggle here; recall to your mind
This rich token. Remember the Green Chapel.
And now, come on, let's both go back to my castle
And finish the New Year's revels with feasting and joy,
                                        not strife,
                    I beg you," said the lord,
                    And said, "As for my wife,
                    She'll be your friend, no more
                    A threat against your life."

"No, sir," said the knight, and seized his helmet
And quickly removed it, thanking the Green Knight,
"I've reveled too well already; but fortune be with you;
May He who gives all honors honor you well.
Give my regards to that courteous lady, your wife—
Both to her and the other, those honorable ladies
Who with such subtlety deceived their knight.
It's no great marvel that a man is made a fool
And through the wiles of woman won to sorrow;
Thus one of them fooled Adam, here on earth,
And several of them Solomon, and Samson,
Delilah dealt him his death, and later David
Was blinded by Bathsheba and bitterly suffered.
All these were wrecked by their wiles. What bliss it would be
To love them but never believe them—if only one could!
For all those heroes were once most happy and free
And the greatest thinkers that ever walked this side
                              of Heaven.
            Yet these were all defiled
            Through faith in lovely women;
            If I, too, was beguiled,
            I think I must be forgiven.

"And as for your girdle," said Gawain, "God reward you!
I'll take it and gladly, and not for the gleaming gold
Or the weave or the silk or the pendants on its side
Or for wealth or renown or the wonderful ornamentation
But instead as a sign of my slip, and I'll look at it often
When I move in glory, and humbly I'll remember
The fault and frailty of the foolish flesh,
How tender it is to infection, how easily stained;
And when I am tempted to pride by my prowess in arms,
A glance at the sash will once more soften my heart.
But I'd like to ask one other thing, if it doesn't displease you:
Since you are the lord of the land where I've visited
And received such splendid welcome (for which may He
Who sits on high upholding the heavens repay you),
What is your true name? I'll ask nothing else."
"I'll tell you truly, Gawain," the other said,
"I'm known in this land as Bertilak de Hautdesert.
Through the might of Morgan le Fay, who lives in my castle,
Well versed in the occult and cunning in magic
(Oh, many the marvelous arts she's learned from Merlin,
For she dallied long ago with the love
Of that crafty old scholar, as all your knights are aware
          at home—
       'Morgan the goddess' she's called,
       And it's thus she got her name:
       There's none, however bold,
       That Morgan cannot tame—)

"—Through Morgan's might I came in this form to your hall
To test its pride, to see if the tales were true
Concerning the great nobility of the Round Table.
She worked this charm on me to rob your wits
In the hope that Queen Guinevere might be shocked to her grave
At sight of my game and the ghastly man who spoke
With his head held high in his hand before all the table.
It's Morgan you met in my castle—the old, old woman—
Your aunt, as a matter of fact, half-sister to Arthur,
Daughter to the Duchess of Tyntagel, on whom
King Uther got his famous son King Arthur.
But come, I urge you, knight, come visit your aunt;
Make merry in my house, where my servants love you,
And where I will love you as well, man, I swear,
As I love any lord on earth, for your proven honor."
But Gawain again said no, not by any means,
And so they embraced and kissed and commended each other
To the Prince of Paradise, and parted then
                        in the cold;
                  Sir Gawain turned again
                  To Camelot and his lord;
                  And as for the man of green,
                  He went wherever he would.

Now Gawain rides through the wild woods of the world
On Gringolet—a man given back his life
Through grace. Sometimes he slept in houses, sometimes
Not. In every vale he fought and conquered,
But of all that I've no intention to tell.
By now the cut in his neck was whole once more
And over the scar he wore his shining sash
Bound to his side obliquely, like a baldric,
And tied with a knot on his *left*, below his arm,
As a sign that he had been taken in untruth;
And thus he comes, alive and well, at last
To court. What cheer there was when the Round Table learned
That good Sir Gawain had come! The King was joyful.
He clutched him and kissed him, and Guinevere kissed him then,
And many a stalwart knight stepped near to hail him,
And they all asked what had happened, and he told his story,
Recounted his hardships, all his fears and griefs,
The adventure of the Chapel, the green man's actions,
The love of the lady, and, last of all, the sash.
He showed them all the scar on his naked neck,
Left by the Green Knight's ax when he was found
                              to blame;
              He told of his disgrace
              And moaned his fallen name;
              The blood rushed up in his face
              As he showed his badge of shame.

"Look, my lord," said Gawain, holding the love lace,
"Here's the heraldic bend of the brand on my neck,
  The sign and symbol of something valued lost,
  Of the coveting and cowardice that caught me—
The token that I have been taken once in faithlessness.
I must wear this emblem as long as my life may last,
For this sign, once attached, is attached for all time."
The King and the court all comforted the knight;
And laughing gaily, they graciously agreed
That all the lords and ladies of *La Table Ronde*,
And all in that brotherhood should bear a baldric,
An oblique heraldic bend of burning green,
And wear that sign forever in honor of Gawain.
Thus was the glory of the Round Table given to the sash
And what marked Gawain's shame made Gawain's glory
Forever, as all the best books of Romance
Record. These things took place in the days of King Arthur,
As the ancient Book of the British has borne witness,
After bold King Brutus founded Britain,
After the siege and assault was ended at Troy
                              at last.
            And many a man has found
            Adventures such as this.
            Now He that bore the crown
            Of thorns bring us to bliss! *Amen.*

HONY SOYT QUI MAL PENCE

ST. ERKENWĀLD

At London in England no long while since—
Since when Christ suffered on the cross and Christendom was built—
There was a bishop in that place, a man blessed and good,
And Erkenwald, it is said, was that saintly man's name.

In his time the greatest of the temples in the town
Was in part torn down to be dedicated anew,
For the place had been honored as a heathen hall under Hengest,
The king whom the Saxon savages sent over.

They outbattled the Britons and pushed them into Wales
And perverted all the people to be found in that place.
Then was the great realm godless a good many years,
Until Augustine was sent into Sandwich from the Pope.

He preached there the pure faith and planted the truth
And called all the country to Christendom anew;
He took again the temples that were taken by the Devil
And cleansed them in Christ's name and called them churches;

He smashed the idols where they stood and set up saints,
And he changed the names of the churches, and charged them more
        nobly:
What once was Apollo's place became now St. Peter's,
Mohomet's became St. Margaret's or Magdalina's;

The Synagogue of the Sun he assigned to Our Lady,
And Jupiter and Juno to Jesus or James;
Thus did he sanctify and establish for saints
Shrines set up to serve Satan in Saxon times.

What is London now was known as the New Troy,
The master-town it remains to the present day;
And the mightiest minster there a monstrous devil
Owned, and the title of the temple took his name:

For he was exalted above all other idols,
His sacrifice the most solemn in the Saxon lands;
His temple was counted the third in the Triapolitan,
And all the breadth of England had only two more.

Now in Augustine's area Erkenwald was bishop
At beautiful London-town, and explained the law,
Seated, splendid on the throne of St. Paul's Minster,
A temple of the Triapolitan, as I've told already;

And a part was razed to rubble to be reared up anew,
A notable structure for the day, called the New Work.
The plan meant labor for many a whistling mason,
Hewing the hard rocks with sharp-honed tools,

And for many a man with a pick who probed the ground
To find a foundation firm on its footing from the first.
As they shoveled and struck deep they discovered a marvel
Which the keenest of chronicles still record and keep.

For while they were delving and digging down deep in the earth,
They found, formed in a floor, a huge, fair tomb,
A crypt of thick-carved rock, craftily wrought
And garnished about with gargoyles, all of gray marble.

The three bolts of the bier-pit, which bore up the coffin,
Were handsomely fashioned of marble and finely polished,
And the listel band was embellished with bright golden letters—
But strange old runes were the rows of words that stood there.

The characters stood clean cut, where all could see them,
But men were at a loss to learn their meaning;
Brilliant scholars of the place, men broad of forehead,
Could discover no hint of what devilish secret they kept.

When tidings of the strange tomb swept through the town,
Hundreds of men of high rank came to hover around it;
Burgesses hurried to the place and beadles and others,
And many a master's man out of many a trade.

Young men threw down their tools and went running to the place,
Racing swiftly in a rout, with ringing voices;
So mighty a multitude came there, so many so quickly,
It seemed as though all the world were gathered in an instant.

When the Lord Mayor and his men had examined the marvel,
With the sacristan's assent they shut it off
And offered to unlock the lid and to lift it away
To find out what remains were sealed within.

With that, big workmen walked down into the bier-pit,
Put wrecking bars to the lid and worked the claws under
And caught the lid by the corners with crowbars of iron;
Large as the stone lid was, they soon laid it by.

Then surely any man standing there was struck
With astonishment if he looked for nothing strange:
The inner casket rim gleamed, aglitter with gold,
And there at the bottom of the bier lay a splendid body

Arrayed richly and rarely in regal robes.
His gown was hemmed with glistening threads of gold,
And many a precious pearl was placed upon it,
And an ancient, golden belt bound the body's waist.

On his shoulders lay a large mantle of miniver fur
And woven of camel's hair, with handsome borders;
And on his coif there lay a costly crown,
And the scepter of royalty had been set in his hand.

Spotless were all his robes and without a stain,
Neither mold nor blemish nor the burrowing of moths;
And the dyes were all still bright in their beautiful hues
As though they'd been closed in the casket just yesterday;

And still fresh were the face and the naked flesh
Round the ears and round the hands, where it openly showed
As rich and ruddy as the rose; and the mouth was red,
As though he had fallen asleep in the soundness of health.

It was wasted time to wonder, one to another,
What body this might be that was buried here,
How long he might have lain here, his look unchanged,
And on all his attire no mold; and each man mused:

"A lord like this would surely be long remembered;
It seems clear enough that he once was a king in this country,
Since he waits here buried so deep. It will be a great wonder
If we cannot find some man who can say he has seen him."

And yet he remained unknown, for no man could name him
Either by title or token or ancient tradition;
There was no man seen in that city or spoken of in books
Who had heard of such a man, either highborn or low.

When a week had passed, the word was taken to the bishop,
The plain witchcraft of the body that lay there buried;
For the bishop and all his attendants were away at the time
In Essex, where Erkenwald was inspecting an abbey.

Messengers told him of the tomb and the trouble in the city;
Because of the corpse, such an uproar rang out day and night
That the bishop, to check it, sent letters and, after them, beadles,
And at last he went there himself on his white horse.

When he reached the cathedral known far and wide as St. Paul's,
Many men met him on his mare with a mighty clamor;
He commanded silence, and he did not go straight to the grave
But calmly passed into his palace and closed the door.

The dark of night drove in, and the day-bell rang,
And St. Erkenwald was up in the early morning hours,
Who well-nigh all night long had knelt in prayer
Beseeching his Sovereign Lord, by His holy grace,
To vouchsafe to him some vision, some revelation:

"Unworthy as I am," said the bishop, imploring
In honest humility, "hear my request, O Lord;
Confirm now the faith of all Christians: Allow me to grasp
The full depth of this mystery no mortal mind fathoms."

And so long did he call out for grace that at last it was given,
An answer from the Holy Ghost. And then came dawn.
The minster doors were drawn open when the matins were sung,
And solemnly he made ready to sing the high mass.

The prelate was soon attired in his priestly robes,
And with dignity he and his lesser priests started the service
Of *Spiritus Domini*, for success in the hour
To come; and the choir sang prayers in sweet, clear notes.

Many a well-dressed courtier came there to hear it,
For all the best men of the kingdom attended St. Paul's.
In time, the service ceased and they sang the amens,
And all the honored priests turned at last from the altar.

The bishop crossed the flagstones—lords bowed low—
And, dressed in his gleaming vestments, he visited the tomb.
They unlocked the cloistered crypt with a clatter of keys,
And all who watched him enter were uneasy at heart.

He came to the burial place, bold barons beside him,
And the Mayor, with his guards and his mace-bearers before him;
And the guard of the ancient grave gave a full account
Of the finding of the freakish thing, then pointed with his finger:

"Behold, my lords," he said, "here lies a corpse
That has lain here locked in this place—how long, no one knows.
Yet the color of the flesh and the cloth are unblemished,
Both flesh and the finely-wrought catafalque where he lies.

"We have learned of no man alive who has lived so long
That he can recall in his mind such a king as this,
No, neither his name nor what notable deeds he did;
Yet many a poorer man has been buried, and his grave
Set in our burial rolls and recorded forever.

"And we've searched all these seven long days among old books
And uncovered not one single chronicle of this king.
He has hardly lain long enough yet, from the looks of him,
To have melted so out of mind—save by monstrous power."

"So it seems," said the holy man, consecrated bishop,
"But a miracle among men amounts to little
  Compared to that Providence that the Prince of Heaven
  Wields when He cares to unlock but the least of His powers.

"When all man's might is mated, his mind played out,
  And all man's plans blown apart and he stands with no move,
  Then easily He lets loose, with a single finger,
  What all the hands under Heaven might never hold up.
  When the creature's pieces swerve away from wisdom,
  The Creator can give him support and can cover the loss.

"And so let us turn to our work, and wonder no more;
  Seeking the truth by ourselves, as you see, gets us nowhere;
  Let us all look up to God and implore His grace,
  Who is generous with wisdom and soon sends aid.

"In fact, to confirm your faith and belief in the good,
  I shall show you soon such sure signs of His power
  That all must find him forever almighty Lord
  And eager to furnish your needs if He finds you His friend."

Then Erkenwald turned to the tomb to talk to the corpse,
  And he lifted the dead man's eyelids and leaned near to speak:
"Now, dead man lying here still, lie still no more,
  For Christ has chosen this day to show His joy.

"Be obedient to His bidding, I bid in His name,
  And as Christ was broken on a beam and bled for mankind,
  As you may well know and as we who are Christians believe,
  Answer now my questions; conceal no truth.

"Since we cannot find what you are, inform us yourself
  What man you were in the world and why you lie here,
  How long your corpse has lain flawless, what creed you followed,
  Whether you are raised to bliss or condemned to pain."

When the bishop had spoken all this, and ended with a sigh,
  The miraculous corpse in its casket moved a little,
  And with a dreary sound it drove out words
  With the help of some heavenly spirit sent down from God:

"Bishop," the corpse began, "your command is welcome;
   For both my eyes I would not be held back from speaking!
   The Name that you now name and command me by
   Commands all Heaven and Hell, and the Earth between.

"First, then, I'll tell what estate I held in my time:
   As unlucky a mortal as ever moved on earth,
   Never a kaiser or king, yet no knight either,
   But a judge who judged by the law this land then used.

"I was commissioned and made an executive here
   To sit over weighty causes; I ruled this city
   By pagan law, as second to a prince of high rank;
   And all who attended that prince avowed the same faith.

"It is hard to find human terms for the time I've lain here;
   It is greater than any mere mortal can grasp in his mind.
   After this city was first established by Brutus,
   It was nearly eight hundred years—lacking eighteen—

"To the time when Christ was born, by Christian account;
   From the time of my death, it was three hundred fifty-four years.
   At that time I was justice of the Iter in New Troy,
   In the reign of the noble king that ruled us then,

"The bold Briton, Sir Belin: Sir Brennin was his brother,
   And many were the angry insults hurled between them,
   And many the ruinous wars while their wrath lasted.
   It was then that I was a judge of the Gentiles' law."

Thus the moan from the bier-pit. And among the people
   No word in this world was spoken, no sound arose,
   But all were as silent as marble who stood there and listened,
   And many there were afraid, and many wept.

The bishop then said to the body, "Explain to us now,
   Since you never ruled as a king, why you are crowned,
   And how it happens that you hold in your hand a scepter
   If you never held lands or had liege men at your feet."

"My lord," said the voice of the dead man, "I mean to tell that,
   Though by no command of mine was I buried in a crown.
   I was deputy and judge for a prince of high rank,
   And power over this place was mine entirely.

"I governed this beautiful city in the Gentiles' way,
   And governed in good faith for forty winters;
   The people were treacherous, false, and hard to rule,
   But for all the heartache, I held them to the right.

"And not for woe, or weal, or wrath, or dread,
   Or for power, or bribes, or fear of any man's might
   Did I ever once slip from honor as I saw it,
   Or ever a day in my life draw up false judgments.

"I never declined my conscience for the comforts of life
   By any crafty verdict or cunning deceit,
   However rich the man or however revered,
   Or for any man's personal threats or for pity or pain.

"No man won me from the highway to wandering lanes,
   Insofar as the faith I knew confirmed my heart;
   Though the man had murdered my father, my judgment was fair;
   And I would not lie though my father's life were on trial.

"And because I was righteous and upright and well read in law,
   At my death great sorrow resounded through New Troy;
   All men lamented the day, both the low and the high,
   And therefore to honor my body they buried it in gold.

"In clothes to suit the most courteous in that court
   And a mantle to suit the most noble and humane on the bench,
   They readied my body as they would the chief ruler of Troy,
   And with furs proper to the finest men of my faith.

"And in honor of my honesty, highly renowned,
   They crowned and declared me king of all the justices
   That were ever enthroned in Troy or, they thought, ever would be;
   And because I gave recompense to right, they granted me the
      scepter."

The bishop inquired still more, solemn of heart,
How it might be that, however men honored his name,
His clothes were kept perfect: "Closed in earth, it would seem,
They ought to have rotted, been rent to rags long since.

"Your body may be embalmed; it does not surprise me
That the flesh is not torn or rotted or teeming with worms;
But I cannot grasp how your color or your clothes—
Whatever men's lore—can lie here and last so long."

"No, bishop," the body said, "I was never embalmed,
Nor could any man's craft, then or now, have kept my clothes;
But the all-wise Lord, who has always loved the right,
And who faithfully loves all laws that cling to truth,

"That God who more honors men for remembering justice
Than for all other praiseworthy virtues men practice on earth—
If mortal men for my honesty mantled me thus,
It was He who loves honesty most that allowed me to last."

"Tell us now of your spirit," St. Erkenwald said;
"Where is it set and established, for you served truth well.
He who rewards each man for the works he has done
Might forget small faults and grant through His grace some blessing;

"For the Lord has said, as we read in the sacred psalms,
'The innocent and the righteous shall see My face.'
Therefore speak of your soul, where it shines in bliss,
And make known to all men the might of God's mercy!"

Then he that lay there moaned, and his head turned away,
And he gave a groan from his grave and to God he said,
"O Mighty Maker of Men, Your might is supreme!
How might Your mercy be made to reach me at last?

"Was I not an unknowing pagan, stranger to Your pledge,
A man unaware of Your mercy or the measure of Your virtues,
And in life a man unlettered in all those laws
That You were worshiped by, Lord? Alas, time is long!

"I was not one of the number Your anguish bought
   With the blood of Your body broken on the cross;
   When You harrowed Hell's dark depth and haled others out,
   Your loved ones out of Limbo, You left me there.

"And there sits my soul even now and sees nought but fire,
   Dwindling in the dark death that descended on our father,
   Our first elder, Adam, who ate of that apple
   Which poisoned forever the pitiful blood of man.

"All men took the taint from his teeth, and took in venom;
   Yet mended by Your medicine, man may live,
   Baptized to freedom at the font, with perfect faith—
   But for that we came too soon, myself and my soul.

"What have we won for our works, who loved righteousness,
   Since our souls are hurled down to writhe in the searing lake,
   And sent away from that supper, that solemn feast,
   Where sumptuously men are served who died serving You?

"My soul sits huddled in horror, suffering pain,
   Dim-eyed in the dark where dawn never strikes,
   Hungry, deep in its hellhole and howling for meat
   Long years before supper can be seen, or the Voice says, 'Come in.'"

So movingly did the dead man describe his anguish
   That every man there wept at the words he spoke;
   And suddenly St. Erkenwald cast down his gaze
   And could find no breath for speech, and wept from his heart.

He moved still closer to the tomb and stood by the side,
   His eyelids wet, and he looked at the corpse where it lay:
"O Lord God grant," he said, "that this corpse may have life,
   By Your leave, and allow me to lift up holy water

"And cast it upon this corpse and comfort him thus:
   'I baptize thee by the Father and by His Son
   And by the Holy Ghost'—not a grain of sand longer;
   Then even if he sank down dead I would stand less at fault."

And even as he spoke those words, the water of his eyes,
The tears of his weeping dropped down and touched the tomb,
And one of them fell on the face; and a faint sigh
Came, and the stranger said, "Our Savior be praised!

"Now praise be to Thee, great God, and Thy precious mother,
And blessèd be that hour when her body bore Thee!
And blessèd be thou, bishop, for bringing me freedom
And relief from the loathsome lake where my soul lay lost.

"For the words that you have spoken and the water you brought,
The bright stream of your eyes, is my baptismal font;
The first tear that dropped brought death to all my grief,
And this very instant my soul has its seat at the table,

"For with the words and water that wash away pain
Comes a flash of light, suddenly, low in the abyss,
And sharply my spirit springs upward with unsparing joy
And into the banquet hall where the blessed sit;

"And there a marshal meets her, with marvelous kindness,
And with reverence shows her a room, hers by right forever;
I praise Thee then, dear God, and thee too, bishop,
For bitterness has brought us to beauty at last!"

And then all sound ceased; he said no more;
And suddenly his sweet face sank in and was rotted,
And all the beauty of his body turned blacker than sod
And rotten as the rotted weeds that rise up in powder.

For as soon as that soul was established in bliss,
That other creation that covered the bones corrupted;
For the everlasting life, the life without end,
Voids all that vanity that avails man nothing.

Then was there praising of the Lord and the lifting of hymns:
Mourning and joy in that moment came together.
They passed forth in procession, and all the people followed,
And all the bells of the city sang out at once.

NOTES

1. *St. Erkenwald* is the poem in question. For a brief discussion of scholarly opinion on this subject, see note 47 below.
2. For a discussion of the traditions involved see *St. Erkenwald*, ed. H. L. Savage ("Yale Studies in English," Vol. LXXII [New Haven: Yale University Press, 1926]), pp. xii ff.
3. The poet's work was no doubt rather well known in the west, however, for signs of his influence appear in many of the alliterative poems. See Sir Israel Gollancz, *Sir Gawain and the Green Knight* (London: Oxford University Press for the Early English Text Society, 1940), pp. xiii ff.; R. J. Menner (ed.), *Purity* ("Yale Studies in English," Vol. LXI [New Haven: Yale University Press, 1920]), pp. xix ff.
4. A good discussion of the poet's religious views, particularly as they are expressed in the *Pearl*, is that of Professor René Wellek in "The Pearl: An Interpretation of the Middle-English Poem," *Studies in English*, IV (Prague: Charles University Press, 1933), 17 ff. The theological basis of *Sir Gawain and the Green Knight* has not been carefully examined.
5. See C. G. Coulton, "In Defense of the Pearl," *Modern Language Review*, II (1907), 39. The child in question is the daughter lamented in the *Pearl*. Coulton's argument is that the poet may have entered the priesthood after the death of his wife, who may conceivably have been dead already at the time he composed the *Pearl*. In the poem no wife is mentioned, and the narrator speaks of grieving all alone.
6. See C. G. Osgood's discussion of the character of the author in the introduction to his edition of the *Pearl* (Boston: Heath, 1906). A brief summary of Osgood's main points appears in *Pearl*, ed. E. V. Gordon (London: Oxford University Press, 1953), pp. xli ff.
7. See Sir Israel Gollancz (ed.), *Pearl, an English Poem of the XIVth Century, together with Boccaccio's Olympia* ("Medieval Library" [London: Chatto and Windus, 1921]), pp. xlvi ff. A good brief discussion of the claim for Strode may be found in F. N. Robinson, *The Works of Geoffrey Chaucer* (2d ed.; Boston: Houghton Mifflin Company, 1957), explanatory note to lines 1856 ff., "Troilus and Criseyde," p. 838.
8. Wellek, "The Pearl: An Interpretation . . . ," pp. 8–9.
9. Oscar Cargill and Margaret Schlauch, "The Pearl and Its Jeweler," *Publications of the Modern Language Association of America*, XLIII (1928), 177–79.
10. This view of the poem might stand without casting doubt on the more common view that the poem is somehow connected with the Order of the Garter. See I. Jackson, "*Sir Gawain and the Green Knight* Considered as a 'Garter' Poem," *Anglia*, XXXVII (1913), 393–423. In my opinion the case for *Sir Gawain and the Green Knight* as a

"Garter" poem is by no means strong. The motto added at the end of the poem, *Hony soyt qui mal pence*, is not good evidence. When we understand that Gawain's adventures can be viewed as a test of his tripartite soul (see my interpretation of the poem), and when we understand that it is Gawain's *rational* part that breaks down, we may be inclined to read the motto as, quite simply, an intelligent scribe's comment on the meaning of the work. Such a view accounts for the absence of the "y" in the motto: The scribe's comment is "Shamed be he who thinks evil," not "Shamed be he who thinks evil of it." The baldric is not good evidence either, being the wrong color.

11. For a New Exegetical interpretation of the *Book of the Duchess*, see Bernard F. Huppé and D. W. Robertson, Jr., *Fruyt and Chaf: Studies in Chaucer's Allegories* (Princeton: Princeton University Press, 1963), pp. 32–100. In my opinion Huppé's interpretation is wrong, the Christian piety of the narrator being in fact a comic element in the poem; but Huppé's identification of exegetical symbols is correct and extremely important.

12. For an ingenious Freudian reading of the *Book of the Duchess*, see Bertrand H. Bronson, "*The Book of the Duchess* Re-opened," *Publications of the Modern Language Association of America*, LXVII (1952), 863–81.

13. These aspects of the *Troilus* will be examined in detail in a book I am now preparing, *Chaucer's Poetry: A Commentary*.

14. See D. W. Robertson, Jr., *A Preface to Chaucer: Studies in Medieval Perspectives* (Princeton: Princeton University Press, 1963), pp. 472 ff.

15. Most scholars agree that one of the six stanzas in the fifteenth group of linked stanzas was meant to be canceled or revised out.

16. It has recently been argued that the "garland" in stanza 99 is not, as Gordon thought, "a metaphorical description of the heavenly procession," and not, in fact, a garland at all, but a crown, symbol, like Dante's *ghirlande*, of the New Jerusalem. It is surely both and thus the earliest example of this later conventional image in English poetry. The New Jerusalem and the blessed or the elevated Church are interchangeable terms in exegetical writing, and the shifting symbolic identifications of the pearl image in this poem would support a view of other symbols in the poem as having double or triple meaning. The argument that the procession is not circular carries no weight (there is no evidence either way—except, perhaps, for the moon image, which supports the view that the procession is circular). We are told that the whole celestial city is filled. More important, the shifting imagery throughout, from the mutable to the immutable, the natural to the supernatural (see my interpretation of the poem), justifies the guess that individual pearls (liberated, pure souls), formerly mutable flowers, become, together, a garland of perfected flowers (flowers "figured" out of pearls) and become, finally, the heavenly city itself. Concerned as he seems to be with the Platonic image of unity and completion, the sphere, the poet would be unlikely to miss a chance of introducing one more circle.

17. Augustine, *On Christian Doctrine*, trans. D. W. Robertson, Jr. (New York: Liberal Arts Press, 1958), p. 52.

18. Quoted by Hugh of St. Victor, *The Didascalicon of Hugh of St. Victor*, trans. Jerome Taylor (New York: Columbia University Press, 1961), p. 63.

19. *Ibid.*

20. Donald R. Howard, "Structure and Symmetry in *Sir Gawain*," *Speculum*, XXXIX (July, 1964), 425–33.

21. If we think of the poems in the *Pearl* manuscript as a unified group, then the parallel description of the revels at Belshazzar's court in *Purity* would also tend to cast ironic light over the revels at Camelot. The Belshazzar passage may be sufficient in itself to account for the irony, without recourse to a theory that allusion is involved. But if the concluding section of *Purity* was written after *Sir Gawain and the Green Knight*,

a possibility very attractive in certain respects, and at any rate one we cannot rule out, we are back where we began.

For a brilliant, partly conjectural treatment of ironic allusion and parody in *Sir Gawain and the Green Knight*, see Marie Borroff, *Sir Gawain and the Green Knight: A Stylistic and Metrical Study* (New Haven: Yale University Press, 1962), pp. 52–129.

22. For a discussion of the origins of the story, see the introduction by Mabel Day and Mary S. Serjeantson to Gollancz' edition of *Sir Gawain and the Green Knight*, pp. xx ff.

23. See J. A. W. Bennett, *The Parlement of Foules: An Interpretation* (Oxford: Clarendon Press, 1957), pp. 62 ff.

24. See Professor Day's discussion of the Green Chapel in Gollancz' *Sir Gawain and the Green Knight*, pp. xix–xx. The evidence for this identification of the mound is strong but not conclusive.

25. Bonaventura, *The Mind's Road to God*, trans. George Boas (New York: The Liberal Arts Press, 1953), p. 9.

26. See *Boccaccio on Poetry*, ed. C. G. Osgood (New York: The Liberal Arts Press, 1930), p. 60.

27. See, for example, Augustine, *On Christian Doctrine*, p. 37.

28. There are two main traditions. For Gregory the Great, Jerome, and Hugh of St. Victor, among others, Scripture works on three levels—the literal, the allegorical, and the tropological (in this formulation, the allegorical is a mode of the anagogical); for Bede, Augustine, and others, Scripture works on the four levels I have outlined in the Introduction. The difference is merely clerical, since identical interpretations might be catalogued in either way. It might be mentioned that poets seem to favor the three-level system; at any rate that is the system expounded by Boccaccio, Petrarch, and Dante.

29. See Professor E. Talbot Donaldson's opposition to the method of patristic exegesis in his "Patristic Exegesis: The Opposition," *Critical Approaches to Medieval Literature*, ed. Dorothy Bethurum (New York: Columbia University Press, 1960), pp. 1–26.

30. *The Works of Bonaventure*, trans. Jose de Vinck (Paterson, N.J.: St. Anthony Guild Press, 1963), I, 79–80.

31. Augustine, *On Christian Doctrine*, p. 84.

32. Hugh of St. Victor, *The Didascalicon*, p. 92.

33. For an argument that the poet was very close indeed to his mythic source, see John Speirs' interpretation of the poem in *Medieval English Poetry: The Non-Chaucerian Tradition* (London: Faber and Faber, 1957), pp. 215 ff.

34. Professor Carleton Brown questioned the poet's orthodoxy in an article which, though wrong in its conclusions, is still of interest: "The Author of the Pearl Considered in the Light of His Theological Opinions," *Publications of the Modern Language Association of America*, XIX (1904), 115–53. Brown's argument was answered by Jefferson B. Fletcher in "The Allegory of the Pearl," *Journal of English and Germanic Philology*, XX (1921), 1–21.

35. Henry Savage, *The Gawain-Poet: Studies in His Personality and Background* (Chapel Hill: University of North Carolina Press, 1956), especially the first chapter.

36. See Hugh of St. Victor, *On the Sacraments of the Christian Faith*, trans. Roy J. Deferrari (Cambridge, Mass.: The Medieval Academy of America, 1951), pp. 110–11.

37. Bennett, *The Parlement of Foules* . . . , pp. 130–31.

38. *The Minor Poems of John Lydgate*, ed. Henry Noble MacCracken (London: Oxford University Press for the Early English Text Society, 1911), ll. 99–105 (p. 149).

39. Robertson, *A Preface to Chaucer* . . . , pp. 45–46.

40. *Ibid.*, pp. 50–51.

41. W. H. Schofield, "The Nature and Fabric of the Pearl," *Publications of the Modern Language Association of America*, XIX (1904), 154–215.

42. R. M. Garret, "The Pearl: An Interpretation," *University of Washington Publications in English*, IV (1918).

43. Jefferson B. Fletcher, "The Allegory of the Pearl." Professor Fletcher thought the poem at once an elegy and an allegory, the pearl representing, on the level of allegory, the Virgin Mary.

44. Sister M. Madeleva, *Pearl: A Study in Spiritual Dryness* (New York: D. Appleton, 1925).

45. Professor Wellek in "The Pearl: An Interpretation . . ." (p. 19) writes: "The purely elegiac interpretation makes the poem an unartistic conglomerate, as it degrades the very centre, the debate between the poet and the visionary girl, to a mere digression detrimental to its artistic unity. Nevertheless, it is untrue to say that the personal loss clearly expressed in the poem is a mere device, a mere vehicle designed to convey the revelations in regard to divine grace and the heavenly rewards. All these lessons would, after all, scarcely interest the poet unless they would administer *personal* consolation and reassurement."

46. See Bertrand H. Bronson's discussion of the "fers," *The Book of the Duchess* Reopened," pp. 285–86.

47. For a brief, thorough discussion of the manuscript, see Gollancz' *Sir Gawain and the Green Knight*, pp. ix ff.

48. Perhaps the most useful summaries of evidence pointing to common authorship of all of the poems are those of Professor Menner and Professor Savage in their editions of *Purity* (pp. xi–xix) and *St. Erkenwald* (pp. xlviii–lxxv), respectively.

   There is no scholarly agreement concerning the authorship of *St. Erkenwald*. But as Professor Savage has pointed out, the poem is confidently ascribed to the poet by those who have edited one or more of the poems—in other words, by all who have worked most closely with them. The similarity of themes, images, and attitudes will be obvious to every reader. The conclusive argument, when it comes, will probably be based upon metrical considerations, for only one poet whose work has come down to us handles rhythms in the way they are handled here. The hypothesis of a clever imitator of *Sir Gawain and the Green Knight* simply will not wash.

49. *Pearl*, ed. E. V. Gordon (Oxford: Clarendon Press, 1963), pp. xxxii–xxxiii.

50. Professor Savage in *The Gawain-Poet* has called attention to the extreme importance of the idea of feudal interdependence in the work of this poet and has offered a partial explanation of why that interdependence is more central to the thought of a man from Yorkshire or Lancashire than to the thought of a man like Chaucer "in toun." It is interesting to notice that Chaucer does indeed concern himself with this theme, however. Taken together, the "Man of Law's Tale" and the "Marriage Group" (or, for those who insist upon Skeat's arrangement of the *Tales*, the "Marriage Group" alone) can be viewed as a study of vassal-lord relationships in the home, in the state, and in the total metaphysical order. And Chaucer's comment on "pacience" in the "Franklin's Tale" is exactly the comment of the *Gawain*-poet, as we have seen. Similarly, the comments on "courtesy" in Prologue F to the *Legend of Good Women* and Pandarus' comments on "courtesy" to Troilus show Chaucer's interest in this concept in its extended, that is, cosmic sense.

51. Emblematic identification of the souls of the blessed (or the Church) as both servants and wives of Christ is allowable, not only because both emblems have scriptural sanction, one through the parable of the vineyard, one through the Song of Solomon and Isaiah (61:10), but also because wives are indeed vassals in the feudal system. The basis of the double identification is evident in Bonaventura's insistence that the husband's relationship to his wife and family, i.e., headship, is not to be confused with

342   THE GAWAIN-POET

mastery. While the wife must give her husband respect, the husband must "love his wife as himself." The interdependence of husband and wife, Christ and Church, lord and vassal, thus happens to coincide. (See *Commentaria in quatuor libros sententiarum magistri Petri Lombardi*, d. 32, t. IV, 742a, in *Opera omnia* [Quaracchi Edition, by authorization of the Most Reverend Augustine Sépinski, Minister General of the Order of Friars Minor, 1882–1902].)

52. This is not to deny Professor Gordon's identification of the *Quen of cortaysye* and the *Regina gratiae* of Paul (see Gordon's note to line 432 of the *Pearl*, p. 61), for grace is, I think, included in the poet's extended idea of courtesy. But Professor Gordon's comment on the narrator's lack of courtesy (Introduction, p. xxxiii) is perhaps misleading. Gordon says, "And so the dreamer who has not faith enough to accept Christ's word without visible proof is *uncortayse*, lacking in spiritual sensitivity, though he is as conscious of his manners as Sir Gawain himself." In the first place, the narrator's lack of spiritual sensitivity is secondary to his failure to trust his liege lord; in the second place, although the courtesy of human society ought to reflect the courtesy of Heaven, it does not; and the result, both philosophical and dramatic, is that the pearl and the narrator understand the word "courtesy" in different ways—one meaning feudal interdependence based upon love, the other meaning a negative kind of good manners, an idea which, even in the human situation, is not sufficient. (Sir Gawain's courtesy is not merely negative: it *becomes* negative only at the last, when he is snatching at straws to evade the seductions of the lady.)

53. Savage, *The Gawain-Poet . . .* , p. 21.

54. *Loc. cit.*

55. A good, brief account is that of Hugh of St. Victor, *The Didascalicon*, pp. 64–65.

56. Tropological descriptions of the Fall characteristically equate Adam with reason, Eve with carnal delight (an effect of perverse desire). Cf. Robinson, *The Works of Geoffrey Chaucer*, pp. 70 ff.

57. Bennett, *The Parlement of Foules . . .* , pp. 62 ff.

58. For the purpose of suggesting just how similar the *Gawain*-poet's scheme is to that of Bonaventura, though this is not the place for a detailed comparison, permit me to quote a few passages from the Boas translation (cited above) of Bonaventura's *The Mind's Road to God*, p. 8: "That we may arrive at an understanding of the First Principle . . . we ought to proceed through the traces which are corporeal and temporal and outside us; and this is to be led into the way of God. We ought next to enter into our minds, which are the eternal image [in the sense of mirror image; *speculum* sets up the metaphor] of God, spiritual and internal; and this is to walk in the truth of God. We ought finally to pass over into that which is eternal, most spiritual, and above us, looking to the First Principle; and this is to rejoice in the knowledge of God and in the reverence of His majesty.

"Now this is the three days' journey into the wilderness [cf. the basic metaphor in *Sir Gawain and the Green Knight*]; this is the triple illumination of one day, first as the evening [i.e., night], second as the morning, third as noon; this signifies the threefold existence of things, as in matter, [creative] intelligence, and in eternal art . . . and this also means the triple substance in Christ, Who is our ladder, namely, the corporeal, the spiritual, and the divine."

From Bonaventura the *Gawain*-poet might have taken his Neoplatonic view of Nature as imperfect image, his views on mutable and immutable Nature and Art, his image of the waterway or moat around Heaven, his treatment (particularly in *Sir Gawain and the Green Knight*) of macrocosm and microcosm, his interest in number and color symbolism, his interest in the five senses as doors to the soul, his identification of the tripartite soul and the Trinity (an identification as old as Augustine, of course: Divine complements human part by part, Wisdom fulfilling man's inadequate

rational part, Power fulfilling man's irascible part, and Goodness fulfilling man's concupiscent part). From Bonaventura the poet might have taken also his view of all
Nature as a garden and as phantom and illusion, his Neoplatonic clothing imagery
(flesh as clothing of the spirit, deeds as the outer appearance of character), and much
more besides. Most of these materials, however, were available to the poet in a hundred
places.

Not for the purpose of suggesting influence (this influence has already been suggested) but for the purpose of indicating how speciously easy it is to find seeming
influences, let me mention Tertullian. Many of the ideas held in common by Bonaventura and the *Gawain*-poet are also to be found in Tertullian. In addition, Tertullian's
paenitentia and *pudicitia* (*Treatises on Penance: On Penitence and On Purity*, trans.
William P. Le Saint, S.J., S.T.D. [Westminster, Md.: The Newman Press, 1959]) are
curiously close in meaning to the *Gawain*-poet's *patience* and *purity*. Tertullian's idea of
penitence has a feudal ring throughout, and his word *pudicitia* (translated *purity* by
Le Saint) has a cluster of meanings which might well account for the *Gawain*-poet's close
association of spiritual purity, modesty, and proper dress and table manners. Le Saint
observes that "What we call 'modesty' today is a safeguard of what Tertullian calls
pudicitia; compare *De cultu fem.* 2, where he declares that the virtue of purity (*pudicitia*)
is necessary for salvation, and that this virtue will be preserved by the avoidance of
extremes (i.e. by modesty) in dress and ornamentation." Tertullian, like the *Gawain*-
poet later, condemns impurity as a form of disloyalty—an extreme form of *impatience*
in the *Gawain*-poet's sense—and sees impurity operating on many levels, in the heart,
between men, and in man's experience with Nature.

59. Cf. Bonaventura's image in "The Tree of Life" (*The Works of Bonaventure*, I,
128) of the flowing spring rising up at the foot of the cross, which becomes a river
watering the Paradise of the whole Church; and see the *Pearl*, stanza 55.

60. Cf. Bonaventura's statement that some things merely are, some are and live, and some
are, live, and discern (see *The Mind's Road to God*, p. 11); cf. also Bonaventura's
graduations from matter to intelligence to eternal art (*ibid.*, p. 8) and from the mutable
and corruptible to the immutable and incorruptible (*ibid.*, p. 12).

61. *Cleanness*, ed. Sir Israel Gollancz (London: Oxford University Press, 1921), p. xvii.

62. *Purity*, ed. R. J. Menner, p. lii.

63. For the basis of the equation of Eve and beauty (or the phantom of beauty), see
Robertson, *A Preface to Chaucer* . . . , p. 70.

64. The treatment of Noah as an adumbration of Christ is traditional. Augustine says in
The City of God (New York: Random House, 1950; p. 516) that the ark "is certainly a
figure of the city of God sojourning in this world; that is to say, of the church, which
is rescued by the wood on which hung the Mediator of God and men, the man Christ
Jesus. For even its very dimensions, in length, breadth, and height, represent the
human body in which He came, as it had been foretold. For the length of the human
body, from the crown of the head to the sole of the foot, is six times its breadth from
side to side, and ten times its depth or thickness, measuring from back to front. . . .
And therefore the ark was made 300 cubits in length, 50 in breadth, and 30 in height.
And its having a door made in the side of it certainly signified the wound which was
made when the side of the Crucified was pierced with a spear: for by this those who
come to Him enter; for thence flowed the sacraments by which those who believe are
initiated."

One of the most interesting literary uses of this allegorical reading of the Noah
story is the Wakefield Master's *Processus Noe cum filiis* (see A. C. Cawley [ed.],
The Wakefield Pageants in the Towneley Cycle [Manchester: Manchester University
Press, 1958], pp. 14–28). If we think of Noah as a human, hence comic, prefiguration

of Christ, the exchanges between Noah and his wife become a rich barrage of puns. Noah's wife fares "the wars I the see" (cf. the motif of seeing God with one's eyes in *Purity*); she asks, "where has thou thus long be?" and says, "To dede may we dryfe, or lif, for the," and she declares:

> When we swete or swynk,
> Thou dos what thou thynk,
> Yit of mete and of drynk
> Haue we veray skant!

(Compare with the parable of the vineyard in *Pearl* and notice the ironic opposition of more than enough in heaven—won by bread and wine, or body and blood—and "veray skant.") Noah replies, "Wife, we ar hard sted with *tythyngys new*." (My italics.) And so it continues.

65. One of the bases of this last comparison is Lot's wealth, concerning which Professor Menner offers the following note: "It may be well to call attention . . . to another element in the Hebrew legend of Lot that seems to have been familiar to the poet of *Purity*: Lot's great wealth, which is emphasized at 786, 812, 878, though there is no hint of it in the Biblical passages paraphrased. The only indication of Lot's wealth in the Bible occurs in Gen. 13.6, where it is said of Abraham and Lot 'for their substance was great, so that they could not dwell together.' But in Rabbinical literature Lot's reputation in this respect has been greatly developed. The *Jewish Encycl.* says: 'He was besides very greedy of wealth; and at Sodom he practiced usury (Genesis Rabbah li. 8). His hesitation to leave the city (comp. Gen. 19.16) was due to this regret for his great wealth which he was obliged to abandon (Gen. R. 1. 17).' " (*Purity*, p. 96, note to lines 819–28.)

66. Compare with the stench of Cain's sacrifice in the Wakefield Master's *Mactacio Abel*, and notice that in *Purity* the sacrifices which consecrate Solomon's vessels are explicitly "savory." The association of hell and foul odor is extremely common in medieval literature, as is the association of heaven and sweet-smelling spices. Spices frequently occur as an exegetical type of grace.

67. Early students of the poem recognized this quality. Recent criticism perhaps takes excessive delight in reducing Gawain to a foolish young man and Arthur's court to a place of license. The poet is capable of ambivalence. That the poem does work as a fairy tale is obvious. Arthur's whole court is young (the Green Knight speaks of the knights as "beardless babes"). The tests Gawain faces are, like the tests in fairy tales, ritualistic: by wit, skill, and luck, he must keep absurd bargains merely because they are bargains; and both the tests and the rewards come in threes. To say this is not to discount the comic qualities of the poem or to forget that Gawain's success is, to say the least, not unblemished. And of course it must be added that the folk motifs *Sir Gawain and the Green Knight* has in common with the typical fairy tale are handled here in an extremely sophisticated way. It is generally agreed, if I am not mistaken, that the host's hunting has a good deal of homeopathic magic in it: he renews himself by drawing life from animals. "*That* was no game," the poet says of his sport—as of many activities that might seem games. (See John Speirs, *Medieval English Poetry* . . . , pp. 219 ff.; see also Jessie L. Weston, *From Ritual to Romance* [New York: Doubleday & Company, 1957], especially chapter 2, "The Task of the Hero," and chapter 8, "The Medicine Man.") But this folkloric element, like other such elements, is neatly balanced by a Christian view, in this case Christ's quite different exchange (pointed out in my analysis) of life for life.

68. It is true that the pentangle is an instrument of magic and tends to make Gawain a magician (see Weston, *From Ritual to Romance*, p. 93, and Speirs, *Medieval English Poetry* . . . , p. 230). George Ferguson observes in *Signs and Symbols in Christian Art*

(New York: Oxford University Press, 1954), p. 153, that the pentangle was used by the magicians of the Middle Ages and that, in the secular sense, "the pentagram was used as a protection against the evils of sorcery." All of the dictionaries of symbolism agree, finding even the pentangle of Solomon primarily magical rather than religious. All this does not diminish, however, the validity of the Tolkien-Gordon note to line 620 of *Sir Gawain and the Green Knight*, which identifies the pentangle as "an ancient symbol of perfection." (J. R. R. Tolkien and E. V. Gordon, *Sir Gawain and the Green Knight* [London: Oxford University Press, 1930].) J. E. Cirlot observes that the five-pointed star has since ancient times signified rising upward toward the point of origin and that in Christian symbolism the number *five* "represents the union of the principle of Heaven (three) with that of Magna Mater (two). Geometrically, it is the pentagram, or the five-pointed star. It corresponds to pentagonal symmetry, a common characteristic of organic nature, to the golden section (as noted by the Pythagoreans), and to the five senses representing the five 'forms' of matter." (*A Dictionary of Symbols*, trans. Jack Sage [London: Routledge & Kegan Paul, 1962], pp. 295, 222.)

69. Chaucer, "Romaunt of the Rose," *The Complete Works of Geoffrey Chaucer*, ed. W. W. Skeat (Oxford: Clarendon Press, 1899), ll. 1286–87.

70. Bennett (*The Parlement of Foules* . . . , pp. 177 ff.) has noted that the movement in the garden of Love, in Chaucer's *Parliament of Fowls*, is from light to dark, better to worse, and that while the noble images in the outer part of the garden gild the blackness of Venus, they also stand between the lover and Venus. I take it that a part of Chaucer's point is that love, like the garden of Love, requires more than its sexual center to be good. Artifice, trappings, courtesy, form, keep it from becoming something mean.

71. Compare these lines from lyric No. 66, "I Will Become a Friar," in *English Lyrics of the XIIIth Century*, ed. Carleton Brown (London: Oxford University Press, 1932):

> Frer menur i wil me make
> and lecherie i wille asake;
> to ihesu crist ich wil me take
> and serue in holi churche. . . .

Whether or not Chaucer intended his lines to echo these, Sir Thopas is clearly in the chaste knight tradition—not a tradition which a fourteenth-century poet had to treat with complete seriousness. If Gawain is a virgin, the comedy of the temptation scenes is heightened.

72. For a discussion of the medieval view of virginity, see Sister E. T. Healy, *Women According to Saint Bonaventure* (New York: The Georgian Press, 1955), pp. 138–54.

73. *The Norton Anthology of English Literature*, ed. M. H. Abrams *et al.* (New York: W. W. Norton, 1962), pp. 183–84.

74. Speirs, *Medieval English Poetry* . . . , p. 232.

75. Bertilak may legitimately be associated with other figures as well, among them the druid, fairy, and devil. John Speirs' opinion that the giant is associated with the thunder and lightning god is doubtful. The two images he cites—the lightning-like look and the spark which flies from the horse's hoof—are both extremely conventional.

76. Savage, *The Gawain-Poet* . . . , p. 41.

77. *Ibid.*, p. 43.

78. *Ibid.*, p. 46, and see note 35, p. 46.

79. F. L. Utley, "Folklore, Myth, and Ritual," *Critical Approaches to Medieval Literature*, p. 90.

80. For instance, see J. R. Hulbert, "Sir Gawayn and the Grene Knygt," *Modern Philology*, XIII (1945), 454–60.

81. Perverse concupiscence and irascibility cause Eve's fall, hence man's fall. See Bonaventura's *Commentaria in quatuor libros sententiarum magistri Petri Lombardi*, II, d. 22, a. 1, g. 1, concl., t. II, 517a.

82. Robertson, *Preface to Chaucer* . . . , p. 70.

83. *Ibid.*, pp. 70–75.

84. In their note to line 184, Tolkien and Gordon (*Sir Gawain and the Green Knight*) point out that the cut of the knight's hair explicitly identifies him as an elf-knight.

85. Cf. *Sir Gawain and the Green Knight*, part 4, stanza 17, lines 2390–94, and note the similar view of confession and penance described as the "polishing" of a gem in *Purity*, part 12.

86. Joseph F. Eagen, in "The Import of Color Symbolism in *Sir Gawain and the Green Knight*," *St. Louis University Studies* (n.d.), pp. 23–24, identifies green as symbolic of "regeneration in eternal life, the hope of rebirth and faith in its accomplishment, youth and love, and chastity and contemplation," and associates green with "the beginning of a glowing love for Christ." He follows Professor Hulbert in finding green an indication that the knight is "an Other-World creature."

87. Cf. Eagen, *op. cit.*, pp. 19–21.

88. Cf. *ibid.*, pp. 25–27.

89. Bonaventura, *The Mind's Road to God*, pp. 12–13.

90. Cirlot, *A Dictionary of Symbols*, p. 222.

91. See Savage, *St. Erkenwald*, pp. xliii ff., for a brief discussion. The most recent study of the poet's meter is that of Miss Borroff, *Sir Gawain and the Green Knight: A Stylistic and Metrical Study*, pp. 133–210, which is excellent in some respects (particularly chapter 5, "The Phonological Evidence," a discussion which supersedes all others) but unconvincing in its metrical thesis. Miss Borroff's account is spoiled by her use of a system of metrical analysis too clumsy to handle any rhythms more complex than those in the nursery rhymes or stanzas from Blake upon which she primarily depends for illustration. Her distinction between "major chief stress" and "minor chief stress" is, as she recognizes, arbitrary. (Miss Borroff presents "alternate readings" of numerous lines, giving her major chief stress first to one word, then to another.) Using the same arbitrary distinction, one might make all the lines fit a three-stress pattern if one pleased. The fact is that any metrical system which can account for Hopkins can account for the work of the *Gawain*-poet, and no system can account for the *Gawain*-poet's practice if it fails to recognize that rhyme, alliteration, and sense all infect stress and tend to "spring" the verse.

92. See K. Luick, "Die Englische Stabreimzeile in XIV., XV., und XVI. Jahrhundert," *Anglia*, II (1889), 392 ff.; W. E. Leonard, *The Scansion of Middle English Alliterative Verse* ("University of Wisconsin Studies in Language and Literature," II [1920]), 58–104.

93. Menner, *Purity*, pp. lvi ff.